WAITING FOR AN ORDINARY DAY

WAITING FOR AN ORDINARY DAY

THE UNRAVELING OF LIFE IN IRAQ

FARNAZ FASSIHI

PublicAffairs
New York

Copyright © 2008 by Farnaz Fassihi

Published in the United States by PublicAffairs™, a member of the
Perseus Books Group.

All rights reserved.
Printed in the United States of America.

Map Iraq created by Gary S. Tong from *Night Draws Near: Iraq's
People in the Shadow of America's War* written by Anthony Shadid. Map
copyright © 2005 by Henry Holt and Company. Reprinted by permission of Henry Holt and Company, LLC.

DOONESBURY © 2004 G. B. Trudeau. Reprinted with permission
of UNIVERSAL PRESS SYNDICATE. All rights reserved.

No part of this book may be reproduced in any manner whatsoever
without written permission except in the case of brief quotations
embodied in critical articles and reviews. For information, address
PublicAffairs, 250 West 57th Street, Suite 1321, New York, NY
10107.

PublicAffairs books are available at special discounts for bulk pur-
chases in the U.S. by corporations, institutions, and other organizations. For more information, please contact the Special Markets
Department at the Perseus Books Group, 2300 Chestnut Street, Suite
200, Philadelphia, PA 19103, call (800) 810-4145, ext. 5000, or
e-mail special.markets@perseusbooks.com.

Designed by Pauline Brown
Text set in 13-point Garamond

    Library of Congress Cataloging-in-Publication Data
    Fassihi, Farnaz.
    Waiting for an ordinary day : the unraveling of life in Iraq /
Farnaz Fassihi. — 1st ed.
    p. cm.
    Includes index.
    ISBN 978-1-58648-475-0 (hardcover : alk. paper) 1. Iraq War,
2003—Personal narratives, American. 2. Fassihi, Farnaz.
3. Journalists—United States—Biography. I. Title.
DS79.76.F385 2008
956.7044'3092—dc22
[B]
                                        2008024862

10 9 8 7 6 5 4 3 2

To my mother and my sister Tannaz
for enduring my adventures

To Babak
for turning every adventure into romance

And to my father
whose love sustains me long after he's gone

CONTENTS

CONTENTS

YEAR 2004
If They See Me with You, They'll Kill Me

YEAR 2005
Our House May Never Be Safe for Us

FOREWORD

I FIRST WENT TO IRAQ WHEN Saddam Hussein was still in power in October 2002 as a reporter for *The Newark Star-Ledger*. Then *The Wall Street Journal*, upon hiring me in January 2003, dispatched me immediately to northern Iraq to cover the impending war, before assigning me to Baghdad for three years. Although I wrote stories about politics and the military, my reportage focused on telling stories about ordinary Iraqis and how they coped as their country went from tyranny to military occupation and civil war. My purpose as a war correspondent was to humanize the war that seemed so alien and far away for most readers.

Over the course of my tenure in Iraq, I witnessed and documented a heart-wrenching unraveling of normal life for Iraqis. Despite the widespread coverage the media is giving Iraq, the scope of the war's impact on Iraqis remains scarcely told. In this book, I hope to paint the story of the war through the eyes of Iraqis. I also hope to offer a glimpse of what it was like for a young female reporter to live and work in Iraq during the height of the war.

Iraq defined my career as a young journalist. I felt lucky and thrilled to be given the chance to witness history in the making and to document the biggest story of my generation. On a personal level, the relentless violence I witnessed and the miseries I recorded left a deep scar. For the longest time after leaving the country, I couldn't talk about Iraq without a knot forming in my throat and tears welling up in my eyes. Writing this book has been cathartic, allowing me to lay the memories to rest.

The material here is drawn from my observations, interviews, and interactions with the Iraqi people I met and the articles I wrote for both *The Wall Street Journal* and *The Star-Ledger*.

In September 2004, I penned an e-mail to a group of family and friends that detailed the rapidly deteriorating situation and the dangers journalists were facing. The e-mail eventually made it to the public sphere, where it was posted on websites, forwarded like a chain letter across the globe, and picked up by blogs. It received national and international attention for its uncanny view of the mess in Iraq. It was also the subject of a *Doonesbury* cartoon. (The full text of the e-mail is printed at the end of this book.) Because I was writing to friends, I spoke freely, without the restraints of daily journalism that obliged me to be distant and objective. The emotional and personal tone grabbed the public in a way that my published pieces for the newspaper seldom did. The reaction overwhelmed me. From Australia to South Africa, the e-mail was published in local newspapers, and strangers wrote to me asking, "Is it really that bad in Iraq? We had no idea."

I have written this book in the same spirit as I wrote that e-mail.

FALL 2002

Finding
Baghdad

1

Yes, Yes, to
Our Leader Saddam

My first glimpses of Baghdad are burned deep into memory, as if they belong to a vanished place.

Palm groves swish in a soft autumn breeze, as the muddy waters of the Tigris River stream through the city. The green riverbank is lined with shabby fish restaurants, and the skyline is dotted with an architectural variety of marble palaces, blue-domed mosques, gigantic statues made of steel, colonial houses with engraved balconies, and multistory, seventies-style office buildings. The roads, wide and well paved, are jammed with cars. In a crowded market, peddlers push wooden carts full of fruit and fresh herbs, and a bookstore is stocked with old translated copies of Russian literature and Shakespeare's poetry.

Iraqis are rushing around carrying out their daily chores. Cafés are packed with old men playing backgammon and younger men puffing on cigarettes or hookahs. Iraqi women stroll down sidewalks, peer into shop windows, and lock arms while crossing the streets. Dressed in stylish hip-hugging pants or knee-length skirts with matching colorful shirts, they sport artfully blonde-highlighted hair. From their high-heel sandals, nail-polished toes peep out.

The city pulses with the rhythm of an urban life, almost deceptive in its normalcy.

And then I notice that Saddam Hussein's face is everywhere. In whichever direction my eyes dart, on walls, shops, schools, and commercial buildings, a life-size or larger picture of Saddam Hussein grins down at me. He is portrayed in various outfits: wearing a military uniform, commanding the troops; sporting a mafia-style black hat, firing a shotgun; sitting cross-legged, sipping tea in traditional Kurdish baggy pants and fringy head wrap; and in an Arabic robe, greeting children. And he is always smiling.

Outsize Iraqi flags, green, white, and red, flutter atop government buildings. White banners stretched thin between walls announce in proud, blood-red Arabic script, "Yes, yes, yes to our leader Saddam Hussein."

In a few days' time, Saddam plans to stage a national referendum to counter world opinion about his lack of popularity and strength at home. In America, a United States–led military invasion into Iraq seems imminent. After spending a week sitting idly on a rigid chair in the waiting room at the Iraqi embassy in Amman, faking smiles and exchanging formal, empty greetings with Iraqi bureaucrats, my visa finally arrived. Saddam has apparently decided now is as good a time as ever to allow hordes of international journalists a rare visit (albeit controlled and strictly monitored) to his Iraq.

Once this ancient capital was famed as the jewel of the Arab world; it was a place of discovery, literature, and progress. It's been decades since Baghdad's fortunes reversed. Brutal rulers have gripped its reign, and years of war, global isolation, and sanctions have turned it into a suspended place, trapped between a glorious past and an ever-ambiguous future.

Iraq has long been linked to my own trajectory. During the fall of my fourth-grade year, my little sister Tannaz and I were sprawled on our bedroom floor in Tehran, playing with Barbie dolls, when a thundering sound rattled the windows. My father scooped us up in his arms as he and Mom dashed down the stairs, taking shelter in the basement apartment of a neighbor.

"It's Iraqi war planes," I remember someone saying. "They have broken the sound barrier. We are at war."

Soon after, state radio and television introduced us to the sound of the "red siren" and "white siren," which signaled when war planes were in the sky and when the threat had cleared. In school, we practiced bunker drills, our little feet stomping down the stairs to the dark basement where we huddled together on the ground. My dad taped our windows with huge Xs to prevent smashed glass from flying in the case of an attack. There were nightly blackouts, to our grave disappointment, often right around 8:00 PM, just as our favorite television show, *Pippi Longstocking,* aired. Food coupons for basic goods such as rice and cooking oil were distributed to households, and milk became an extravagance of the prewar days. We rationed gasoline. Days went by without hot water, forcing my mom to boil water and pour it by the potful into the chilly water of the tub to give us our lukewarm baths.

My family left Iran soon after the war began to settle in Portland, Oregon. I eventually returned to Iran with my family, where I attended university and stumbled into journalism by chance by becoming a translator and stringer for foreign correspondents traveling to Iran. Ever since my childhood, I have had an irresistible attraction to my roots in the Middle East and a yearning to make sense of the constant upheavals in the region that shaped my own life from a very young age.

Now, nearly two decades later, I find myself evoking those childhood memories as the driver points out an array of monuments commemorating Iraq's eight-year war with Iran, including a massive replica of Saddam Hussein's fists, about the size of a six-story building, crushing actual helmets of Iranian soldiers seized from the battlefield.

We disembark from Jordan a few hours after midnight in an SUV driven by a burly Jordanian driver who is accompanied by his chatty assistant. Inside the car are enough entertainment and snacks to sustain us for days if we get stranded in the Jordanian desert. There's a flask of hot water, another one filled with Arabic coffee, paper cups, napkins, a plastic bag of pita bread, and the sort of Turkish cookies that resemble small, round sandwiches stuffed with banana cream. In addition to a top-notch radio and CD player with speakers loud enough for a disco, there is a small television screen above the glove box. Easam, the driver, says he makes frequent runs to Baghdad, and the music prevents him from dozing off in the dull landscape of highway in western Iraq, where miles of brown swaths of earth devoid of life yawn endlessly outward. As I settle in the backseat, he puts on an Arabic music video. A popular Arabic pop song blares out and an attractive, busty woman sways her hips.

"You like?" he turns to me and asks. "I have Madonna and Celine Dion, too."

More than anything, the two Western journalists with me and I want to sleep. At the crack of dawn, Easam wakes us up. We have arrived at the Iraqi border, where we negotiate our way through a labyrinth of bureaucracy at customs: we register laptops, satellite phones, and Internet transmitters and bribe our way out of an on-the-spot AIDS test. I repeatedly offer my smiley explanation as to why someone with an Iranian-sounding name was standing before them holding an American passport: I was born in the United States to Iranian parents.

Our destination is the Palestine Hotel in central Baghdad, a tower of gray cement and one of the city's many seventies-style architectural monuments. The hotel serves as a landmark and registration point for arriving journalists.

Easam points out the hotel as it appears in the skyline and reassures us of its luxury, "It's a four-star hotel. Very nice. Good location, you can find taxis easily."

"Can we go out on our own?" I ask. "Won't we have government minders? Do you think people will talk to us?"

"Yes, yes," he replies, pausing and then adding, "But this is Iraq. Everyone is afraid of Saddam."

The building looks gloomy, even from afar, like a piece of neglected furniture. The rooms are caged behind balconies that are slightly angled and covered by geometric panels. We wind around Ferdous Square, which is littered with dilapidated cars run down by almost a decade of sanctions. In the middle of the circle, atop a patch of green, is a giant statue of Saddam Hussein. One hand raised, he is saluting, dictator style.

Inside, the hotel lobby bristles with excessive Middle Eastern decoration and kitsch art-deco furniture and light fixtures reminiscent of the hotel's better days. From within a tribal tent at the entrance, colorful carpets are sold. Traditional abayas made of fine camel hair and long hand-embroidered dresses dangle from hangers. There is a newspaper kiosk that sells only Iraqi newspapers owned by the government and a handful of postcards from Babylon, dating back to the 1970s. The hotel souvenir shop has a window display of the usual items—clunky silver jewelry, lapis boxes, and hand-carved knives—but it's the Saddam memorabilia that stands out. Lighters, wristwatches, alarm clocks, bumper stickers, plates, and jugs depicting his face are for sale. An art gallery next door has a few canvases of Iraqi landscapes tucked away among the dozens of brightly painted portraits of Saddam.

The Ministry of Information, which assigns minders and translators to journalists, has conveniently set up a desk in the lobby. A middle-aged man, Mr. Alla Khalil, shakes my hands warmly and scans his list for my name. He is short, with a patch of shiny, black-dyed hair and a thick, bushy moustache. The Saddam-style mustache is in vogue in here; practically every man, young or old, seems to sport one.

Mr. Alla is constantly interrupted by a bevy of international journalists streaming in and out of the lobby with inquiries about their permits for filming on the streets or whether a press conference has been scheduled.

Mr. Alla's first question of me is whether or not I have a satellite phone. "Before we check you in, we have to seal your equipment and take it away from you," he says in a flat voice. "You can pick it up on your last day here."

Then, like a skillful matchmaker on a dance floor, Mr. Alla checks my name off his list, grabs me by the hand, and walks me over to a small crowd of Iraqi men hovering nearby, government minders assigned to monitor each reporter as well as double as translators.

"Miss Farnaz, these are our translators. What language do you need? English or Farsi? We have many translators, Spanish, Russian, and French," Mr. Alla explains.

"English is good. I write in English," I say.

Eventually, I'm matched with a smiley middle-aged high school English teacher named Mr. Nuri, who is new to the job. His lack of experience as a person who monitors and reports our every move and the fact that no one in the ministry has ever heard of the newspaper I represent, *The Newark Star-Ledger*, allow me a great deal of wiggle room in the days to come. I quickly discover that reporting in Iraq requires a great deal of patience. Official interviews are seldom granted and accurately gauging the mood of the public is challenging in the presence of a minder, who reports back to the ministry. When we do man-in-the-street interviews, Iraqis eye Mr. Nuri suspiciously and praise Saddam. I can't continue to press the issue until I get a satisfactory, truthful answer. I am acutely aware that my questioning can get Iraqis into trouble.

The day I arrive at the Palestine Hotel, a much sterner young man from the group of minders whisks me away. He leads me through a maze of stairs and hallways and up an elevator to a room on the ninth floor, where confiscated satellite phones are stored. I have no choice but to surrender my equipment and watch him jot down its serial number. He is polite but firm and ignores my attempt at casual talk. He informs me that there is a reliable Internet café at the Rasheed Hotel, where I plan to stay, but most electronic-mailing websites like Hotmail and Yahoo! are blocked. To work around that problem, the information ministry will issue me a temporary e-mail from their government servers, from which I can file my stories and they can easily monitor the content.

Before I finally settle in my room on the second floor of the notorious Rasheed Hotel, decidedly the most luxurious and modern establishment in the country, my roommate, journalist Vivienne Walt, a more seasoned colleague who has been to Iraq before, warns me against getting too comfortable: "The room is tapped, the phone line is tapped. They are listening to everything we say. There is a secret camera in the ceiling. You must change with the lights off and only in the bathroom."

For the rest of my stay, Vivienne and I develop a schoolgirl method of communication, giggling and passing notes to each other while sitting two feet away. Often we returned to our room at the end of a day's reporting to discover our suitcases opened, clothes rifled through, our notebooks misplaced.

On that first night in Baghdad, I set out on my own for a stroll around the hotel. No one seems to notice me quietly walking out of the hotel lobby. The streets are well lit, and small groups of Iraqis are roaming around. I notice a family eating at a hole-in-the-wall eatery that serves roasted chicken; the mother scoops up bits of chicken with a piece of bread to feed her toddler perched on a rickety table. The father chats away with the cashier as they watch a small television screen broadcasting a marathon of singers praising Saddam. I have been here only a day and I already feel cut off from the rest of the world. There are no cell phones, and dialing any number, domestic or international, from the room is forbidden. One must call up the hotel operator, surrender the contact, and request a connection, yet another of the regime's clever tactics to monitor foreign guests.

Satellite dishes, common in the rest of the Arab world, are nonexistent in Iraq, and with no access to round-the-clock news channels like CNN, BBC, or even Al-Jazeera, journalists are left in a disassociated cutoff zone. The state owns and operates all media, strictly filtering the flow of information, particularly broadcast news. On TV, reruns of Arabic soap operas, music videos from the 1980s, and brief news clips of Iraqis jumping up and down on camera, holding framed posters of Saddam to their hearts, and pledging their devotion to the regime dominate.

"Victory is yours, oh Saddam, with our blood and with our soul, we sacrifice ourselves for you, oh Saddam. . . ."

The Rasheed Hotel is surrounded by government landmarks. Directly across the street is the Convention Center, home to the Iraqi parliament, and down the road is the notorious Assassin's Gate, a massive arch leading to Saddam's palace compound from which he resides and rules. The Foreign Ministry and the Ministry of Information are each a few blocks away. I am surprised at the lack of extra security in the streets. There are only policemen guiding the traffic and soldiers standing guard at the entrance of some buildings.

For dinner I join Vivienne at an Italian restaurant on Arasat Street, an upper-middle-class neighborhood of two-story houses with front gardens and low walls. The restaurant, Saj al-Reef, feels out of place with its cozy red and white checkered tablecloths, fine dinnerware, and the faux antique clocks and ceramic plates that decorate its walls. Around us, well-to-do Iraqi couples and families chatter away and dine on pasta. A man in a tuxedo plays Frank Sinatra tunes on the piano and we are served salad in a tortilla-style bread shell and green lasagna Bolognese. Ever since Saddam invaded Kuwait and decided he was a devout Muslim, alcohol has been forbidden in restaurants and only Christian liquor-store owners are allowed to sell their goods. We have sneaked in our own bottle of red wine, which the waiter cheerfully cracks open and pours.

On the way back to the hotel, without a minder, we try to chat up the hotel taxi driver, who speaks enough English to offer his sober point of view. He won't give us his name. He says he is in his late forties. When we ask him what he thinks of the referendum and whether he will vote for Saddam, he looks at us from the front mirror, takes one hand from the wheel, and makes an impassioned speech about how voting yes for Saddam is really a no for President Bush. He asks plaintively why America wants to attack Iraq. "For what?" he demands. We ask him what he thinks will happen if the United States declares a war on Iraq.

"We will fight very hard. Not just the army but the people, because we don't like foreigners to tell us what to do. There will be a lot of blood; you will see."

2

Nobody in Iraq
Wants War

The dining room of the Nassers' home, where I'm attending a birthday party for their oldest son, is lit by tall, beige candles. The air is heavy with the scent of roses and white jasmines, which had been picked from the garden and are tastefully arranged in a crystal vase. My host is Sabah Nasser, a retired businessman in his early sixties, whom I recently met at the hotel. Sabah gestures to his guests to sit. The table is covered with an old, hand-embroidered lace cloth and laid with a silver teapot, white china teacups, and a big heart-shaped sponge cake that Nasser's wife, Marie-Rose, has baked. Marie-Rose and Sabah both come from well-to-do Catholic families and are more sophisticated and Western than most other Iraqis I've met. They live in a lovely two-story villa, with high ceilings and mosaic floors, set in the middle of a garden shaded with date palms and pomegranate trees. A short, white fence draped in scarlet bougainvilleas and white jasmine separates their garden from the street.

The guests tonight include a handful of family members and close friends: older son Ayad, who is turning thirty-one tonight, and his wife, Aseel, who is seven months pregnant with their first child; younger son Ziad and his fiancée, Rana; Aseel's parents; Sabah's brother Nosrat and his wife, Theresa; Sabah's childhood friend Riad El-Taher, a British Iraqi who is visiting the country at the invitation of the Iraqi government; and me. I've been granted a unique treat: an invitation into an Iraqi home, far from the lurking stares of my minder. As a gift I have brought a big bottle of Johnnie Walker Black Label whiskey purchased in the duty-free shop in the Amman airport. Sabah holds up the bottle and declares to the guests, "Look, it's an original Johnnie Walker."

I have a notebook in hand, but I've already agreed to the condition that we will only discuss daily life. Like all Iraqis, the Nassers are wary of the repercussions of opening their home to an American reporter, and they agree to do so only after Riad approves of my visit.

The Nassers have one daughter, Ghada, who recently migrated with her Iraqi priest husband to Sweden, where she has applied for refugee asylum. Ghada's presence is frozen in the Nassers' house through framed pictures on practically every table.

Ayad Nasser is quiet and reserved, speaking only when someone asks him a question. His younger brother, Ziad, who sports a goatee and is wearing jeans, is far more outgoing and often makes the family laugh by telling jokes. He attends to his young fiancée with loving devotion. The brothers, both graduates of Baghdad University's school of engineering, gave up on jobs in their field because the salaries were so low. After graduation, with the help of their father, they each opened shops selling buttons, ribbons, hair accessories, and lingerie. Earlier in the evening, over vodka and berry-juice cocktails and a bowl of crispy potato chips, I ask the young couples about jobs, economic survival, and future plans. It strikes me that for young Iraqis here, unlike for Americans who have mapped out their life goals at a young age, surviving simple day-to-day life is considered an accomplishment.

"We don't pay attention to anything; we look just in front of us, not left or right, just to live a quiet life," Ziad says.

On the wall above the television are framed graduation portraits of the Nassers' three children. "Sometimes I think my diploma was only so I could take this picture for my parents. What can I do with my education?" Ayad asks.

When I ask them about the war, their anxieties are pragmatic. Ayad is worried about the collapse of infrastructure when his wife delivers their baby. Ziad wonders if his shop will survive a war and whether he can save enough money to get married.

For the young generation, Iraq's economic isolation has meant being shopkeepers instead of engineers and living at home even after they are married and have children. Ziad tells me that attending restaurants and clubs is beyond the economic reach of the middle class. Even throwing parties at home is an expense saved for special occasions. In the past decade, the value of the Iraqi currency, dinar, has plummeted, but salaries have remained the same. Before 1990, one dollar was worth one-third of a dinar. Now it's worth 2,000 dinar.

Ayad's wife Aseel is twenty-six, with a pale face, greenish gray eyes, a resigned, shy smile, and short, stylish hair. She is a civil engineer and works for the Baghdad municipality eight hours a day. Her monthly salary is $12.50. Not even enough, she says, to buy a pair of shoes or have a dinner at a restaurant. Not enough to feed the couple. The consecutive wars and sanctions have created a society almost entirely dependent on food coupons and subsidies by the government. Even upper-class families like the Nassers rely on subsidized food.

"An average couple with one child would need about five hundred dollars a month to live a very simple life," says Ayad. "Our living standards have decreased since the sanctions."

Low income has forced both sons to live with their parents. After Ayad got married, Marie-Rose and Sabah offered the newlyweds their master bedroom upstairs and relocated themselves to a room adjacent to the kitchen because "every new couple needs privacy, you know what I mean?" Marie-Rose giggles as she gives me a tour of the house. Ziad also plans to bring his bride home after his wedding.

Gathered around the dining table, the guests start singing "Happy Birthday" in Arabic. They sing in abandon, swaying left and right. Their voices rise and fall and the tune, identical in melody to its English counterpart, sounds strangely melancholy. When the singing subsides and Ayad blows out the candles, everyone cheers. He turns to kiss Aseel, who puts her hands on her belly and tells Ayad to make a wish.

"I wish for my baby to be healthy. And I wish there is no war and we all live in peace," says Ayad.

"Inshallah [God willing]," everyone says in unison.

"Now let's not talk about war anymore. Who wants cake?" Marie-Rose says cheerfully, piling slices of cake onto plates, which she hands around.

Marie-Rose is gregarious and warm; at fifty-nine years old, she is a retired accountant and spends her days cooking, fussing about her husband and children, and watching soap operas with her sister-in-law. As we sit around the table and munch on our cakes, the cheerful mood of the evening slowly evaporates as we turn to the subject of war. No matter how hard people deny or pretend, the agony of war looms large, stalking Iraqis like an invisible intruder and quietly seeping into every conversation. I'm sitting next to Marie-Rose when she leans over and whispers that her biggest fear is that if American bombs fall on Baghdad and the battle drags on, their sons will be drafted. Unbeknownst to her family, she has contacted a local midwife to deliver their first grandchild at home in case Aseel's delivery date in late November coincides with bombing. Taking a deep drag on her cigarette, she puts down her teacup.

"You see, when bombardment starts there will be no electricity, no water, no gas to drive her to the hospital," she says, her eyes filling with tears. "All I want is to have my children around me and live a normal life. But war after war after war. Why won't they just let us be? What have we done? It's so unfair."

The modern history of Iraq is a bloody tale of twenty-three coups, numerous attempted revolts, and brutal military rulers. Saddam came to power on a pan-Arab nationalist fervor derived from the Baath party movement. After muscling his way into the presidency, he maintained his grip on power by ruthlessly murdering his opponents (including members of his own family), torturing prisoners, and crushing any ethnic dissent by the country's Kurdish population in the north. There, he sprayed chemical gas on Kurdish mountain villages and murdered thousands of civilians. In the south, he executed Shiites and dumped them in mass graves. Saddam's egomania drove him to invade Iran and Kuwait, cost his country over a million lives, billions of dollars of debt, and sanctions that eliminated the once-vibrant Iraqi middle class and created a welfare society completely reliant on government subsidies for basic food. Iraqis often remind me of abused children, with an utter lack of drive or sense of control over their destinies. War and its happenings—sanctions, an overriding veil of oppression—have become a way of life. Almost all Iraqis I meet recall memories of the last war, forty-five days of air strikes in 1991, when a U.S.-led military coalition forced Saddam to withdraw his troops from Kuwait.

Then the Nassers' house sheltered forty-two relatives, five of them children. Mattresses were spread on the first floor. Without water or power, the family cut trees from the garden to feed the fire for cooking. The men walked to the Tigris for water and dug a ditch in the backyard for a toilet. The Nassers rationed their food, feeding the kids first while they themselves took turns eating, often skipping two meals a day. To save on gasoline, they rode bicycles. The telephone lines were cut for over three months and electricity was available for only a few hours a day.

"It was a terrifying experience," Marie-Rose tells me. "And we are afraid this time it will be much worse." She pauses for a few seconds and glances around at her family. "God is great," she continues. "Nobody in Iraq wants war. This is very scary and everyone is very, very worried. How shall I explain, like we are living under siege or in prison all the time."

A frequent complaint I hear from Iraqis is about how much they've suffered as a result of the UN-imposed sanctions that have created a crisis in the country's health-care system. Marie-Rose was diagnosed with an overactive thyroid gland about four years ago and lost over thirty pounds. The iodine capsules she required were in short supply, so she begged a cousin traveling to Jordan to regularly bring her supplies. But when her cousin's trips ended, so, too, did Marie-Rose's dose of medication. Her doctor put her name on a government list of recipients for medications imported under the oil-for-food program, but nine months would pass before she could receive benefits. During that time, she was hospitalized twice.

Sabah, sixty-two, has a bachelor's degree in business administration from South End College in England. Nostalgically, he recalls how he passed his A- and O-level studies with flying colors at the elite all-male high school Baghdad College. It was customary of affluent Iraqi families to send their children abroad to England or America for higher education.

"Everyone respected us then; when you said you were Iraqi, it meant something dignified. Now, look at us; we cannot even travel next door to Jordan easily, and no one will give us a visa to visit a Western country. They treat us like dogs," Sabah says.

When Sabah returned from England, he met and fell in love with Marie-Rose. She was college educated, with a degree in accounting, and spoke fluent English. Together, they held steady jobs and raised their three children, living in the house that Marie-Rose inherited from her father, weathering the tumultuous times of war. Most of Marie-Rose and Sabah's relatives, including all her siblings, have long left Iraq and made lives in the United States and Europe. But the Nassers refused to leave despite the fact that they were well educated, spoke fluent English, and had support from a network of relatives abroad. On a few occasions when I am at their house, one of their anxious relatives calls. One day it is Marie-Rose's brother, Hekmat al-Khouri, calling from Columbus, Ohio. She clutches the handset and utters words of endearment while wiping her tears.

"Habibi [my dear], we miss you," she says. "I wish we were together." She reassures him that the family is safe, failing to tell him how scared she is of war.

When she hangs up the phone, she turns to me and says, "I wish I could remind Bush there are people living in Iraq. We have lives, get married, have babies, go to work. All you hear is America talking about Saddam, Saddam, weapons, inspectors, war, bombs. Nobody talks about the Iraqi people. You can't dehumanize an entire country like that."

Now retired, Sabah runs a kebab restaurant on a busy Baghdad street. He spends his days reading or visiting with friends at an antique shop. They play cards, chess, and backgammon, talk politics and sip Arabic tea from tiny cups. In the evening Sabah supervises the kebab restaurant, but like his sons, he complains that business has decreased dramatically in the past few weeks.

"People are not coming out to eat as much," says Sabah. "They are all waiting for bombs to fall."

Sabah's older brother, Nosrat, is deaf, but he can read lips if you speak to him slowly. Almost every day around lunchtime, he gets dressed and walks across the street to the Nassers' and spends the afternoon with the family. He's never been taught standard sign language, but he's created his own gestures and is eager to communicate with me in a way that is both amusing and touching.

When I slowly say, "I'm American," he lifts one hand like a torch and the other like a crown. I am puzzled. Sabah steps in to decipher, "Statue of Liberty." Then he points to my hair and makes a confused face. "He is wondering why you don't have blond hair, then, if you are American," explains Sabah. "Not everyone has blond hair and blue eyes in America," I say.

Sabah shouts, "Father, mother, from Iran." His brother makes circles around his head like the turbans of the mullahs who rule Iran. I crack up with laughter. With his index finger Nosrat traces the number 1979 on his palm and blows a kiss into the air. "He is saying Iraq was very good then," explains Sabah. Then he writes 2001 and sticks out his tongue and puts both his hands around his throat as if he is suffocating. Sabah doesn't offer an interpretation for this one. Lifting his arm, stretching out his right hand, saluting (pretending he is Saddam), and making waves with his arms like an airplane flying in the sky (bomber jets), he makes a quiet *boom boom* sound with his lips.

"War?" I ask. He nods, pressing his right hand on his heart and leaning back a little, pretending to fall from a gunshot.

"You see," says Sabah, "even the deaf can't escape the thought of war."

Nosrat's wife, Theresa, is a quiet woman who looks at least a decade and a half older than her forty-two years. From Lebanon, without children of her own, she helped raise the Nassers' three children, babysitting them every day while they worked. Affectionately called Mama Theresa, she is a seamstress who sews clothes for all the women in the family and for a circle of clients. When she takes me to her house, I notice that her sewing machine is old and rusty; she bought it in the 1970s, and her fashion magazines, from which women pick styles, are at least two decades old. She charges her clients about five dollars for a blouse and fifteen dollars for a dress.

"Since the sanctions, women can't find any nice ready-made clothes in the shops because imports from Europe and America are banned," she says. "So we buy textiles and do it all ourselves, by hand."

She offers to make me some clothes fit to my figure but I say I don't have enough time here, maybe next time. She then hesitantly asks me if I can bring her some up-to-date fashion magazines if I visit Iraq again, especially the German *Burda*, which has ready-to-make patterns she can cut out and copy.

Theresa pulls a curtain back from a closet to reveal a pile of emergency goods she has been stocking for the war. There are plastic jugs of water, canned food, rice, beans, lentils, macaroni, flashlights, and batteries.

"I am using the money I make now for this," she adds.

Although I have promised not to discuss politics with the Nassers, I can't avoid asking their opinions about Saddam's referendum. About 11 million registered Iraqi voters across the country—minus the Kurds in the north—were asked to answer yes or no to a single question on the ballot: whether they want to reelect Saddam as their president for the next seven years. Little doubt exists about the results. For one thing, there are no other candidates; opposition parties have been banned since the 1970s. For another, voters are assigned numbers that correspond to the cards on which they mark their votes, so that a voter's choice could be traced. In 1995, a similar referendum was held, and 99.96 percent of Iraqi voters answered yes to securing Saddam's presidency. The official voting age in Iraq is eighteen. Voting is not mandatory, but the ruling Baath party has strongly encouraged people to cast their votes this time around. In interviews with Iraqis at polling stations, markets, and in Baghdad streets, I've encountered a dogmatic fervor for the regime that strikes me more as rage at America than real love for Saddam. In every comment about the referendum, America's name is intertwined with Saddam's and voting for him is declared an act of defiance against the war rhetoric of the United States and Britain.

In a popular bookstore on Tahrir Square, a busy commercial thoroughfare, the thirty-year-old owner, Hayder Abdul Karim, tells me, "Nobody will vote no. We will all vote yes because we love our president and because America wants to destroy Iraq."

The Nassers are no exception. From the parents to the children, they tell me that they were so angered hearing President Bush speak of a regime change in Iraq that everyone of voting age showed up early at the neighborhood polling station to wait in line to put a check mark in the yes box on the ballot. They tell me Saddam symbolizes nationalism and the defiance of Western powers. When I press them on Saddam's role in dragging them into the eight-year war with Iran and the invasion of Kuwait, which led to Operation Desert Storm in 1991 and resulted in UN-imposed sanctions, they fault the West, foreign meddling, and the U.S. desire to control Iraq's oil reserves.

"Voting yes wasn't so much yes to Saddam as it was no to Bush. 'No, you don't tell us how to run our country,' and 'No, you don't tell us who should be our president,'" says Sabah.

On one afternoon, I huddle with the Nassers around their old television set and watch a forty-minute broadcast of Saddam's latest speech. In a rare live television appearance, during his inauguration ceremony Saddam thanks the 11.4 million registered voters for giving him 100 percent of the vote in the October 15 national presidential referendum.

If Allah Almighty, in his great wisdom and for reasons beyond our comprehension, decides to put you again to the test of fighting on a large scale, then the Almighty, the nation, and history will expect you to deliver an effective stand. Afterward the enemy will fall on his face, despised, condemned, and defeated, while your banner, the banner of God Is Great, will continue to fly high on its nest, dignified and honorable. The road of blood takes you to more blood, and he who tries to shed the blood of others must expect his blood to be spilled.

Sabah moves closer to the screen and jacks up the volume. "He is saying Americans are being aggressive against Iraq for purposes of oil and Israel," he explains to me. "He is saying a lot of people in the world are with the people of Iraq."

They are surprised when I openly agree with some of their criticism of the United States and the Bush administration. Even in private, no one here dares to criticize the regime and hardly anyone admits that there are real problems in Iraq. I can't figure out if this stems from loyalty or denial. I am floored at how successful the regime has been with ingraining its version of truth into the Iraqi psyche. In conversations, nothing seems the fault of Saddam Hussein; Iraq is the eternal victim of Western powers after its oil and strategic geographic positioning near the Persian Gulf. This conspiracy-laden theory and sense of victimization is widespread in the Middle East, and it's commonly believed that a larger American, British, and Israeli hand is always at play shaping the political and social fabric of the Middle East according to its interests. History has unveiled enough evidence to support this idea—the CIA-funded 1959 coup in Iran that overthrew the democratically elected government of Prime Minister Mohammad Mossadegh and reinstalled the autocratic regime of Mohammad Reza Shah Pahlavi offers a potent example.

"Look, nobody is naive enough to think the Bush administration is coming to save them from the tyranny of Saddam," says Riad al-Taher, the British-Iraqi friend of the family. "The Americans are doing it for their own self-interest, and this makes people much more supportive of this regime," he said. Riad believes that Saddam's republic of fear is a homegrown phenomenon and that Iraqis only respond to fear and force. "Democracy won't flourish here with the change of the regime. This society is used to being ruled with fear and power. You have to demonstrate your power by showing you actually mean it for people to respect you."

I met both Riad and Sabah Nasser through my roommate Vivienne—who randomly ran into Riad at the Jordan border crossing—in the coffee shop of the Rasheed Hotel. Riad introduces himself to me as the chairman of an organization in Britain called Friendship Across Frontiers that aims to promote dialogue and peace with Iraq and lobbies for lifting the UN-imposed sanctions. On first impression he strikes me as a nationalist, even perhaps a regime loyalist eager to deter any military action against his home country. Riad is tall, dark-skinned, and well built, and his stylish clothes and leather shoes are giveaways that he lives abroad. Sabah, in contrast, is short and pudgy, with thick white hair and big blue eyes obscured by prominent glasses. He usually wears gray or brown suit trousers, a checkered shirt, and square-toed loafers.

We sit and chat in the café, with its dark blue velvet art-deco chairs and dim lights. As we sip Arabic coffee, I listen to the customary passionate debate offered by almost all Iraqis against the prospect of an American military attack. Riad lists the potential threats after the ensuing mayhem of an invasion and the policy crises that the United States will face in the Middle East.

Sabah clings to hope that the United Nations will step in to prevent war and Arab leaders will unite behind Saddam. All week he and his family have listened to the BBC and the Voice of America, which serve as their main source of news in the country. When the waiter isn't looking, he leans forward and in a barely audible whisper asks if I have any newsmagazines like *Newsweek* or *Time*. The third person in a week to request American magazines from me, Sabah offers yet another sign that despite praise for Saddam and his government, people don't trust the regime's censored information.

"The news this morning was good," says Sabah. "America won't attack Iraq until the UN Security Council allows it. I heard Colin Powell say war will be the last resort. Of course, we don't really believe what the Americans say," he adds. He estimates that the chance of an attack has dropped from 100 percent to "shall we say, 80 percent."

Riad doesn't hide the fact that he is sympathetic to and connected with the Iraqi regime. At one point he offers to secure an interview for me with then foreign minister Tariq Aziz. He boasts of arranging a visit to Iraq for antiwar members of the British parliament, including George Galloway, and Irish senators.

21

Years later, Riad's name is mentioned in association with the United Nations' oil-for-food program scandal. He is accused of receiving approximately 2 million barrels of oil while he was working as the Iraq consultant for Irish oil firm Bula Resources and making hefty payments of hundreds of thousands of dollars to the Iraqi government on its behalf, according to Western and Iraqi media reports.

At Sabah's house, I always assume Riad is closely monitoring my conversations. I have no way of knowing if he will report on me, but I'm mindful of the possibility and pick my topics carefully. On my numerous visits to the family's house, Riad advises me to ditch my driver and minder. He dismisses my anxiety as unfounded paranoia. When I tell him that my room is routinely searched, he laughs, assessing it as normal.

I grow accustomed to being ambivalent about my daily plans with my minder Mr. Nuri and my young driver, Ahmad. I tell Mr. Nuri to wait for me for an hour or so in the hotel lobby as I disappear for most of the day. I often return to find him dozing off in one of the lobby's big leather chairs.

When I approach he opens his eyes to scold me. "You have planted me again, Miss Farnaz," he says as he lifts his arms above his head. "I have grown leaves."

Riad usually sends his chauffeur to the hotel to whisk me away to Sabah's house in Adhamiya, a neighborhood that after the invasion will become a major battlefield between the Sunni insurgents and American forces. From the backseat of the black Mercedes, I make mental notes of all the landmarks we pass: the July 14 Bridge over the Tigris, a four-lane highway, the palace of Saddam's son Uday, right turn outside the exit, a square with a giant stone replica of an Arabic coffeepot and teacups, a bicycle shop and a right turn onto an alley directly across a riverfront mansion. I memorize these places because I'm almost certain the United States will invade Iraq. I need signs that can lead me to the Nasser family.

3

No Problem between Sunnis and Shiites

Early in the morning we set off for the holy twin cities of Najaf and Karbala, approximately 100 kilometers (about 60 miles) south of Baghdad, where two of Islam's most revered imams are buried. The sites attract thousands of Shiite pilgrims a day, many of them from Iran, Afghanistan, and beyond. Negotiating permission to travel on short notice was no easy task, as the government likes to dissuade reporters from venturing to the countryside, where monitoring is limited and interactions with Iraqis are less predictable. Requests to tour Shiite regions are particularly frowned upon because the population, which makes up nearly 60 percent of Iraq's 24 million, has a history of conflict with the ruling Baath party. Shiite animosity toward Saddam is no secret. In his twenty-three years of rule, the only incidents of domestic uprising have been led by Shiites, several times in Karbala and Najaf. The only real political opposition challenging the regime was in the form of Shiite clerics and Islamist Shiite political parties. These parties have long been outlawed and banned. The government and its secret police agents have been swift in crushing such uprisings, murdering prominent clerics, jailing their supporters, torturing their advocates, exiling tens of thousands of their sympathizers, and forcing other leading political dissidents into neighboring Iran.

The twin cities symbolize what the Sunni ruling class likes to deny: the oppression of the Shiite majority and its tendency toward political

Islam. So it's no surprise when my late-notice request to visit the cities is met with a good deal of resistance and shaking heads at the foreign press office of the Ministry of Information. It typically takes a few written requests, a detailed account of one's itinerary, and several visits to the chief, Mr. Hillal, to gain approval. I show up at his office late in the afternoon to make my case.

"I'm Iranian; I am a Shiite Muslim. I promised my grandmother I would go to Karbala," I tell him.

Mr. Hillal seems amused by this request; he eyes me up and down and says there is not enough time to organize a translator or issue an approval. I told him I would travel with the authorized team from *The New Yorker* and share a translator. Mr. Hillal pauses to consult with several men who are sipping tea with him. Like a number of bureaucrats I've encountered as a foreign correspondent, Mr. Hillal flat out denies my request with the thinly veiled excuse that I would simply be disappointed.

"It doesn't matter. I'd still like to go," I insist.

Throwing his best punch, he tells me: "You don't have the proper clothes for visiting the shrines. You can't go dressed like this." I am wearing black capri pants and a tailored short-sleeve blue shirt.

In my bag is an abaya, the head-to-toe black covering devout Arab women wear, which I have bought this afternoon as preparation for visiting the shrines. I pull out the rumpled piece of black nylon fabric from my purse.

"You mean I need this?" I ask.

A smile breaks out on Mr. Hillal's face. "You are a clever girl. Okay, I will let you go tomorrow if you put this on right now and let me see if you know how to wear it."

Asking me to model my Islamic hijab in his office is an inappropriate and creepy request, but it's too late for me to back down. I slip the cloth on my head and stand up before him.

"Now turn around. Very good." Without another word he signs a piece of paper authorizing my visit and stamps it with the government seal.

I have long wanted to visit the shrines, enticed by stories my grand-father had told me as a child about Imam Husayn's famous battle in the desert of Karbala in 680 CE. According to legend, Husayn, with seventy-two of his aids and family members, fought soldiers of Yazid, the second Umayyad caliph. The defining split in Islam dividing Sunni and Shiite is over the rightful successor of the prophet Muhammad. Shiites believe that Husayn's father, Ali, who was married to the prophet's daughter Fatima, inherited the dynasty and the faith. Sunnis claim it was the caliphs upon whom the mission was bestowed. In the battle of Karbala, Imam Husayn and his companions were massacred and beheaded in a brutal, bloody siege, their heads placed on staffs and paraded through Kufa and Damascus. Villagers living near the battlefield retrieved and buried their fallen bodies, whose deaths marked the legacy of martyrdom in Shiite Islam. Like his son's, Imam Ali's life came to an abrupt end when he was stabbed in Kufa while praying. Ali had instructed that upon his death, his body be mounted on a camel and set loose into the desert. His final resting place should be the first spot where the camel kneeled.

Initially, the burial sites of Ali and his son were nondescript tombs, but by mid-eighteenth century they had been transformed into glorious shrines that exemplified Islamic art and architecture. Deeply religious Persian sultans dispatched their most prized artists and calligraphers to grace the walls and ceilings of the shrines. Each shrine contains a treasure room that houses hundreds of priceless manuscripts and antiques of the Islamic golden age, bejeweled swords, daggers, ornamental boxes, and tiaras—gifts from royal Islamic courts from Persia to Constantinople.

Within the walled courtyard, which is adorned with blue mosaic tiles bearing golden calligraphy, we see hundreds of pilgrims praying, sleeping, and picnicking on flatbread and cheese in the shadow of the big golden dome. Occasionally, the words *"Allahu Akbar* [God is great]" are called loudly before a funeral procession. Men carry a wooden coffin draped in green cloth, and women wail behind them. It is considered a blessing for the soul if a corpse is taken around one of these shrines in loops, and the body is finally laid to rest at a huge Shiite cemetery nearby. Women clutch their toddlers to their chests, and the elderly limp alongside them.

We are eager for the chance to talk to some ordinary Shiites, but the minder brushes off our request by suggesting it would be impolite to disturb the pilgrims during their prayers. When we ask him if we can speak with the imam, the custodian of the shrine, he shuffles a few times between us and an office tucked away in a corner of the courtyard.

In the Karbala shrine, Shiites have come to pray. There is an air of melancholy here. Above one of the arched entrances, a tile within the blue and white pattern has been replaced with one that bears the image of Saddam Hussein. There are no pictures of Muhammad or his sons-in-law Ali and Husayn anywhere on the walls. In Islamic tradition, iconography is banned in mosques and holy shrines. I point this out to our minder, and he shrugs, offering a ridiculous explanation, "It's because President Saddam loves the Shiites and the shrines."

The pretense of solidarity with Shiites is more a gentle reminder that Saddam is the sole ruler of Iraq. Saddam bans Shiites from practicing Ashura, the ceremony that marks a ten-day period of mourning for Imam Husayn. In addition to limiting the opportunity for large, dramatic gatherings, the strict control of Shiite religious rituals is a way of keeping this mostly poor and underprivileged population marginalized. The Ashura rituals are intense and hypnotic: Men wearing black headbands walk in a procession, rhythmically beating their chests with chains. Some use daggers to make incisions in their shaved heads. Women watch from the outskirts of the crowd. Both men and women attend the mourning sermons, which are dramatic recitations and reenactments of the murder of Imam Husayn. Children carry jugs of cold water, which they splash on the men in the procession and offer up to them to drink.

Ashura is more than just a religious ceremony. It's a celebration of collective Shiite identity. In my secular household, Ashura was the only Islamic ceremony that my otherwise nonreligious relatives observed in Iran. Once a year, during the ten days leading up to Ashura, my grandfather oversaw a massive cooking production of *gheymeh polo*, a stew made of lamb meat and lentils served on white saffron rice, which was served by the plateful to poor families, passersby, and neighbors. Once, when I was about eight years old, my paternal grandmother took me to a *rouzeh* (the Ashura mourning ritual) with her, covering my head in a small black lace scarf, the kind that Sicilian mafia widows wear, and knotting it neatly under my chin. I wiggled uncomfortably on the floor next to her and pressed my hands against my lips to suppress the urge to giggle at the sight of such melodramatic displays of grief. My grandmother was mortified, shooting me disapproving looks and raising her eyebrows. Then she took my hands and whispered, "Stare at your thumb. Stare at your thumb carefully and hard. You will see the *mosibateh* [tragedy of] Imam Husayn and stop laughing." Even at that young age, I remember being astonished that my worldly grandmother with a college degree in Persian literature and a successful career as the principal of an elite Tehran school could believe the massacre of Imam Husayn and his family over one thousand years ago would play itself out on her granddaughter's thumbs.

Such is Ashura's hold on the Shiite psyche, a mixture of faith and superstition deeply indoctrinated by family, school, and society. In Shiism, imams are the necessary channels through which we must approach God in order to receive redemption from our sins, miracles for our woes, and blessings for our souls. And you are never closer to achieving these goals than when you stand at the site of an imam's tomb, where the imam's divine powers can encompass your soul.

My foreign companions, writer Jon Lee Anderson and photographer Thomas Dworzak, are forbidden from stepping inside the shrine because they are not Muslims. But I want to have a peek. Inside it is glorious and opulent. The insides of the giant wooden entrance doors have been gilded in gold and hand painted with delicate miniature flowers. The walls and ceilings are made of tiny, mirrored mosaic tiles that catch and reflect the light, multiplying images into eternity and producing the effect of an enormous kaleidoscope. I sweat under the burdensome abaya, which also causes me to trip over my feet and constantly slips off my head. I am very surprised that, unlike Iranian shrines, the shrine at Karbala is not segregated, and men and women participate in customary rituals (those that the regime allows) alongside one another. I inch closer to the gold-encased tomb and run my hands along its outer edge. The whiff of the rose water being splashed on pilgrims catches me. A young boy hands me tattered pieces of cloth the deep green of Shiite Islam and motions for me to rub it on the walls for blessing. I mimic the rituals carried out around me: I circle the shrine, caress the tomb gently with my fingers, press my forehead to the cool marble of the walls, and kiss the doors upon leaving. When I take out my camera and start snapping clandestine pictures of people praying, the minder, who is accompanying me, gives me a scolding frown. "That's not allowed," he says.

When I come out, I find Jon Lee and Thomas still waiting to see the imam. Finally the minder says it's a waste of time to hang around, as nobody has time today to talk to us. We drive to Najaf and briefly stop in the massive Shiite cemetery adjacent to Najaf, where our frantic minder hurries us along.

Throughout the day, I had exchanged a few stolen sentences with two people. Both times my minder rushed over, terrifying them into silence with his icy stares. On both occasions I spoke Farsi. My first encounter was with a young Iranian woman in the courtyard of the Imam Ali Shrine in Najaf.

"Salaam. Excuse me, are you from Iran?" I asked.

"Salaam. Yes, are you too?" she replied.

"Yes, but I'm here from America. I'm a journalist. Who are you here with?"

"I'm here with my husband's family. We came with an organized pilgrim tour from Tehran," she said.

"So have you had any interaction with Iraqis? How do they receive you?"

She shook her head, "*Na baba* [No way]. We were warned that we can't talk to anyone or step away from our group. They are watching us all the time. It's worse than Iran here."

I knew what she meant. In Iran, it takes about two seconds to gauge the pulse and the mood of the public as all, from taxi drivers to passersby, are eager to speak their minds about the regime. Before I could ask the woman more, I was interrupted by my minder, who came to tell me it was time to leave.

The second conversation I had was with a shopkeeper selling textiles just outside the Imam Ali Shrine in Najaf. His colorful shop with its bolts of velvet and silk intrigued me. After asking if I was Iranian, he switched to Farsi, which he'd learned from years of serving Iranian customers. After we exchanged greetings, he offered me a bottle of cold soda, which I gratefully accepted. He told me that his name was Ali Asghar, he was thirty-seven years old, and he was a native of Karbala. He had deep blue eyes and curly brown hair, and his family had owned this shop for over twenty years. They import fabric from China and Syria.

"Our business has improved a lot since Iran and Iraq agreed to allow pilgrims to travel here," he said.

I leaned over the counter and asked him in Farsi, "So are there any troubles between the Sunnis and Shiites here? Do they bother you?"

"No, no," he replied, his blue eyes widening. "No problem between Sunnis and Shiites. We are all brothers. No problem between Shiites and Saddam. No problem."

When my minder came to ask what we were talking about, I told him textiles. But Ali Asghar was visibly nervous. He reassured the minder that we were done speaking and that I was just about to leave.

▨ ▨ ▨

The opulence on display in the shrines is nowhere to be found in the streets. Karbala and Najaf are run-down and shabby. The roads are interrupted by puddles of sewage and potholes. Donkeys pull carts full of vegetables, and old men clad in long Arabic robes sit on the roadside, selling small bananas and trays of pastries dipped in sugar. The city has low buildings, many made of mud bricks, and narrow, unpaved alleyways.

The experience of the shrines sharply contrasts with our visit to Tikrit, Saddam Hussein's hometown in the Sunni Triangle, which resembles an affluent California suburb, its wide, well-paved streets lined with palm trees. The commercial buildings sport elaborate stone facades, while residents live in villas flanked with gardens and balconies. On the banks of the Tigris is Saddam's notorious palace compound. When Saddam refused entry to UN weapons inspectors to search the palace in February 1998, a breakdown between the United Nations and Iraq ensued, and a decade of sanctions followed. The UN inspectors believed Saddam might be hiding weapons of mass destruction in the Tikrit palace compound, a suspicion that was later invalidated when the Americans arrived to find only large, tacky, gold-plated furniture within. Saddam wanted to surround himself with people he could trust, and since a large part of his government hailed from Tikrit, it offered a degree of built-in security. Since the early 1970s, Saddam had fortified his position by recruiting members of his innermost circle from his tribe and young, loyal officers from his hometown.

We tour Tikrit and its surrounding areas on a visit organized by the Ministry of Information on the day of the referendum. When our busload of journalists passes the palace compound, we crane our necks, half standing to get a glimpse of its interior.

The minder announces, "No one really knows, but we hear that one of Saddam's wives [he has three] and his son live in this palace. His relatives also live in these palaces."

Unlike Karbala and Najaf, in Tikrit we are allowed to linger for a while. Everyone is willing to talk to us, and our minders are more than eager to translate. When our two buses, packed with journalists, arrive at polling stations, thousands of men, women, and children swarm around us chanting praise for Saddam. One woman shoved her newborn, bundled in a blanket, in front of a camera lens. By the ballot box, several people poked needles into their thumbs, smearing blood on the ballot as a pledge of support for Saddam. It's a formidable show that feels hard to believe.

I finally grab a middle-aged couple for a chat. Khalil Wahab is forty-eight years old and a retired army officer who fought in Saddam's army in both the Iran-Iraq war and the Gulf war. He and his wife arrived at the polling station at 9 AM. He, like most of the Iraqis I encounter here, is pro-Saddam. "Saddam is a true nationalist. He stands up to the West and to Israel. He has provided a lot of social services for our town. We have good hospitals, schools, and infrastructure. He has changed our lives for the better."

I wonder if Mr. Wahab has visited the Shiite south recently, where the good life Saddam created is sorely missing. "So are you willing to fight another war?" I ask.

"What kind of a question is that? Of course, yes. I will sacrifice my life for my country." He pauses for a second, shifting from foot to foot. "We don't want war. We really like peace. We know war, and it's a terrible tragedy."

A chorus of approval echoes from all the people interviewed: Saddam is the father of our nation, and we will die to protect him. In the afternoon, we are driven about an hour or so north to a tiny desert village called Atouz. The tribal chiefs have erected a massive tent near a polling station, and a hundred or so men from the tribe, all dressed in traditional Arab attire, are seated in rows of white plastic chairs. There are no women present. I sit next to an elderly man, Sheikh Sabah al-Aslan, chief of an ancient tribe called the Aslan, with more than a hundred thousand members scattered around the Salahedin district in northeast Iraq. He affirms that his tribe is ready to fight.

"We will all side against the Americans," the sheikh, who wears a long white traditional dress, gold bracelets, and a thin camel-colored robe trimmed with gold, tells me. When I ask him whether he ever thought there would be Western-style elections in Iraq, with more than one candidate on the ballot, he tells me no, "because Iraq is different than the West. Its religion, culture, and other aspects of life are different. We need a strong leader."

Which, I wonder, is the real Iraq? In my short stay here, I've seen two starkly different sides: the Shiites' dead silence, seeking salvation from the imams, and the Sunnis' roaring devotion to Saddam. Back at the Rasheed Hotel, I pose this question to Wamidh Nadhmi, a professor of political science at Baghdad University. My conversation with Wamidh is the most

31

candid I've had in Iraq. To avoid being overheard by hotel staff, who walk past us every few minutes with a tray of sweets, we both lean forward in our chairs and practically whisper as we sip coffee.

"The Shiite strongholds, especially in the south, are not happy with the situation at all," Wamidh says. "You also have many people who are liberal democrats and leftists and rightists. To pretend the entire nation loves Saddam Hussein and voted for him is an exaggeration at best and a lie at worst. Iraqis have always been intellectuals and thinkers, and of course there are voices of disagreement.

"People feel alienated from the government because they are not consulted about anything. They are called upon to elect, called upon to join the army, called upon to cheer. No one is ever called upon to give their opinion. People here are living double lives. The same person who feels deeply dissatisfied and marginalized will sing songs to praise the regime because he wants to keep his life and feed his family. There are no pure revolutionaries or radicals here, and on the other hand, there are no pure supporters either. Things get mingled in between."

I ask Wamidh about political dissent in Baghdad and whether he sees any political fervor building up among his students. In Iran, the biggest threat to the regime comes from college student activists critical of the regime's claim over a populist revolution that meant to replace a tyrant with democracy. But there's no criticism in Iraq.

"The climate is too dangerous, the risks too high for such open and direct discussions about the regime; but the students find other ways."

As an example, Wamidh points to a lively debate about the lack of democracy in the Arab world in a thesis dissertation of a candidate for a PhD in political science. "It was a provocative subject. We were really arguing about this regime but without really touching on it directly. The 'Arab world' idea provided a safe umbrella for discussions."

Why, Wamidh wonders, doesn't the Bush administration confront or punish Saudi Arabia, Egypt, or Syria for their harsh treatment of dissidents or for their lack of democratic reforms? "If you say Saddam is a dictator, I agree with you," he continues. "But show me one example of democratic regime in the Arab world. Saddam was America's best friend until 1990. What has changed? He's still the same guy with the same policies. He was no less of a dictator back then. And if they remove Saddam from power, who will they put in his place? The people the Americans are talking to haven't stepped foot in Iraq for decades; they are completely out of touch."

If Iraqis are hesitant to discuss their true opinions on Saddam's regime, they make up for it by voicing anxiety over what or who will come next. Even in Iran, student activists and reformist dissidents are always quick to distance themselves from foreign opposition groups, whom they dismiss as opportunists out of touch with their country. I find that this sort of bitterness runs far deeper than the question of political leadership. Similar to Iranians, the Iraqis who stayed behind feel that they have endured much hardship and suffering. Those with cash and better connections left the country. They resent the idea that expatriates should be rewarded for abandoning their country. The Iraqi expatriate opposition is a mishmash of ethnic and political groups with equally diverse goals and visions of how to rule a new Iraq. Its leaders include Jalal Talabani and Massoud Barzani, heads of two major Kurdish parties known for their long separatist struggles with Baghdad; Ahmed Chalabi, a banker who heads a London-based coalition called the Iraqi National Congress; Ayatollah Mohammed Baqir Hakim, head of the Supreme Council for the Islamic Revolution in Iraq, a Shiite Muslim group based in Iran; Ayad Alawi of the Iraqi National Accord, a Sunni Muslim organization reputed to have links with the CIA; and Adnan Pachachi, a former Iraqi official reported to be a favorite of the U.S. State Department.

Almost unanimously Iraqis tell me that America will initially win the military war but will face a fierce resistance for establishing peace. The exiled opposition, with its varying agenda, will pull Iraq further apart.

4

If You Like It,
I Can Make You
a Good Price

I have found a tranquil sanctuary in Baghdad, in the heart of the bustling commercial Rasheed Street. I escape to Beit al-Iraqi, an old Ottoman mansion that has been transformed into a center for Iraqi art and culture. Here I recline on a big wicker chair shaded by banana and palm trees, in a courtyard perfumed by hibiscus and violet. Along the Tigris, I spend hot afternoons, which wear off into breezy sunsets as the pace of the gallery ebbs and flows. Iraqi artists and intellectuals leisurely drift in and out, providing me a rare chance to socialize. Visitors are served a tasteful tray of refreshments that include cookies stuffed with walnuts and dates, a hot pot of brewed mint tea, and fresh lemonade flavored with rose water. It is the only place in Iraq where I feel joyfully free and unchoked by the paranoid psyche of Iraqis who fear Saddam. Occasionally foreigners wander in to check out an exhibition or to buy souvenirs. Each room displays a specific Iraqi handicraft: baskets woven from palm leaves, handwoven tribal carpets and textiles made of goat and camel hair, brilliantly painted ceramic tiles.

Amal al-Khudeiry, in her late sixties, owns and operates the center, which was built by her father at the turn of the twentieth century as a family residence. When I first stroll in to introduce myself on the recommendation of a friend, Amal greets me with a tight embrace.

"I feel like I've known you all my life. It must be because you are from the East. The heart connects, you know," she says.

Before traveling to Iraq, I was anxious as to how Iraqis would react to my Iranian heritage, given the countries' history of opposition. But so far, my encounters have been pleasant. Even the hotel staff members go out of their way to tell me of the kinship between Iranians and Iraqis. When they learn that I spent part of my childhood and young adulthood in Iran and still have close relatives living there, my American identity starts to fade. I'm no longer viewed as a westerner from a privileged nation with little understanding of their sufferings and traditions.

I admire Amal's feisty independence and her desire to preserve her culture. The day I meet her, she is wearing an elegant brown skirt and shirt and a beautiful silver necklace made of round balls. Amal, who was raised in a wealthy Sunni household, has led a privileged life, attending elite Baghdad schools run by missionary American nuns before going abroad to universities in England and Switzerland. She is a widow and the mother of a son, who lives in Dubai. She has dedicated much of her adult life to tracing and preserving folk art and to empowering poverty-stricken women. Her shoulder-length chestnut-brown hair is always well styled. When she gets sad or angry, usually when we are discussing the possibility of war with the United States, she presses her lips tightly together. Amal's fluency in foreign languages and her worldliness don't amount to much love for Western countries. In her younger days, she felt idealistic about the West, about its democracy, free press, and respect of human rights. Over the years, the wars she's lived through, and particularly the double-standard foreign policy of the United States toward the Middle East—where ideals are overlooked in favor of interests—have stripped her bare of that idealism.

"My love attraction to the West has ended. My generation was so much more connected to the West. We came back to our country and brought with us the idealism we learned in the universities abroad, but none of it has materialized."

She is outspokenly patriotic, and it's perhaps because of this trait that she mingles freely with the small foreign community in Baghdad, frequently hosting diplomats and the staff members of foreign nongovernmental organizations for classical music concerts, poetry readings, lectures, and exhibitions at her center. She is seemingly unafraid of the regime's punishment for unsupervised contact with foreigners. Amal insists that she has nothing to hide and her contact with foreigners is strictly cultural.

When we talk about politics and the overall situation in Iraq, Amal offers no answers, only a barrage of questions. "Tell me, can you bring democracy with bombs and guns? Do they think Iraq is a backward country like Afghanistan? Americans can just do whatever they want? Do they even know Iraq? How to rule it? Their Iraqi advisers have not been to this country for thirty years. Tell me, what do they know of our suffering? Would the Americans like it if some other nation went and told them what to do, how to rule the country, live their lives? What have we done to deserve this?" Her eyes well up with tears as she takes a deep breath and steadies herself against the wall. Her assistant, a young woman who is a university art major, rushes over and hands her a glass of cold water. "Relax, sit down, *khaleh* [auntie], sit down," she says to Amal.

Amal takes a few sips, sits next to me, and continues, "I am not scared, not really. I am very worried about what will become of our future. I have worked so hard to rebuild my life here. I have twice renovated this center by borrowing money from family and friends. People's livelihoods depend on this place; what am I going to do? Where will I get the money and the energy to start from scratch if everything is destroyed? Every time we try to do something, to move on, to live our lives, we are threatened and stopped."

As Amal descends into rage, her tough nationalist demeanor quickly disappears. A vulnerable old woman, whose entire existence is intertwined with a way of life that may soon cease to exist, emerges in its place.

Beit al-Iraqi was the first of its kind when it opened in 1987. During its first years, Amal traveled to remote villages around the country, seeking folk handicrafts and offering villagers incentives to preserve their dying arts. She bought as many pieces as she could and encouraged villagers to send their goods to her center. As word spread in remote communities, old men and women and young artists arrived at her doorstep with their art. Eventually Amal began holding weekly classes for underprivileged women to teach them sewing, weaving, and embroidery. Many of the women lacked education and income. They were widows of Iraq's many wars, faced with heading households of children. Under Amal's guidance, Iraq's artistic society began to emerge. Villagers formed an association for craftsmen and craftswomen; architects founded a society for urban preservation; collectors of stamps, currency, and calligraphy formed interest groups.

Amal's center, which caters to foreign clients, serves as a vital life link between Iraqi artists and the outside world. In the 1950s, Iraqi artists studied in Europe and Turkey and imparted their knowledge to a generation of younger artists upon their return. But sanctions and isolation have left Iraqi communities cut off from the rest of the world.

"Iraqi society is dynamic and ferocious," she tells me. "We are not all divided along the stereotypical lines the West likes to portray. We have thousands of years of culture and history. It's our only asset, and it's what pushes us to the future."

After meeting Amal, I visit an array of privately owned art galleries and state-run museums. Here I discover a thriving vein of abstract modern paintings and sculptures that makes no reference to the country's tormented history of war and suffering. Political art is virtually nonexistent.

Baghdad's art scene is divided into two groups: a cluster of rickety wholesale shops selling arabesque landscapes and Saddam portraits, and a strip of privately owned galleries showcasing art by promising young artists and old hands. The former is located in Sharaa Aswa, a middle-class neighborhood, where all artists are men whose work is often ugly and unoriginal. Most of their time is spent painting Saddam, whose iconographic proliferation is part of his personality cult. One of the artists I speak with paints as many as a dozen portraits of Saddam a week. He charges fifty dollars for the life-size portraits, most of which are purchased by the government, hotels, and the army. The government has even sponsored an annual contest for the best likeness of Hussein, and a giant exhibition of the entries is held each year in Baghdad. With a dearth of local sales, artists have been forced to send some Arab landscapes to Syria and Jordan.

The more upscale art galleries are located on Abu Nawas Street near the Palestine Hotel, where old houses with high ceilings and whitewashed walls showcase abstract and figurative paintings by up- and-coming young artists. Surprisingly, the private gallery owners refrain from hanging state propaganda-style portraits of Saddam. The art they showcase is mostly composed in earthy reds, browns, and oranges and pastel blues and greens. Despite the lack of overt political messages, this art offers relief from a shifting regime.

When I visit galleries, the curators' eyes follow my steps. When I linger at a stall to admire a piece, their sense of anticipation is unmistaken. "If you like it, I can make you a good price," they all say.

I visit Baghdadi Center, an antique store run by one of Sabah's friends, a sixty-seven-year-old Shiite named Adel Baghdadi, whose family has owned the business for two generations. When I ask the price of an old handwoven kilim, unique to Iraqi tribes, Adel responds with poise and dignity.

"It's fifty dollars, but I can give it to you for thirty-five."

Too guilt ridden to accept a discount, given my relative wealth, I buy two for one hundred dollars. Every Friday afternoon Adel holds an auction. Recently most of the auctioned goods have been from Iraqi families rather than dealers. Everyone is desperate for cash.

"We used to travel to Iran, Turkey, and Egypt and shop for antiques. This is the 1970s I am telling you about, because now we feel like we are in prison. We can't go anywhere, because it's very, very expensive, and nobody will give us visas. But before the war, Iraqis were proud people. We held up our heads very high when we traveled," Adel tells me with a worried expression.

When he is wrapping up my carpet, he wishes me a good trip back to the States. We shake hands. "I hope there is no war, and you all remain safe," I offer.

"Our destiny is in God's hands, but for now we are very afraid of America," replies Adel.

Before my trip ends, Amal and her assistant give me a whirlwind tour of Baghdad. As we stop at landmarks and museums, Amal narrates the historical importance of each site. We eat kebabs, grilled tomatoes, and fresh baked bread in a caravansary, a roadside inn that was once a stopover for merchants en route to China on the Silk Road. As I hear the lull of Amal's voice, I think to myself that she is clinging to Baghdad the way one holds tightly to a loved one who's about to die.

The Americans
Call It the New Iraq,
but the Iraqis Call
It the Situation

5

Sulaimaniyah,
Northern Iraq

I *have been* in Iraq for the buildup of the war and the aftermath for almost three months. I am here with my partner, Babak Dehghanpisheh, a correspondent with *Newsweek* magazine. We met at a dumpy hotel called Hotel Success in the middle of the war in Herat, Afghanistan, in 2001. Babak is half Iranian, half American. Like me, he left Iran when he was ten years old, after the revolution and war. On one of our first dates, we survived a near-stampede in an overcrowded and overcharged refugee camp by pressing our bodies together as the crowd shoved us this way and that. Babak grabbed me and instructed, "Hold on to me, and don't let go." At night we'd sometimes sit on our balcony holding hands, our heads covered with helmets, watching AK-47 tracers light up the sky. Babak chopped wood and fed a fire in an oven to keep us warm at night. We read Persian poetry and literature from antique, handwritten volumes we found in a Kabul bookstore and told each other our favorite fairy tales from our childhoods. Our connection was intense; we fell in love against the backdrop of chaos and misery from one war zone to the next. When the drum roll to invade Iraq began beating in Washington, we knew we wanted to cover the war. I joined *The Wall Street Journal* as Middle East correspondent and was immediately dispatched to northern Iraq. Babak had arrived the previous week.

It's spring in Kurdistan. Yellow daffodils dance in the wind on rolling hills carpeted in fresh grass.

Today, April 9, 2003, Baghdad fell to American troops. Saddam is toppled.

The Americans have finally completed the unfinished task of the first Gulf war.

When I step out of the elevator of the Sulaimaniyah Palace Hotel where we have been staying, the cleaning ladies are shrieking with joy. They are holding each other's hands, waving towels in the air, doing the Kurdish dance: one step forward, one back in unison, a mini kick in the air as shoulders jiggle up and down. A cart of clean linens sits abandoned in the hallway. Images of Baghdad even I can't believe skip across the TV screen. A dancing crowd in a Shiite neighborhood is ripping down a poster of Saddam Hussein; another man slams his sandals on Saddam's picture. The regime no longer controls the capital. One of the cleaning ladies grabs my arm, stuffs a pillowcase into my hand, and starts waving my arms up and down, motioning for me to dance with her.

"*Zoor khosheh, zoor zoor khosheh* [I am very, very happy]," she repeats over and over in Kurdish. "Saddam *tamam* [finished]." She then kisses my cheeks. "I thank you. I thank you. Thank you, America. Thank you, Mr. Bush."

She drags me to the balcony of one of the rooms facing the street, and together we twirl our pillowcases in the air, jumping from joy. Below us, in the square leading to the bazaar, a spontaneous celebration erupts. Cars honk their horns, shotguns fire into the air, lively Kurdish music blasts, shopkeepers hand out sweets, and hundreds of men and women dance on the sidewalks and children clap and wave a makeshift map of Kurdistan, which includes land in the Kurdish areas of Iran, Syria, Iraq, and Turkey. When two SUVs carrying American Special Forces slow to a halt, people grab the sleeves and hands of the American servicemen, yelling in English, "I love you!" and "Thank you!"

The Kurds could not have wished for a better outcome for this war. The military end to the invasion was swift. Saddam didn't direct his mortars and bombs to the north, as everyone feared. The Kurds' land, stretching over mountains and rivers in northern Iraq, was spared from a ground invasion by American troops and a much-dreaded intervention by Turkish forces. Kurdish hatred for Saddam runs deep. An ethnic group of roughly five million, the Kurds were brutally persecuted under Saddam's regime for seeking independence and autonomy from the central government in Baghdad. One of Saddam's most notorious, well-documented atrocities was gassing the Kurdish village of Halabjah in 1988—instantly murdering five thousand innocent residents, many of them children and elderly. Over seventeen months, Saddam's helicopters sprayed poison gas across more than two hundred towns and villages across northern Iraq in a ruthless sweep that destroyed livestock, farms, and agriculture. As part of Saddam's cease-fire agreement with coalition forces, a "no fly zone" was established in the north to protect the Kurds against the regime, and an autonomous Kurdish zone came into existence and flourished.

Now the Kurds are free. Saddam is gone.

Several hours after the news breaks, a crowd charges into the lobby of our hotel, gathering around a big-screen television broadcasting live images of Ferdous Square in Baghdad, where American troops are wrapping a rope around Saddam's statue, covering his face with an American flag.

"I have been waiting for this moment for thirty years," says Rahman, a forty-five-year-old man sitting next to me. "I never thought I would see it in my lifetime and never even dared to dream it."

The statue comes crashing down. The crowd cheers and jumps to its feet. Around me, Kurds are crying, laughing, clapping. What will happen next? I can't help but think that what comes afterward will be more important than the day's celebrations.

6

Kirkuk

The city is burning. Government buildings are ransacked. Shops and markets are torched and set ablaze. Walls and doors of commercial properties are axed apart. Swarms of men, many wearing baggy Kurdish pants, wave guns or wooden sticks and sporadically attack the first car or building in sight. A manic expression is frozen on their faces.

The mayhem is unmatched by anything I've seen in my experience as a war correspondent. I watch in disbelief as a crowd storms a school, strips the blackboards off the walls, breaks up wooden desks, and smashes the classroom windows. At Kirkuk's main hospital, looters shove patients off beds, pull IV needles violently out of their arms, and carry out whatever equipment they can muster. The highway leading out of the city is packed with trucks and vans loaded with looted merchandise. Some of the items are useful, but many are absurd gains; the pumping machine from a gas station, or a broken X-ray machine. The Kurdish Peshmerga soldiers manning the checkpoint entrances in and out of Kirkuk make no effort to stop the looters.

We have rushed here amid a chaotic scene of thousands of Kurdish Peshmerga fighters dashing, on foot and in cars, across the frontline hills that separate northern Kurdish areas from Iraq proper. By morning we have received news that Iraqi forces have abandoned their bases. So much for Americans and Kurdish commanders controlling the Peshmerga takeover of Kirkuk.

The Kurds call Kirkuk the Jerusalem of Kurdistan. Like Jerusalem, the city has captivated many hearts and eluded all who have laid claim to it. Kirkuk's recorded history, which extends to the fifth century BC, has, like the rest of Iraq, been plagued by ethnic, religious, and tribal rivalries. Once, Kurds were the dominating population of Kirkuk. For more than eighty years, various Sunni Muslim–dominated governments of Iraq forced the Kurds and Turkomens, a smaller Iraqi minority, out of Kirkuk. Saddam formalized the process with an "Arabization" policy that prohibited Kurds in Kirkuk from property transactions or from registering for marriages or businesses. Under Saddam's regime, Kurds were required to change their ethnicity from Kurd to Arab on all official documentation. But with an Arabic name, a Kurdish man or woman could enjoy the same rights as other Iraqi citizens.

It has long been the Kurdish dream to reclaim Kirkuk and declare it the capital of an imaginary Kurdistan, a land connecting the Kurdish-inhabited areas of Iran, Iraq, Turkey, and Syria.

When Kirkuk fell today, April 10, 2003, the Kurds took over with a vengeance. Celebrations soon gave way to anarchy and chaos.

Around noon, we are standing in the town square, watching Kurds riddle murals of Saddam with bullets and bring down his statue, and a middle-aged man approaches us for help. A Christian pharmacist named Esmat Yousef, he had been held at gunpoint by Kurds demanding his car keys.

"This is a very critical time now, and we are happy Saddam has fallen, but we live in fear. The Americans need to restore law and order right away, before it's too late," Yousef warns us.

But the American forces are strangely absent. I spot a handful of American Special Forces only twice today: once at the Kirkuk governor's office, where senior Kurdish commanders and their entourages have swiftly taken control, and once at the oil fields near the city outskirts.

When Babak and I drive to the city's oil fields, some of the largest in Iraq, we find them completely deserted. The ground is littered with tanks, guns, and military artillery left behind by the fleeing Iraqi army. We cautiously walk toward a fence near the pipelines. A team of four or five

American Special Forces guys appears as if out of nowhere, jumps out of unmarked SUVs, and runs to the pipelines to examine them. With them, we kneel to check for damage to the pipes, when we come under fire.

"Duck, duck your heads; lay on the ground; crawl to your cars!" one of the Special Forces guys shouts at us. We hit the ground, then run half bent to our cars, our movement slowed by the weight of flak jackets and helmets. The Special Forces team fires back. We can't know if it's Iraqi soldiers hiding in the distance or armed looters. The shooting subsides only when our car speeds out of sight.

When night falls, the smells and sounds of the fallen city are overbearing. Ash- and gunpowder-filled air makes us cough. Families who were celebrating the fall of the regime earlier in the day are now barricaded behind locked doors. I dictate my story to my editor on a satellite phone, repeating each sentence several times in order to be heard above the sounds of explosions, screaming, gunfire, and breaking glass. At night, we sleep on the floor of a Kurdish family's house because the city's two hotels are overbooked with reporters. Rahman, our Kurdish driver, sleeps in the car to ward off looters. The same frightening cycle repeats itself in each Iraqi city as coalition forces advance. From Basra to Baghdad and now to Kirkuk, the U.S. assault leads to the regime's collapse, and celebration turns into looting and mayhem.

I am furious when I hear that Defense Secretary Donald H. Rumsfeld in Washington D.C. defended the Americans' lack of interference with Iraqi looting by dismissing it as being part of a free country. Rumsfeld quipped, "It's untidy. And freedom's untidy. And free people are free to make mistakes and commit crimes."

7

Tikrit

Saddam's hometown fell to the American marines with a whimper. Contrary to expectations, Saddam's Republican Guard troops and the residents of his hometown neither put up a fight nor celebrated. When Americans rolled into the city, they were met with deafening silence and closed doors. When we arrive a day later, the city looks almost devoid of life. Shop windows are shuttered. Saddam's murals still loom large over the city at every traffic light and smaller posters of him dangle from every lamppost. The bronze statue of him riding his horse stands proudly in the town square.

Graffiti in blue paint on a wall reads in Arabic, "We love you and are loyal to you, our leader Saddam."

Outside of a mosque, a black banner bears the names of Iraqi "martyrs" who died fighting the Americans in the past few weeks. The atmosphere is tense. We encounter our first scary situation almost immediately upon reaching the bridge that leads to Saddam's palace, where the U.S. marines are bunkering down. The bridge is bombed out; one side has collapsed into the river, and now only one car can pass through at a time. As we approach, a mob of angry Arab men carrying sticks and AK-47s makes its way toward our car. Within a few minutes, we are swarmed. They smash the sticks and rifles against the windows, shouting in Arabic, "Infidels, we will kill you! America, go home!"

We are paralyzed with fear.

"*Sahafi! Sahafi!*" we manage to shout, using the Arabic word for "journalist," but to no avail.

Our Kurdish translator, Ranj, cracks open his window an inch, yelling in his accented Arabic, "*Sahafi* Swedish! *Sahafi* Swedish!" Babak and I certainly look nothing like Swedes, but it's the first neutral country that springs to his mind.

The mob picks up on his Kurdish accent, screams, "Kurds! Kurds!" and begins banging harder, firing into the air. On the other side of the bridge, the marines notice the commotion and rush to our rescue. They disperse the crowd and guide our car safely into Saddam's palace compound.

The marines we speak to report on the population's sullen and hostile reaction to them. Already a car bomb has been discovered—and defused—planted in a car on the same bridge we have just crossed.

After touring Saddam's palaces like Alice in Wonderland and picnicking in one of Saddam's rose gardens on M.R.E. (Meals Ready to Eat) from the soldiers, we drive around the city, against the marines' advice. Further up the road, away from Saddam's palace, we notice Americans driving truckloads of weapons out of Salahedin Military Hospital. Following the trucks, we discover that an entire wing of the hospital is packed from floor to ceiling with tens of thousands of AK-47s, machine guns, and other artillery belonging to the Iraqi army. One room stores hundreds of gas masks and atropine injections, used to treat victims of a chemical attack. A few Iraqi doctors hang about, watching marines pile the weapons onto trucks. They appear completely unfazed at their army's decision to use a hospital as a weapons warehouse.

"It's normal," says Dr. Bassem Mohammad, a forty-five-year-old pathologist who bunkered down at the hospital for the duration of the war.

When I ask him what he thinks of the Americans' arrival in Tikrit, he dismisses it as damaging. "All Iraqi people think this is an invasion," he tells me. "It's insulting. Any human being would like to change a bad system himself, not have another army come and do it. Our future is gloomy."

We knock on the door of Iraqi general Ahmad Tikriti, a thickly built man with a bushy moustache; after he answers, we invite ourselves inside.

Over dark, bitter tea, Babak and I chat with the general about the fight in Baghdad and his feelings for Americans. Until the day Baghdad fell, he had been commanding a unit in the city. It wasn't until the chain of command broke and his underlings abandoned their posts that he realized it was all over. The general also fled, walking and hitchhiking up to Tikrit. We are shocked when the man begins to cry, repeating in broken sobs that his country was "defeated, and not liberated," and that he is "watching the end of Iraq."

When he composes himself, General Tikriti asks why Americans are in Iraq. "They destroyed our country, ruined our government and everything we had, and now we have to thank them? We don't want them here. *Khalas. Tamam. Yallah.* [The end. Finished. Go.] Go back."

On our way back to the palace, we stop to chat with three men standing outside a shop. Ali Jabouri, the forty-year-old shopkeeper, has come to check on his property. He points to the pictures of Saddam still hanging above the cash register and says, "We don't want anyone to touch those pictures and statues of Saddam. They are memories of Saddam. He was brave and courageous. America is occupying our homeland. It's come into our city and our homes. They are not liberators. They are monsters."

"Will you give the Americans a chance? Maybe things will be better than before," I ask.

The younger man standing next to him, with black eyes and a black unibrow, looks at me intensely. His name is Ahmad Aboudy, and he is thirty years old. He says, "The people now are waiting for what will happen next. If soldiers stay longer, yes, Iraq will be Palestine. Intifada will happen here. Jihad will happen here. But it will be larger than Palestine. Bigger than the Americans can imagine."

On day two of Tikrit's "liberation" Sunnis are throwing around profound words like *intifada, jihad,* and *resistance.* I underline these words in red in my notebook at night. I've been reporting in the Arab world long enough to recognize that the minute such wobbly ideas are put into action, the American efforts in Iraq will be futile.

8

Baghdad

T*he American military* is on full display. The troops have taken over some of the city's most renowned landmarks: the Republican Palace compound, the Convention Center, the Rasheed Hotel, and Baghdad's international airport. Americans patrol the streets and highways in big convoys of Humvees or loner tanks. The roaring tanks leave permanent imprints in the cement. For some reason, this particularly irks my newly hired translator-and-driver team, Haqqi and Munaf, two young Sunni men who are street-savvy, story-smart, and amiable.

"Look, Farnaz, look," Haqqi points out to me each time we see a tank. His voice fills with anger. "They are destroying our roads. They are ruining our city. Who will fix it? Why do they do this?"

"Americans don't care. They are not here for us. They want their own benefits. Why the only place that wasn't destroyed is the oil ministry? They couldn't stop the looters destroying our museums, libraries, and other buildings? They don't care," Munaf adds in his calm voice as he steers the car to the side to let the tanks pass.

Haqqi is *The Wall Street Journal's* principal translator and office manager. Plumpish, light-skinned, of medium height, and slightly buck-toothed, Haqqi has a receding hairline, a round, pudgy face, and a patch of white hair the size of a quarter, which is a birthmark. At twenty-six, he displays a pride grander than his age. Haqqi, who comes from a Tikriti clan, enjoyed a privileged life alien to most of his countrymen. His father served as an ambassador in Turkey, France, Hungary, and Pakistan, and so Haqqi was educated in international schools. While his conversational English is impeccable, his written English is peppered with grammatical mistakes. His mocking sense of humor and open resentment of Americans are tiresome, and occasionally I lose my patience with his constant complaints. Munaf is our main driver. At twenty-five, he has movie-star good looks; he is tall and well built, with a boyish smile and a genuine kindness that makes you trust him immediately. Munaf was a gifted student, and finished first in his class majoring in chemistry. He aspires to become either a medical doctor or a researcher. On the subject of Americans, Munaf is ambivalent. On principle he is opposed to the occupation, but he also sees that opportunities have opened up for his generation with the fall of Saddam.

Listening to these men, I realize the Sunnis will never be won over in this war. It is still early enough in this adventure that the prospect of a better Iraq is still a possibility, but I am yet to meet a Sunni willing to give the invaders the benefit of a doubt.

In these early days, we see the American soldiers move about the capital with ease and confidence. Sometimes the soldiers park their cars at intersections and venture around the neighborhoods on foot for hours, shaking hands with residents or exchanging greetings with a few who speak English. It's not uncommon for soldiers to lean nonchalantly on their military vehicles, machine guns slinging from their arms as they hand out candies and chocolate bars to bemused Iraqi children. On a few occasions, I even spot the soldiers buying sodas and snacks from Warda, a supermarket that's newly stocked with imported Western goods from Amman, Jordan.

Postinvasion Baghdad simmers with the excitement of newfound freedom and stagnates with an underlying sense of loss and defeat.

The city is decidedly more free-spirited than I remember from my last visit before the war. Iraqis are no longer afraid to tell me what they think—be it good or bad—about the war and its aftermath. I notice that when they talk, their shoulders are relaxed and the pitch of their voices ebbs and flows. The formerly panicked looks and tensed neck muscles at the mere mention of Saddam's name have vanished.

Satellite dishes are mounted on rooftops by the dozen as the nation slowly opens itself up to the world. Every morning, hordes of Iraqis flock to the hotels where American journalists and nonprofit organizations' staff members are staying and form long lines outside American military bases to hunt for jobs and contracts.

Former employees of the information ministry—whose jobs under the former regime mostly involved the minding and monitoring of journalists—have reinvented themselves as agents of a free press. In the new Iraq, they offer their services as translators, guides, and assistants.

Baghdad, one of the Arab world's most ancient capitals and one that stirs Arab pride the world over, has fallen to a foreign army. The lingering sense of defeat announces itself in the bombed-out, dilapidated government ministries and institutions scattered around the city. The dissolution of the armed forces is physically expressed in the ruins of the capital. Religious leaders are stepping up to fill the hollow vacuum left by a collapsed government. Shiite clerics are replacing secular technocrats—the Baathists now deposed. The streets are policed by neighborhood volunteer task forces commissioned by local mosques. Every home is now armed.

At the gun market, machine guns, hand grenades, and rocket-propelled grenades are piled up neatly on the sidewalk like knickknacks at a garage sale.

The United States now controls Iraq. It has invaded an oil-rich Muslim country in the name of democracy and freedom. It has vowed, to the world, that Iraq will be molded into a shining example of unity and an Arab democracy in a region that's rife with autocratic rulers. The Americans call it the New Iraq, and the Iraqis call it the Situation.

This Isn't
the Way It Was
Supposed to Be

9

I Can Bring
Back the Dead

The wooden door of Abou Mouaya's house creaks open as Haqqi and I
step inside a darkly lit room adorned with Quranic verse. Haqqi tells
me that the name Abou Mouaya means "mirror man," a nickname for a
person with the supernatural power to locate the missing and recall the
dead. The house has three rooms and a small kitchen. The living room,
sparsely furnished with a wooden bench and a sofa chair, doubles as a
waiting area during the day for the anxious clients who arrive in hordes.
From the ceiling, a fan hangs motionless until electricity, cut off in regular
intervals, whirrs it back to power. The air is stifling hot and heavy with the
smell of sweat and feet and the residual smoke of cheap cigarettes. A stack
of shoes is piled next to the door (it's customary in the Arab world to remove
one's shoes before entering a house). The women sit together on the floor,
their legs folded beneath them and their long skirts and abayas stretched
like puffed-up tents over their curves. Some bounce restless kids—all
boys—on their laps. (Abou Mouaya uses preadolescent boys as mediums
to channel his visions). It's only May, but desert summer heat has arrived.
I fan myself with my reporter's notebook, and Haqqi and I ask the families why they are here.

One old man is desperate for news about his twenty-year-old son,
Rafaat, who left home on April 7, while the war was raging in Baghdad,
and still hasn't returned. A young widow in tears beats her chest as she

wonders aloud about the fate of her husband, Mohsen, who vanished in 1980 after Mr. Hussein's government arrested him on charges of involvement with a Shiite political party plotting to topple Saddam. A middle-aged taxi driver from a Baghdad suburb admits that he is a little ashamed hearing other people's stories since he only wants to find the blue Toyota Corolla that was stolen from him at gunpoint last week. In these early weeks after the collapse of regime, chaos defines each day. Hope and despair are close cousins as people scramble to improvise. Every Iraqi I meet is searching for something or someone. One day, we come across a procession of mothers howling and holding up pictures of their missing sons as they wander like gypsies outside prisons, hospitals, and the city's main morgue. In a plot of land near the town of Hilla, where Shiite mass graves were unearthed, we stand in a corner and watch a man dig up unmarked graves with his bare fingers, pushing aside the dirt to fetch the skeletal remains of his younger brother.

No one can accurately account for Saddam's victims because his regime did not log its crimes. The scopes of the regime's crimes against humanity, for which Saddam will eventually stand trial and be executed, are mind-boggling. During twenty-four years of rule, Saddam committed genocide against his own people, murdered political and ideological opponents—including his family members—and scores of clerics. Prisoners were brutally tortured and hundreds of thousands of people went missing. Of his citizens he required the kind of blind loyalty that allowed no room for questioning his motives.

After Saddam's fall, the depth of the regime's crimes is told as Iraqis step forward. No interim government is yet in place, although the Iraqi opposition groups returned from exile will soon form a temporary governing body, the governing council handpicked and supervised by Americans. The Americans aren't much of a help to desperate Iraqi civilians since they are much preoccupied with conceiving a plan for their occupation. By all accounts and anecdotes, there seems to have been very little planning for the postinvasion period. Each day, in each interview, and at each press conference, it becomes clearer that the Americans are making up the rules as they go along.

The same is true of the Iraqis. I'm impressed when we discover a grass-roots movement led by former prisoners calling themselves the Committee of Free Prisoners, in an abandoned villa in the Shiite suburb of Kadhimiya. Volunteers scour former intelligence offices and neighborhood Baath headquarters to retrieve any documents that might offer clues to the whereabouts of the hundreds of thousands of people who are missing. The files are sorted by date and by crime and stored in stacks in the villa's basement. Some files provide details on the individual's date of execution and place of burial. Most criminal charges are as vague as "links to Iran," or "travel to Kurdistan." After a file's contents are read, a list that matches the names of victims to places of burial goes up on the wall. On any given day, a quiet procession of hundreds of Iraqis streams in and out of the garden for a peek at the list. When all roads have been exhausted and no answers found, they flock to Abou Mouaya.

Abou Mouaya is a thirty-seven-year-old, tall, thin man, a chain-smoker of unfiltered skinny cigarettes, whose given name is Seyed Nezar Alaadin. Although his title, Seyed, suggests he is a direct descendant of the prophet Muhammad, he is not a cleric. His clairvoyance, as he tells it, was passed to him from his father and grandfather, who used ancient Islamic methods and verses from the Quran to hypnotize their subjects before tapping their "inner souls." In an interesting way, Abou Mouaya's career mirrors the troubled political landscape of Iraq. During the bloody Iran-Iraq war, Abou Mouaya's business boomed as distraught mothers and wives of soldiers came to him to ask after the missing men. When Saddam began cracking down on Shiites and Kurds in the 1990s, arresting and executing thousands, he labeled Abou Mouaya's metaphysical methods satanic and banned him from accepting customers. He turned all but his best customers away and was careful never to go near cases of political prisoners. After the collapse of the regime, Abou Mouaya prepared himself for the surge of clients he reckoned would once again seek him. For forty-eight hours, he locked himself in a room to fast and meditate and re-cite the al-Baghareh verse of the Quran, which he credits with evoking mystical powers. In strict Islamic terms, magic and fortune-telling are for-bidden. But these are desperate times in Iraq, and people cling to what-ever hope they have. Abou Mouaya's clients line up outside his house from the early morning hours and knock on his door late into the night.

Haqqi and I are called into the numinous room, and Abou Mouaya, dressed in gray cotton Arabic attire and sporting a thin goatee, greets us with a handshake. As he holds on to my hand, I feel a chill rush through me, as if I've been stripped naked before a stranger. His back resting against the puffy cushion of his chair, Abou Mouaya rolls amber rosary beads between his fingers. A bright green cloth encrypted with verses from the Quran, which he uses to cover the faces of child mediums, rests on his knees. His piercing black eyes stare into mine as he nods his head, mur-muring a quiet chant in Arabic as Haqqi explains why our story would benefit from spending half a day watching him at work.

Abou Mouaya asks gingerly if I have any special requests before he sees the next client. "Is there any dead person the lady wants to connect to? I can bring back the ghost and pass messages. Is the lady married? Is there a fiancé? I see a tall man in her life. I can help the relationship flourish by giving you a good spell. It's a chart drawn from the Quran that you carry with you at all times or leave in the pocket of the man's shirt. You don't have to tell him. I have given it to many people before."

I try to imagine Babak's face if I returned to the hotel with an Iraqi love spell. Haqqi is suspiciously silent, staring down at his feet. I stumble on my words, searching for a polite way to decline without offending. I tell him that American journalists aren't allowed by their news organiza-tions to mix personal issues with working. I add that I am also looking for some Iraqi families I befriended before the war and I will surely seek his help if I fail to locate them. He seems pleased with my answer and calls out for his next client.

Zeid Hashem, a middle-aged man with deep wrinkles and hollow eyes, sits across from Abou Mouaya and explains in a labored, emotional voice that his son is missing and if his family would be grateful to confirm where he is. His wife sits next to me, her hands rubbing together nervously. The couple's seven-year-old son, Hassan, sits on the floor beside him, while Abou Mouaya covers his face with the cloth and begins a hypnotic recital of a Quranic verse. He pauses and then chants a mantra for ten minutes. The boy's head drops and his arms dangle weightlessly along his side as he falls into a deep trance.

"Your brother is in this room; say hello to him. Make contact with him. Can you hear him?" asks Abou Mouaya.

The boy nods his head as the mother takes a deep breath. The father's eyes widen in disbelief.

Haqqi, looking unsettled, whispers, "*Besemellah alrahman al rahim* [In the name of God, the compassionate and merciful]."

"Where is your brother? Ask him where he is."

"He says he is in Basra. Inside a camp."

"Who took him there?"

"The Americans. He says the Americans."

The father jumps to his feet. The mother puts her hands across her mouth.

The boy opens his eyes with a jolt. Abou Mouaya looks at the parents and says, "Now you know that he is alive. Inshallah, he will be released soon."

"I believe him," says the mother as she leaves the room. "This is the first time anyone has given us any news about my son. Abou Mouaya knows more than the police. He knows more than the Americans."

Haqqi, with a half-outraged, half-mocking voice I've become accustomed to by now, turns to me to say, "See, I told you, you cannot trust the Americans. They don't tell you the truth."

Like the Iraqis who are looking for their missing loved ones, one of my missions is finding my own Iraqi friends. The phone lines are down, and some of the landmarks I remember have been destroyed. I pencil a map of Rasheed Street and surrounding areas in order to give my driver Munaf clues on how to find Beit al-Iraqi, Amal al-Khudeiry's art center. He looks confused.

"Are you sure? But the area you are describing is destroyed; Rasheed Street is looted. Most of the shops are destroyed. There is nobody there now."

The day Munaf and I drive through the narrow labyrinth of the once-thriving commercial district the scope of devastation visible at every turn is chilling. Rasheed Street is eerie in its emptiness. We pass the wreckage of smoldering buildings, mangled remains of cars, and streets littered with rubble, burnt paper, ash, and broken glass. When I get out of the car at Beit al-Iraqi, Amal's art center, I am rendered speechless.

The center is half crumbled. The roof is gashed with a craterlike hole. The walls are riddled with bullets. The windows are smashed. The wooden doors are swung out into the middle of the street. Ash and dust cloak the mosaic floors. Two of the pillars in the garden are collapsed onto the palm trees. The furniture is slashed. I recognize a few antique pieces, including the old window with hand-painted glass I once wanted to buy.

For the next few days, Munaf and I visit Baghdad's ransacked museums, inquiring about Amal's whereabouts. One gallery owner assures me she is safe and unharmed. Another tells me she was forced to evacuate her house, a two-story villa on the banks of the river in the wealthy Sulaikh neighborhood after it was partially destroyed in the American bombardments of Operation Shock and Awe.

Finally, I score a solid lead when the director of the arts and archaeology board tells me he is a close friend of Amal's and can pass along my message. I scribble down a note with the address of our guesthouse asking Amal to look me up as soon as she can.

Two days later, a haggard Amal, with black circles under her eyes and hair pulled back into a tight knot, appears at the front desk of the hotel. We embrace and she breaks into tears.

"Did you see what they did to my gallery? It's all gone. Everything is destroyed. The paintings, the window you liked, the carpets, the tiles. I told you to take that window; I told you. Do you remember what a nice time we had there?" Amal can't contain her rage as she tugs my sleeves. "This is what they call liberation? They are savages, barbarians. They stood aside and watched our city get looted and destroyed. They allowed these animals to run loose. Saddam, Saddam was better than they are. Where will I get the money to rebuild my life?"

I tell her that the American military is talking about compensation for Iraqi civilians who suffered collateral damage. I advise her to write an inventory and take pictures of the wreckage before cleaning it up. She seems mildly encouraged but understandably cynical. "They tell me it's too soon right now because none of the departments are organized. It's too soon for them and too late for us."

To locate the Nasser family's house, Munaf circles Adhamiya, a predominantly Sunni enclave, which will later become the bastion of the insurgency, for three hours. I hand him a page torn from my old notebook on which Marie-Rose wrote directions in Arabic. We stop and ask directions from passersby about a dozen times. They seem amused that an American reporter is looking for her Iraqi friends.

Finally we spot the house. It looks just as I remember. The garden has gone a little dry, the grass has yellowed, and the flowers are rangy. I swing open the garden gate and call out to the Nassers. When I knock on the main door, one by one the family files out of the house. They weren't expecting a guest; Sabah is wearing pajama pants; Marie-Rose is in a long, flowery, cotton housedress; Aseel hands me the new baby daughter, born before the war. From across the road, Mama Theresa, married to Sabah's deaf brother, Nosrat, hears the hubbub and rushes over to greet me, as does her husband, who in his special sign language presses his palms against his heart and points to me.

Everyone is safe. Nothing is damaged.

"*Alhamdullelah, Shokran Alameen* [Thank God]," they say.

The family endured the war by staying put in their own house. The food and water they had stored lasted them the three-week invasion. Aseel stuffed the baby's ears with cotton puffs to prevent her from waking up at the sound of bombs in her sleep. Money is scarce. Sabah's restaurant and the sons' shops have been closed since the war, and the family's savings are thinning out.

Weeks after Baghdad's fall, the city's basic urban infrastructure—electricity, clean water, and sanitation services—is dysfunctional, and fuel and phone lines remain unrepaired.

When the phone lines went dead, cutting off the family's communication with their relatives, Marie-Rose's nerves caved in. She smoked up to a pack of cigarettes a day and insomnia kept her sitting at the kitchen table quietly crying late at night. Marie-Rose's eyes fix on the antenna of my large Thuraya satellite phone. She hasn't spoken to her daughter Ghada, living in Sweden, for over a month.

"Is that a mobile phone? Can you use it to call Ghada? Just one minute to tell her we are safe?" she says.

She goes back inside the house and brings out a notebook, the telephone numbers of her relatives abroad listed alphabetically according to country of residence. We dial Ghada's number in Sweden, then her brother in Ohio and sister in California.

A desperate plea to use the satellite phone occurs every time I step out to the streets. Often I don't know how to explain to strangers that I can't share my phone, which costs a small fortune to use and is paid for by the newspaper. Haqqi usually responds by saying the phone doesn't get good reception in this part of town or that the battery is low but on a few occasions, particularly when older people beg to call their children, I don't have the heart to say no.

Like most Iraqis, the Nassers are tough and have an inherent knack for accepting what comes their way as fate or "God's will." Marie-Rose emphasizes the Iraqi approach to events beyond their control by pointing to her forehead and telling me, "Whatever is written on your forehead, it will happen. It's all here. God wrote it."

The Iraqi ability to accept destiny and succumb to all manner of events as God's will is a powerful coping mechanism honed by decades of fiercely totalitarian rule. Under Saddam, individual thinking was shunned. Personal choice was unthinkable, and straying from the regime's script often ended disastrously. Such a systematic demoralization of individual identity offers Iraqis a convenient tool for exonerating their collective consciousness for what happened under Saddam. In the mind of an average Iraqi, they are without fault. It was the regime. It was Saddam. It was his circle. It was his commanders. And at last, when all arguments are exhausted, it is God's will.

The Iraqis I meet hardly discuss or reflect on the tormented past, even now that they can. When I press them on what they think of the revelation of the regime's crimes or whether they feel any remorse, most often they shrug, telling me there is no point in living in the past. How, I wonder, do you begin to heal a nation when there is no acknowledgment of culpability or forgiveness on the part of sufferers? Coming to any one consensus on what actually happened under Saddam is difficult, particularly since Iraqis who don't feel a strong sense of nationalism associate instead far more closely with their ethnic tribe or religious sect.

I track down Wamidh Nadhmi, the political science professor who was an outspoken critic of Saddam's regime. His house is just a few doors down from Amal's, on the bank of the Tigris. When Babak and I arrive at his door unannounced, his son takes our cards and reemerges a few minutes later to guide us through a living room elaborately decorated with antiques and old photographs. Wamidh, whom we find sitting on a large mosaic terrace above the water, is clearly disgruntled. In an interview that takes more than an hour, he never smiles, even when he is offering us tea and dates.

"This isn't the way it was supposed to be after Saddam. We did not bargain for an American occupation. We are not pleased to see Americans making excuses for allowing the looting and destruction," he says. He complains about the suspension of life's routines: because the university canceled the spring semester, he has no classes to teach, his children don't go to school, and he spends his time devouring the news on the new satellite channels and analyzing it with a circle of Sunni friends.

I am a little startled by his anger. I expected Wamidh, the only advocate of regime change that I had met in Saddam's time, to be more forgiving. "But you told me you despise Saddam and crave a more open society, democracy. Don't you think no matter what happens Iraq is better off with Saddam gone?" I press him.

"Look, anger for Saddam doesn't translate into support of American occupation. Why don't your people understand this? If there were a normal situation, with an Iraqi government in place, a functioning army, and no occupation, then I would be a lot less skeptical."

It's remarkable that as fatalistic as Iraqis tend to be, they can't swallow the American occupation of Iraq as destiny. That the American military patrols their roads and raids their homes is not a test of God's will but an injustice enforced by a self-serving foreign power. When I relay this to the few Americans I know at the Coalition Provisional Authority, the administrative body ruling Iraq, they dismiss such comments as marginal.

But the more I speak to Iraqis and Americans, the more I am aware of a widening gap and a strong disconnect between Iraqi reality and American ideology. It's astounding that the Americans seem so oblivious to their surroundings, with an inherently selective eye for what's occurring in Iraq. The occupation appears doomed from the start.

On Wamidh's balcony the whirring drove of an American patrol boat interrupts our conversation. Two seated soldiers peer into gardens and balconies through their binoculars. Impulsively, I raise my hand and wave. As the boat nears, one of the soldiers waves back. On each side of the boat, two soldiers point their machine guns out at invisible enemies.

"See, that's the occupation you are waving at," Wamidh says, scolding. "They do this at least twice a day, in the morning and at night, disturbing our peace. They want to remind us they are in control of our country. Democracy at gunpoint! Change with the force of tanks! Liberty with bombs!"

The American military boat disappears down the broad curve of the river. The sun sinks behind the dark silhouettes of palm groves, casting a rosy glow across the brown waters of the Tigris. A flock of birds flies by, collective wing tips twinkle in the light. At times, Baghdad reveals an almost biblical beauty.

▨ ▨ ▨

By the end of summer 2003, we have moved into the Hamra Hotel. Although *hamra* in Arabic means "red," the hotel consists of two indistinguishable white cement towers separated by a courtyard and a large, pristine swimming pool. An assortment of lounge chairs, a swing that seats three, and plastic chairs and tables surround the swimming pool, the favored gathering spot for war hacks. The lobby's cafeteria is decorated with retro furniture and large circular light fixtures. It serves light snacks and Western dishes like soggy spaghetti Bolognese and dry, breaded chicken breasts, and in the mornings they spread a pleasant breakfast. To the right of the garden, a pseudo-Chinese restaurant with fancier table settings and a piano bar cooks up an Arab interpretation of Chinese dishes: bland, overcooked chicken and meat swimming in gravy. Iraqi cuisine leaves much to be desired. Thankfully, there is a good bakery in the hotel that sells a variety of delicious sugar cookies, miniature croissants, spinach pies, and pizza bites.

We have taken two corner suites at each end of the fifth floor in the second tower, where we work and live for now, until we sort out a more permanent residence. The suites are decorated with simple, light-colored wood furniture: a long sofa, two chairs and a coffee table, and a small dinner table. I have fashioned the table into my desk and put a whiteboard above it, with emergency numbers for staff and my editors in New York and a large map of Iraq that I had sent from the States. (Saddam, who didn't like maps, banned them. The only map I have found in Baghdad dates from 1971, the year of my birthday.) A row of all-purpose white cabinets lines the wall and a credenza for storing books, knickknacks, and the white china dishes of the hotel sits beside it. In war zones, a few homey touches to one's environment can be transformative. Babak and I treat the hotel room as our private sanctuary. We buy a carpet, plants, candles, and some cushions and throws to add color to our living quarters. In place of the cheap printed copies of Monet on the walls, we put up several framed Iraqi pieces of artwork. We replace the hotel's coarse towels with our own and shove the brown bedspread in the bottom drawer in favor of a puffy comforter.

I have accepted the newspaper's offer to be stationed in Iraq for the foreseeable future. I will be joined for a year with a colleague from our Washington bureau, Yochi Dreazen. He and I will share the responsibility of running the bureau and finding stories. Babak and I feel remarkably lucky at our mutual posting and make the best of it by trying to introduce little doses of domestic life into our days. Occasionally, when a work night ends early, we pretend to go on a date. I wear a summer dress and heels, and he puts on black slacks and a freshly ironed shirt. We hail a taxi from the lineup of cars in front of the hotel and go to Arasat Street. After peeking in the windows of newly opened shops, we eat at a nice restaurant. Our favorite is Nabil, which serves decent food and offers a comfortable atmosphere. Sometimes we go out in large groups with our journalist friends, many of whom we know from Afghanistan. We order big meals, laugh out loud at each other's quirky anecdotes, gossip, and stay well past midnight drinking bottles of arak, a medicinal-tasting liquor that's been mixed with water, and cheap Lebanese wine. On weekend nights we have rowdy parties around the hotel swimming pool, where we dance, chase, and shove each other into the pool. We sing along as one of our friends, BBC radio reporter Quil Lawrence, plays our favorite songs from the 1980s on his guitar.

With an endless supply of fascinating subjects and a great appetite for my stories back home, reporting from Iraq continues to be rewarding. And I cherish my personal life. It's remarkable to share this amazing experience with Babak.

Every so often my girlfriends and I designate an Iraqi girls' day out, which usually consists of spending a leisurely morning browsing shops or art galleries and lunching at the Saj al-Reef Italian restaurant. On one such day Catherine Philp and I sneak into a small all-women's beauty salon for a pedicure. It's a modest place with only two beauty chairs facing a rectangular mirror and an old stand-alone hair dryer. On the counter is a basket filled with rollers, a vase with fake red roses, and an assortment of nail polish and makeup. The walls are decorated with posters and magazine clips of Egyptian and Lebanese pop stars.

The women eye us with curiosity and ask endless frivolous questions: How come our families allowed us to travel to Iraq alone? Are we married or single? Do we have children? Do we have boyfriends? Do our parents know and approve of our relationships? How come we are not wearing makeup and don't have blond streaks in our hair? What is the fashion in London and New York these days? Where did we buy that linen skirt and those platform sandals?

Catherine and I settle onto stiff chairs and two young women squat on stools before us. We dip our toes into red plastic bowls. Halfway through the pedicure with still one foot to go, electricity cuts off. It's over 110 degrees outside and within a few short minutes the heat becomes unbearable. "Normal, normal," says the owner, waving her hands dismissively. "We have two hours of electricity and six hours of blackout every day. What is taking the Americans so long to fix it? After the last war, Saddam fixed our electricity in one month. One month! America, with all its engineers and top technology, can't fix our electricity? They are doing this on purpose. They want us to suffer."

Inevitably the conversation shifts from frivolous hair-salon chitchat to hostile interrogation. The faces of the women, bent toward us, are no longer friendly. Catherine and I leave, with a half pedicure and no nail polish.

I've made a tradition of having lunch with Sabah's family every Wednesday. Spending time with the Nassers, who treat me with great love and care, is soothing. "You are like family," they often say, and I know they mean it. I float freely in their house, chopping vegetables with Marie-Rose in the kitchen, analyzing the day's news with Sabah, and playing in the garden with the baby.

In anticipation of a postwar reconstruction boom he reckons will be hitting Baghdad any day, Sabah has closed his kebab shop and opened a paint company. On my last visit, he hands me a stack of one hundred business cards and sheepishly asks me to pass the word to the Americans and foreigners I know.

"There will be lots of foreign companies coming to Iraq; they will open offices and rent houses for their employees. The Americans are also expanding their bases. I am very hopeful that my business will do well, and I can make some money with the reconstruction," he tells me.

There is a sense of eager anticipation for progress and improvement. Even when I stop by Amal's house for afternoon coffee, I notice that her bitterness is slowly decreasing as she busies herself with the task of refurbishing. Meanwhile, she's moved back to a small studio space upstairs near her study, where she can lock herself up from intruders who try to break in every now and then. She still hasn't found sufficient funds to restore her art center. She keeps a thick folder on her desk and asks me to review some of the proposal letters and project outlines she has prepared to submit to various aid agencies that focus on art and culture. "I must go on, one step at a time, if not for myself, for others who relied on the center for their livelihood," she tells me.

The local artists, even villagers from out of town, have tracked her down and occasionally drop off their paintings, embroidered shawls, or woven baskets. She sells each item for twenty dollars or less, and I seldom leave her house without buying at least one gift for someone back home.

With my Iraqi staff I've settled into a smooth routine. We have two drivers and two translators. They show up at the hotel by 8:30 every morning with all the day's newspapers. By the time I have my coffee, check e-mail, and read some clips, my translator Haqqi will have browsed through the papers, marking any article worthy of a follow-up story or a revealing quotation by someone of note. We have a story meeting and make a list of interviews we need to do and places we must visit before we venture out. We have a small staff, many of whom are related and all of whom are—unintentionally on our part—Sunni. There is Munaf, our handsome driver, and his father, Abu Munaf, who resembles the Egyptian actor Omar Sharif and has a gentle, caring personality. Before the war,

Munaf was studying chemistry; his father was a pharmacist. We have two translators: the ever-charming and gregarious Haqqi, who managed the guards at the Vietnamese embassy and occasionally translated for the staff using his fluent English, and Munaf's cousin, Amer, who is a master in greasing deals. They've all left their chosen profession because they can make more money working with us. Work is often a refuge. We have electricity, gas, hot water, and air conditioning in summer. We can afford the hefty black market price of oil required to keep the generator humming twenty-four hours a day. But most of all, in our office and with us, the staff feel shielded from the insecurity of raids and arbitrary arrests by the American military. When they complain, it's always about the difficulty of day-to-day life.

10

We Will Be Strong,
Absolutely Strong

By fall of 2003, a Shiite awakening is under way as an unintended consequence of the American invasion. The Americans have reversed decades of Sunni supremacy in Iraq and have offered Shiites the chance to mend the thin fabric of their tattered society through layers of clerical networks. Saddam did not allow Shiite clerics a prominent position in society; they were sidelined to religious centers and prohibited from conducting any social work and from speaking publicly. Now the clerics are spreading Islamic conviction and shaping public opinion through civic services and grassroots activism, a method tested and proven by their counterparts in Iran and Lebanon. Many of these young clerics are either students or fresh graduates of Najaf religious centers, with little field experience. They are shepherded into their task by more senior and older Ayatollahs with close ties to the greater Shiite world and deep pockets. (It is customary in Islam to pay religious tax based on your income and capital. Devout Shiites donate the funds to senior clerics, known as *marjayat,* whose teaching they follow.)

This unappeased hunger for a thriving Shiite society is most noticeable at small neighborhood mosques and the offices of local clerics. I have made a habit of visiting one such place at least once a week. I time my visits for early afternoons, after the clerics have finished a round of morning duties, eaten their lunches, and completed their midday prayers. My Shiite encounters occur at the office and residence of Ayatollah Seyed Hussein al-Sadr, an elderly high-ranking cleric with a gigantic black turban, pudgy cheeks hidden under a thick white beard, and a very round belly. He is an avid supporter of the war, quick to say that the American and British invasion freed Shiites and achieved the impossible task of removing Saddam from power. But he grumbles about the heavy-handed role Americans have taken in Iraqi politics.

"The Americans have absolutely saved the Iraqi people from a regime that no one else could free us from," he tells me the first time we meet. "But Iraq should be ruled by Iraqis chosen by the people, not handpicked by the Americans."

As far as Shiite clerics go, Seyed al-Sadr is an invaluable asset to the Americans. By blood and connection, his feet are firmly placed in both Shiite camps. He boasts of being a *wakil*, or official Baghdad representative of the Iranian-born Grand Ayatollah Ali Sistani, the most powerful and influential of all Shiite clerics, whose orders are adhered to by tens of millions of Shiites worldwide. Seyed Sadr is also a second cousin to the young rebel cleric Moqtada Sadr, who is quickly gaining a name for himself from his politicized Friday prayer sermons, which are loaded with anti-American rhetoric. In negotiations with Moqtada, Seyed Sadr is always at the forefront.

One day, as I sip tea and watch Seyed sign a stack of letters, he casually mentions that the day before, the coalition administrator Paul Bremer visited him. During another visit he recounts the menu served at a luncheon he hosted for Secretary of State Colin Powell at his house. Seyed Sadr tells me that these meetings were authorized by Ayatollah Sistani, who has refused to meet Americans face-to-face, in part because he doesn't want to lose credibility with his followers.

"The Americans like to come and see me. I tell them what Seyed Sistani wants and they listen very carefully. Iraq's future belongs to the Shiites. We are now getting very organized. I have dispatched my men everywhere in Baghdad, to schools, to hospitals, to municipalities. These clerics must bring back civil order and control the neighborhoods. They must gain the trust of the public. You see, under Saddam we couldn't do any of this. But now we are free. Do you know what it means for Shiites to be free?" he asks me. "It means we will be strong. Absolutely strong. The wind is now blowing in our direction, and we must sail very far."

Seyed Sadr's office is located in a north-facing house on a residential block of the sprawling Shiite suburb of Kadhimiya, far from the hubbub of the area's revered shrine and strip of gold and textile shops. Usually we park our car at the tip of the road so I can throw on a black abaya. Despite my Middle Eastern features, according to Haqqi, the two giveaway signs that I'm a foreigner are my shoes—comfortable black leather flats—and my multipocketed blue reporter's satchel. Munaf concludes that the way I walk offers another hint of my foreign status.

"You look Iranian but walk like an American," he says. "You are always looking around at everything and everyone. Arab women look down and don't smile at strangers."

I am in *hijab* not to disguise my identity, but out of respect for the clerics. Often in this neighborhood we pass women returning from the grocery store with plastic bags spilling with fresh herbs and vegetables. Little kids kick a plastic ball and ride around the dusty streets on their bicycles. At Seyed's office, a guard waves us inside past a small courtyard and into the library.

The guard, his skin wrinkled from sun, pokes his head inside and shouts to a room full of young clerics, "Seyed Hashem, Sheikh Haydar, come. Sahafieh Iraniehi is here."

Seyed Hashem Mousawi and Sheikh Haydar al-Nassrawi, two young clerics at the helm of Seyed Sadr's network, are my friends here. Usually I meet them in the library. The library, with its wraparound floor-to-ceiling mahogany bookcase, holds an impressive collection of Islamic manuscripts, religious texts, and poetry. A row of wooden chairs is lined up against the bookcase, interrupted with individual coffee tables topped with glass.

I'm drawn to this place. Here I can speak with the clerics and am guaranteed to meet an interesting cast of characters, while I sit for several hours in the library. They have become accustomed to my presence and introduce me to other visitors as an Iranian journalist, a fellow Shiite, who happens to work at an American daily newspaper. And they never leave out the sentence "She goes to Iran every year," as if that automatically makes me sympathetic to the Islamic Republic's regime.

Seyed Sadr always receives me in a narrow hallway between his library and his residential quarters. The hallway is spread with a red Persian carpet and a few thin mattresses covered in white cotton sheets. He sits on a cushion in the far corner, with a copy of the Quran, a prayer book, the day's newspaper, and an appointment calendar before him. Refusing to tell me his exact age, he says he is in his early seventies. He is half amused and half disapproving of my presence in Iraq and the influence of a secular Western culture in my upbringing.

"What does your father say about you being here in Iraq?" he asks me.

"My father passed away a few years ago," I tell him.

"May Allah bless his soul. Then what does your brother think?"

"I don't have a brother."

"Then what does your uncle think? Isn't there any man in your family who speaks for you?" he growls back.

On many occasions I leave without seeing Seyed Sadr and am content to sit in the library and talk to the junior clerics who fill me in on the latest political gossip. My favorite cleric is Seyed Hashem. He is tall and lanky, and when he walks, his white robe flaps around him like wings. Until very recently, Seyed Hashem, who is in his late twenties, was an unassuming student at a prominent seminary in Najaf, learning how to interpret and adapt religious texts for contemporary life. He was born in Baghdad and left for Najaf after graduating from high school. At the seminary, he woke at the crack of dawn to pray and study; he attended lectures by other clerics and consumed books voraciously. He kept a picture of Ayatollah Ruhollah Khomeini, the father of the Iranian revolution, hidden under his mattress. But for the most part, he stayed clear of politics and focused on how to become a good Shiite cleric. At best, Seyed Hashem's visions of his future included an honorary completion of *hawza* studies, a devout wife, and a return to a small Shiite religious center, called a Husseinieh, in Baghdad where he would quietly lead Friday prayers. He did not dare contemplate the possibilities that have opened up to him now, or the leading role he has come to play in the Shiite grassroots movement.

When President Bush gave his forty-eight-hour warning for attacking Iraq in March 2003, Seyed Hashem abandoned his small room at the religious seminaries and took a rickety taxi ride back to Baghdad to stay with his family. Nearly a month later, when the regime had fallen and the Americans had taken control of the capital, he postponed his return to school and turned to Shiite activism. At Seyed Sadr's office, Seyed Hashem quickly gained recognition for his calm, earnest manners, his quick thinking, and his ability to mobilize volunteer task forces.

Now Seyed Hashem dedicates himself to his civil work with the same energy he once poured into his religious studies. He creates outreach programs, sending clerics door to door to take surveys of the Shiite population's demographics and their most immediate needs. He appeases those needs by sending jugs full of clean water, sacks of rice, and clothes, fuel, and money. When word got to him that the most pressing concern among Shiites was lack of security, Seyed Hashem organized neighborhood patrols. His team collected looted goods, which were returned to the rightful owners. In the absence of a judiciary, the clerics formed ad hoc religious courts, settling ownership disputes and issuing marriage and divorce licenses. They were dispatched to run hospitals and government institutions, filling the void left by the collapse of the state. Seyed Hashem says his men now control four hospitals, including a mental institution, a dozen schools, two universities, and several banks.

"As religious men we have many responsibilities. We are living in emergency times now, and Seyed Sistani says we have to control the situation because there is no government, no security, and we don't want the Americans to take over everything."

All the while, Seyed Hashem appears quite pleased with the Shiites' awakening. He is often contradictory in his views of religion and state, desperately wishing for Islam to penetrate all aspects of Iraqi life and yet mindful of its stifling impacts. He is also acutely aware that the empowerment of Iraqi Shiites is fulfilling a promise larger than Iraq.

"Shiites in the rest of the Arab world are looking to see what will happen with us. It's very important we don't let them down. If I have a choice, I will choose an Islamic government. It doesn't have to be as strict as Iran. Everyone should be free to express their opinions and live according to how they like. We don't want to tell other people what to do or force them to be religious. But I still believe that for Shiites, the thing that matters most is the sharia law. Islam teaches you about everything: politics, justice, social behavior, even marriage."

There are sides of this Shiite revival that remind me of Iran's experiment with Islamic theocracy. The seeds of Iran's 1979 revolution that deposed the dictatorial monarchy of Shah Mohammad Reza Pahlavi were sown by the promise of democracy. The popular uprising gradually transformed into an Islamic movement and little by little, the clerics injected Islamic rule into our lives. The day that the Shah left and the people declared victory, my relatives stuck their heads out of the living room window of our fourth-floor apartment, waving Iranian flags and singing the national anthem song, "Ey Iran," an ode to Iran's glory and a declaration of utter devotion by its citizens. They rushed down, skipping the steps three for one, to dance in Tehran's main throughway, Vali Asr Street, with a jubilant crowd. In preparation for Imam Khomeini's return from exile in Paris, my aunt and uncle played the revolutionary song "Khomeini Ey Imam" on the cassette player all day, encouraging me to memorize the words for the occasion. When Khomeini's wife was receiving visitors at a villa in the upscale Darous neighborhood in northern Tehran, my grandmother took us to pay our respects. When it was our turn to greet Mrs. Khomeini, who was sitting on the floor, we knelt down to kiss her cheeks and welcome her back to Iran. My grandmother gave me a gentle nudge that landed me in Mrs. Khomeini's lap. Afterwards she declared I had been blessed.

My family did not fit the average profile of revolutionaries, nor did they consider themselves as such. Both my parents hailed from privileged backgrounds. My father was a Qajar aristocrat and my mother came from a prominent merchant family. After American educations, they returned to Tehran, where they found prestigious jobs. My father, an architect, designed commercial and military buildings for the navy, and my mother, a trained interior designer, worked at Tehran University. As a dashing young couple, they were fixtures of Tehran's social scene, dancing at openings of exclusive nightclubs, sitting in the front row at fashion shows, and sipping champagne at decadent parties with attendees as glamorous as Elizabeth Taylor.

When revolutionary fervor and promises of a democratic republic swept the country, my parents were caught in the swell. But the regime quickly turned against people like them, and their idealism faded to disillusionment. In sweeping rounds of what the regime called *paksazi,* or cleansing, scores of technocrats and professionals lost their jobs because they were deemed either too Western or too secular. My father came home one day from work and announced his name had turned up on one such list. At the height of his career, he no longer had a job.

In that first year of the Islamic Republic's birth, the regime had an inalterable effect on my family. The same uncle who had practiced revolutionary songs with me and slept on the airport highway, waiting to greet Khomeini upon his arrival, was imprisoned for three years. Family properties were confiscated in the regime's attempts to take away from the rich and give to the poor. I returned home from school one afternoon to find my mother's eyes swollen and red from crying, because my fourteen-year-old cousin had been sentenced to two years in prison after a teacher caught her with anti-Khomeini leaflets in school. My grandmother, who had rushed to greet Mrs. Khomeini, cried for days when a close relative, who had been a prominent general in the Shah's army, committed suicide in his prison cell on the eve of his execution date.

The British-style elementary school I attended was shut down and educational establishments were segregated. Our new transitory public school sent home a written advisory that wearing a scarf was now mandatory, even for elementary school girls. One afternoon when my mom drove us to our weekly ballet lessons, we found the door of the dance school sealed with the logo of the revolutionary court. The dance center, which was seen as responsible for the spread of indecent and un-Islamic values, was indefinitely suspended. Soon after, the state officially banned music and dance. When my mom and I went to our local photo store to develop film, we were asked by the shopkeeper, a man we'd known for years, to leave. A decree had been issued that shops were not to serve women who weren't wearing *hijab*. Much like post-Saddam Iraq, neighborhood mosques, clerics, and volunteer task forces of zealously religious men and women were at the forefront of shaping Iran's postrevolution life. Like Iraqis, my family struggled to contend with these new boundaries. They turned to local mosques and pleaded with influential clerics to free my uncle and cousin from prison and sought religious courts headed by clerics to reclaim the family's many confiscated properties.

Iran is still grappling with whether democracy is compatible with theocracy. The Iranians brand their system of governance an Islamic Democracy, a notion that I see is extremely appealing to Iraqi Shiites. Iran has largely given up on the early dreams of exporting its theocracy across the Middle East. Instead, it works through clerical networks and charity foundations, in countries like Lebanon and Palestinian territories, to graft its workable model onto religious activism and grassroots social movements.

Iraqi Shiites have a romantic attachment to Iran that is in part one of identity, in part a result of Iran's accomplishments in achieving theocratic rule. Very few of the young clerics I meet at Seyed Sadr's office have actually traveled to Iran, and they are stunned when I tell them that not everybody in Iran is happy with the government's performance. But nonetheless, Seyed Hashem insists he feels a deep loyalty to Iran and its ruling clergy.

"For Shiites, Iran has been our only friend, a best friend. When Saddam was persecuting us, where was America? Where were the countries of the Arab league? They didn't lift a finger for us. But Iran is like a brother. It gave us funding for *hawza*; it protected our political parties and leaders."

Every time we leave Seyed Sadr's office, Haqqi and Munaf grumble all the way back to the hotel. At Seyed Sadr's office they stick out in their jeans and colorful checkered shirts and their clean-shaven faces.

"They are turning Iraq into another Iran," Haqqi says with a hint of snottiness that stems from his privileged Sunni upbringing. "They promise us democracy, but why are they allowing the clerics to become so influential?"

"They took Iraq by gun and are now handing it on a silver tray to Iran," Munaf says. Munaf is a devout Muslim: he doesn't drink, and he prays when the call to prayer is announced. He comes from an educated middle-class family with strong values and, as the oldest son, feels responsible for sharing the financial burden of running the household. But he is still uneasy about the ascending power of Shiite clerics and worries that the newfound social freedoms could slowly evaporate.

Most of the Sunnis, just like Haqqi and Munaf, are puzzled at America's chumminess with the Shiites, given their strong ties to Iran and their preference for a conservative, Islamic society.

Americans must hold tightly to the small number of friends they have in Iraq. Shiite clerics are an important source of stability. The coalition simply can't afford to lose the Shiites, an oppressed majority that is by and large thankful for the invasion. Ayatollah Sistani grudgingly tolerates America's presence. In exchange Americans turn a blind eye to how the Ayatollah and his underlings are laying the foundations of a clerical authority. For better or worse, in his forceful calls for democracy, Sistani is empowering the Shiite masses and limiting the possibility for America to determine Iraq's political future. While the rival Shiite movements may differ on whether the Americans should stay, they share the same goal of ensuring that the Shiites rise to power.

Friday prayers are becoming a showcase of Shiite power. In Baghdad, the largest prayer gathering is in Sadr City's Mohsen Mosque, which is adorned with life-size murals of Moqtada's father. Sadr City is a sprawling slum that's home to some 2.5 million Shiites, or roughly 10 percent of Iraq's population. Sadr City is named after Moqtada's father, Mohammad

Sadiq al-Sadr, a beloved cleric who was murdered with two of his sons by Saddam in 1999.

The worshippers stretch for miles beyond my sight. Rows and rows of men stand shoulder to shoulder on prayer rugs rolled out on the hot cement toward Mecca. Haqqi and I conclude that at least fifty thousand people have gathered so far. A group of armed watch guards with postcard-size pictures of Moqtada pinned to their shirts attempt to bring order by shouting directions to new arrivals. When the guards approach us, they scold me as a distraction. We diffuse the complaints and stand in a corner in the back of the crowd.

Several loudspeakers are erected on the wall and rooftop of the mosque. Traditionally a *khutbah*, or sermon, is delivered in two parts between the prayers. Its tone is one of practical Islamic teachings. Iran, however, successfully transformed Friday prayers from religious gatherings to weekly political platforms where worshippers vent their frustrations by chanting slogans in between prayers while the imams deliver heated political rhetoric. A similar scenario unfolds in Baghdad every Friday.

The voice of Sheikh Kathem al-Naseri bellows with rage, "The people are like toys in the hands of the Americans! They are interfering with our future and putting in place a government that is loyal to their interests. Don't look at what we have as liberty and freedom. I say to you, the faithful people, that the Shiites are the majority, and our new government must be Shiite. But the Americans don't want to give power to Islam. But I tell you that *hawza* is the voice of the people. *Labeik, labeik, ya hawza, la Sunni, la Shiites, wahda, wahda Islamiyah!*"

The crowd responds in a frenzy, raising fists, punching the air, and shouting in unison, "*Labeik, labeik, ya hawza* [Yes, yes, hawza]!" And "*La Shia, la Sunniya, wahda wahda Islamiya* [Not Sunni, not Shiite, Islamic unity]!"

Unlike blasé Sunnis, the Shiites greet foreigners with enthusiasm, and soon a group of about a dozen men forms a circle around Haqqi and me. A middle-aged man named Mohsen says he will only follow the orders of

Sistani, who has so far not declared a jihad against the Americans. An engineer named Abbas who sees the clerics as pure at heart and free of corruption believes *they* should be ruling Iraq.

A young man named Hussein elbows his way to the front of the crowd to face me, asking, "Are you American?"

"Yes," I respond, having no reason to conceal my identity.

"Then I have a message for Mr. Bush. Can you tell him for me?"

"I don't communicate directly with the president, but what is it you want to say?"

"Mr. Bush, when the Americans came to Iraq they took Saddam out and their aim was to make Iraq a secure country. But until today we have no security. The entire basic infrastructure is destroyed. Mr. Bush, your country is very strong. It is a superpower, so why don't you fix everything for us? I want to tell you Mr. Bush, either secure our country properly, or leave us to do it ourselves by depending on the *hawza*."

Iraqis think of America as an ultimate superpower, incapable of making mistakes. Iraqis can't comprehend that the reasons behind deteriorating security, the lack of electricity, and the decline in prosperity are largely a result of the incompetence and cluelessness of the Americans rather than any deliberate intention.

On my next visit with Seyed Hashem, I ask him to explain to me how the Najaf *hawza* operates it. In Arabic, *hawza* translates as "a center for religious learning." Colloquially the word also refers to the collective and intricate web of *mujtahids,* or Grand Ayatollahs; the religious training schools; the senior clerics, or *ulama,* who teach there; and the younger apprentice clerics. The first seminary opened in Najaf in the eleventh century, and for two centuries it was regarded as the prominent seat of Shiite learning. Saddam's crackdowns on the Shiites led to the *hawza*'s decline, as clerics and students migrated to the Iranian city of Qom. Now Najaf is only home to about twenty or so religious seminaries, paling in comparison to its thriving rival in Qom, which houses several hundred schools equipped with computers and digital libraries. Students of *hawza* enter the seminaries as young as their early teens. Sometimes completion of rank can take up to a decade as students learn about religious science, Arabic literature, Islamic jurisprudence, theology, and even Greek philosophy.

Najaf seminaries are traditionally under the supervision and guidance of a senior cleric, who is responsible for funding the schools, paying instructors' salaries, and providing a small stipend for the students. Controlling the seminaries is regarded among the Shiite elite as a significant and highly sought-after position, since the seminaries train the next generation of religious and community leaders. In Najaf, Moqtada Sadr now controls every single seminary, a position he muscled to gain after the regime's fall.

"How did this happen?" I ask, bewildered.

"He claimed he is the rightful heir because all the seminaries were under his father's leadership until he was killed by Saddam," answers Seyed Hashem, shaking his head. "Seyed Sistani can't dispute him, because he is Iranian and can't lead Najaf's schools. But we are very worried about whether Moqtada will use the schools for his political ambitions."

To date, Iran has been the only country in the world where the theological schools have determined the course of politics. Now that Saddam is gone, the seminaries in Najaf are vying for a similar role. I'm determined to get inside one of the schools and head south to spend a week in Najaf with Haqqi and Munaf.

Based on Seyed Hashem's recommendation, we pick Najaf's oldest and most prominent theological seminary, Ayatollah Seyed Muhammad Kathem Yazdi School, a 150-year-old religious learning center tucked away in the back alleys of Najaf, near the Imam Ali Shrine. Decades ago, the Yazdi School was famed for its impressive list of Islamic scholars and senior Ayatollahs. It was the forefront publisher of the latest interpretations of Islamic texts and boasted of producing prominent Shiite leaders and schooling the sons of the Shiites with Islam's best-known names. Moqtada Sadr, who has been studying there for the past five years, now holds a weekly seminar on religion and politics.

Najaf is a city simmering with such an economic boom that Baghdad seems bleak in comparison. The clerics flaunt their turbaned heads with newfound confidence as they hurry past shops packed with customers and restaurants catering to the wave of pilgrims arriving by busloads from Iran. Haqqi pauses to ask directions to the Yazdi seminary school and leads me through a labyrinth of narrow dirt roads until we reach an old wooden door beneath a turquoise-mosaic archway bearing the school's name.

I had imagined a Shiite seminary to be somewhat dreary. But stepping inside the Yazdi School, I find an architectural gem modeled after Persian palaces of Isfahan. When no one greets us in the foyer, we pass through a narrow passageway connecting the outer area to the interior, where classes are held. At the center of the rectangular courtyard are a single palm tree and a shallow blue pool. The school is strikingly symmetric, with carved wood and geometric and flower mosaics of deep blue, yellow, and green. At the far end of the courtyard is a rickety wooden ladder that leads upstairs to student living quarters. The school is quiet and only a few classes are taking place in tiny rooms elevated half a foot above the ground. I peek through an open door at a group of young clerics, who sit cross-legged around an instructor. Their textbooks are mounted on individual wooden holders.

As usual, my presence, as a woman, causes a stir. The instructor motions for one of his students to see what we need.

Sheikh Aghil Ibrahim's thin camel robe sweeps the dusty ground as he steps down from the class. He is easily convinced to sit down for a chat in a shaded corner of the courtyard. When he speaks, his voice thrills with enthusiasm. Enrollment in the school has more than doubled this year compared to previous years, when students shied away from it because secret police raided the seminaries routinely and dragged students to interrogations. Ibrahim is excited by the preponderance of religious and political books, banned under Saddam, that are being imported from Iran, Syria, and Lebanon.

"You are witnessing a golden era for Najaf's *hawza*," he says, adjusting his black turban. We are joined by a second student, wearing brown pants and a black button-down shirt, who introduces himself as Riyadh Taeb.

He explains that he has not yet reached the level of a sheikh, which will allow him to wear a turban and a cloak. I ask both men to tell me about the biggest difference between the seminaries now and during Saddam's time.

"Without question, it's the freedom to talk about politics and religion," Ibrahim tells me. "Before, we studied hundreds of volumes of religious Islamic texts and listened to interpretations of Quranic verses. But there was never any debate about the role of religion in politics. Now it's all we talk about."

"The clerics in Qom are famous for interpreting how Islam should merge in society and politics. We are trying to do the same here," adds Taeb. "We all go to the Friday prayer because the imam talks about how to behave toward the Americans and the role of *hawza*."

"What do you think should be the role of *hawza* in the new Iraq?" I ask them.

"It's every Shiite's ambition to have an Islamic country," Sheikh Ibrahim says. He points to a large poster of Ayatollah Khomeini pinned to the wall next to one of the senior Ayatollah Sadr.

"Do you think that's a realistic goal?"

"Yes, why not? Seyed Moqtada tells us we are the majority, we have been underrepresented for years, and this is our time. What is wrong with what he is saying? Isn't it time for Shiites to rule Iraq?"

When it's time for recess, Sheikh Ibrahim takes me to an office in the front foyer and introduces me to Hajj Heydar Salkhi, an Afghan instructor who has taught at the Yazdi School for thirty-two years. Hajj Salkhi speaks candidly with me about the rivalries for control of the seminaries and about the clerics' sentiments toward the Americans. He tells me that more and more of the younger clerics are gravitating toward Moqtada and his radical politics. Moqtada's office also pays a stipend of about twenty dollars a week to each student.

"Sistani does not control any of the schools now. Sistani is a *mujtahid;* he can give a fatwa for what is *haram* and what is *halaal,* but he can't really publicly stand up to Moqtada. At the end of the day, Sistani is Iranian and Moqtada is Iraqi."

The cleric leans closer toward me. "The Shiites don't say this publicly to anyone but amongst ourselves we say God sent Bush to save us from an oppressor." He pauses for a few seconds to register the impact of his confession on my face. "I always say a silent prayer for Bush every day and for his wife and children."

"Why won't you say it publicly?"

"Because if we say so, then the population will turn from us and say clerics have sold their souls to the Kafir Americans. We want to appear to be with the people. Sistani told me last week that he doesn't support the Americans publicly, because he wants to keep them on their toes. He wants them to know that if they take one wrong step the *marjayat* will turn against them. This is our strategy to prevent the Americans from getting too comfortable here. We are worried they may stay in Iraq for many years."

The answers to fundamental questions regarding Iraq's future remain hazy. When pressed on what kind of vision the senior clerics and Shiite politicians foresee for Iraq, their answers fall in three general categories: Islam as the principal religion of the state, Shiites holding the majority of seats in government, and the establishment of sharia law (although less strict than in Iran).

When I put the same question to a circle of students and the future leaders of the Shiite community at the Yazdi School, they offered a more specific list.

> We want an Islamic government.
>
> We want all Muslim women to wear *hijab*.
>
> We want alcohol to be banned across Iraq.
>
> We demand that sinful things like cinema, music, and dance be forbidden.
>
> We want whatever is written in the Quran to be our law.
>
> We want a Shiite political leader to rule Iraq.

11

The Sunnis
Are Like Sheep
without a Shepherd

The office of the mayor of Fallujah is hot and noisy, and crowded with men in blue Iraqi police uniforms, American military desert camouflage, and tribal gold-trimmed cloaks. Wearing an ill-fitting mustard-colored suit, Mayor Taha Bedawi sinks behind his huge desk and greets the arriving delegation. Iraqi technocrats have an affinity for oversize furniture and often fill modest spaces with ornate pieces that look cartoonish outside anything other than a palace. From the corner of my eye I notice several framed certificates on the wall behind Mayor Bedawi's desk. They are certificates of appreciation from the U.S. Third Infantry Division and an endorsement letter from the CPA. Mayor Bedawi prides himself in having cooperated with the Americans thus far. Today as on every Wednesday, at 11 AM, the mayor hosts a meeting between Americans and important community leaders like tribal chiefs and religious sheikhs. On the agenda, the mayor tells me before the meeting starts, is "Security, security."

He adds, "It's very complicated because we don't see things the same way as Americans do. When the Americans talk about securing Fallujah, they want to arrest everybody who is opposed to their presence. They want our police and tribal leaders to turn over the mujahideen. But for us security means we want Americans to leave the city and not drive their tanks down the road. We want them to stop turning their weapons on our people. So, you see, we have a problem because we can't agree on the definition of security."

Like many Iraqis cooperating with the American enterprise here, the mayor is finding it a crushing task to balance the conflicting interests of Americans and Iraqis, in his case, the residents of Fallujah.

It's nearly six months since the Americans arrived, but hostility is spreading in the Sunni areas. The Americans are understandably jittery about the growing insurgency and the increase of hit-and-run attacks targeting the coalition forces. While no more than usually a mortar here, an ambush there, such attacks are still enough to kill or severely injure soldiers. Reports have surfaced of fundamentalist Islamist groups linked to al-Qaeda, with robust foreign funding operating in Fallujah. Lately the city's mosques have blatantly called for jihad. There is no shortage of angry men heeding their call. Leaflets pasted around the town square warn fellow residents of reprisal for cooperating with foreign troops. Mayor Bedawi complains about "foreign fighters" crossing the border from Syria, who bring in cash to pay off new recruits. He has heard talk of insurgent training camps cropping up in remote Sunni areas.

The Americans see the insurgency as a tactical inconvenience that must be dealt with swiftly and heavy-handedly in order to restore calm and order. They go about the task with sweeping house raids and roundups of men of fighting age, in waves of arbitrary arrest. But from the onset, the insurgency eludes them. It's a hodge-podge of nationalists, former Baathists, Islamists, and criminal gangs. An insurgency fueled by ideology and a deep sense of injustice is different from one driven by political aims. The more the American military presses, the more the ideology strengthens. Perception weighs more heavily than truth in Iraq. For the Americans, the Iraqis fall into two simple categories—the good guys who cooperate and the bad guys who fight them. For the Iraqis, it's a fight between the occupier and the occupied. To the Americans it's terrorism; to the Iraqis it's resistance. Americans see defensive killings, while Iraqis see unprovoked murder. The cycle continues to backfire, blurring progress as it unfolds.

In Fallujah, the fragile relationship Mayor Bedawi has been carefully fostering between Americans and local leaders has grown frayed. Recently American soldiers from the Third Armored Cavalry Regiment opened fire on Iraqi policemen packed into three vehicles outside a hospital here, killing ten police officers. The Iraqi police were chasing a suspicious car on the highway when they crossed paths with Americans, who opened fire. The Americans say the soldiers came under attack from a nearby truck. By the time the Americans issued a statement of apology and declared it an accident, it was too late. The funeral procession turned into violent riots in which the crowds chanted for revenge. Imams at local mosques declared the slain police officers martyrs and called on brave young men to join the resistance in their honor. Angry constituents showed up at the doorstep of the mayor's house and office demanding an end to his amicable relationship with the Americans and accused him of treason. In order to mollify the mobs, the mayor convinced Americans to pay the families blood money, a compensation fee dictated by the Islamic sharia law paid to victims' families after a member has been killed. But the trouble didn't disappear.

"It is a big, big crisis," says Mayor Bedawi as he rubs his forehead. "Sometimes I don't know what to do anymore. What to say to change how people feel. I hope the Americans are listening to us. We are telling them that the society here is very tribal, it's very traditional. Normal people don't want to see any Americans here. They are not Muslims; they are not Iraqis. At the end, they are foreign occupiers."

Fallujah is an easy drive, less than an hour from Baghdad. It's a dusty, flat city with lush green farmland and deep groves that curve around the bank of the Euphrates River. With the main highway between Jordan and Baghdad passing through the city, there is a constant buzz of commercial travel. A string of shops, gas stations, and fast-food kebab eateries caters to truck drivers and travelers. Before traveling here, Haqqi advised me to wear a long-sleeve loose-fitting shirt because the Sunni population is the most conservative in Iraq, with the largest number of mosques and minarets in all of the country. Haqqi and Munaf, who are both Sunni, are visibly more at ease here than in Shiite cities.

When we pass the governor's compound, Munaf points to Arabic graffiti on the wall that proclaims, "U.S. Army will pay blood for oil," and "People of Fallujah, we must revenge from the Americans." At the main square in town, Munaf stops to inspect leaflets plastered on the walls. It is a warning from insurgents to local motorists to keep at least fifty meters' distance between their vehicles and American military convoys. "It's from the mujahideen; it says we plan to attack all military convoys. Therefore, stay away, because we do not want to harm Iraqis," Munaf explains.

"How very kind and considerate of them to give advance warning of killings," I sarcastically retort, half expecting Haqqi and Munaf to share my outrage. But they stare at me in cold silence.

"American military is a fair target. They are not ordinary people. They are soldiers in uniform at war with our country. So what is wrong with attacking them? What are we supposed to do, just sit and watch them rob Iraq and humiliate us day after day?" Haqqi says, shrugging his shoulders.

"Everybody thinks killing civilians and Iraqis is *haram*. But American soldiers are different. They are occupying our country. It's a natural human desire to stand up against such a thing. We have the right," Munaf says.

"We don't see these guys as insurgents or terrorists. This is an *ihtilal* [occupation] and they are *moqawama* [resistance]," Haqqi says.

I ask the question I dread to know the answer to. "Would you guys ever fight? Would you join the resistance?"

"We are trying to make a difference by helping you tell the truth. We think this is a better way," Haqqi responds, and Munaf nods his head in agreement. I ask them if they know anyone who is a member of a resistance group. They tell me no, but then they add that if they did, they probably would not tell me.

Before today I had never discussed with my staff their feelings about the insurgency. It's unsettling and somewhat upending to discover they applauded the attacks against the American military, and view them as justified.

Haqqi and Munaf are neither religious zealots nor anti-Western. They are not unemployed or disenfranchised. Their generous monthly paychecks come from an American organization. They spend their days catering to Americans. They are cordial when they interact with American soldiers. They like practicing American slang, which they pick up from us and from watching sitcoms like *Friends*. They listen to Western and Arabic pop music, and they like to party and dance. Both of them want to travel and see the world. They want to save money to buy a car and want beautiful girlfriends. Intellectually they understand that the insurgency is destabilizing their country and halting progress. Yet, an intuitive sense of pride stirs them to support the resistance. I can't help but think that if the insurgents are succeeding in tapping into the nationalist sentiments of Iraqis like Haqqi and Munaf and winning their sympathy, if not their cooperation, the Americans have lost the heart of the battle.

With several hours to kill before a meeting with a tribal sheikh, we tour the city, chat with shopkeepers, and eat lunch at Fallujah's famous kebab eatery. Sitting in the back family section, I get a few curious glances from other patrons when they hear us speaking English, but they smile back when our eyes meet.

After lunch we drive to the outskirts of town to visit Sheikh Khamis al-Hassnawi, the chieftain of the Bu-Issa tribe, one of Anbar province's largest and most influential Sunni tribes.

The sheikh has eight sisters, nine brothers, and three wives. He considers himself the authoritative patron of at least a hundred thousand immediate tribal members. The men in his tribe, all of whom are armed, provide him with a small militia. The sheikh proudly introduces his eldest son, Malek Khamees, a handsome twenty-three-year-old who is being groomed as a successor in the ways of tribal politics and feudal leadership. With hawkish eyes, deep wrinkles, and an austerity that comes from firm-handed rules, Sheikh Hassnawi looks much older than his sixty-six years.

Freshly pressed white *dishdashah* made of fine cotton and handmade expensive leather sandals reveal his wealth.

Sheikh Hassnawi receives me in his *mathif*, a grand marble mansion built for the sole purpose of receiving guests and subordinates. A sleek black Mercedes Benz, the sheikh's favorite car, is parked out front. When I ask the sheikh about his residential quarters, he points off in the distance to a place hidden from view, telling me of his three houses, one for each wife. I mortify Haqqi and Munaf by asking the sheikh how he divides his time among his wives, and whether they get jealous. He laughs. "I try to be fair but the ways of the heart are not always equal. All women are jealous, don't you agree?" he tells me. When I admit that I would probably kill any husband who took another wife, everyone bursts into laughter.

We sit in a reception hall large enough to hold a football game, on throne-like chairs upholstered in scarlet fabric and littered with gold-trimmed cushions. Tribal custom requires that hospitality precede business. A servant enters the room ceremoniously, carrying a huge silver Arabic coffeepot—the type that looks like an hourglass with a pointy lid and curvy handle—and one tiny cup. He pauses for a few moments in front of each of us, puffs up his chest, and pours the thick dark liquid into the communal cup. I gulp it down like a shot, and as I've learned from the staff, shake the cup in the air to indicate I don't need a second helping. After the coffee we are invited for dinner. Sheikh Hassnawi orders his servant to kill and roast a lamb and prepare the traditional Iraqi meal of *qouzi*—lamb served with rice garnished with raisins and caramelized onion. When we say we can't stay for dinner because we don't want to travel after dark, the Sheikh instructs the servant to prepare guest bedrooms. I notice Munaf's tense smile. When my eyes catch his, he moves his eyebrows up and down to signal that he doesn't think it's appropriate for me to spend the night here. Despite my longing for adventure, we decline.

The sheikh tells me that Iraqi tribal leaders have by tradition and necessity always been aligned to the central government. He explains that this pledge is not so much a matter of loyalty but of survival and patronage and that Iraq can't be ruled without the support of tribal leaders. From the

Ottomans to the British, the chieftains played a key role in stabilizing the public as the majority of Iraqis belong to one of the country's 150 tribes spread across the landscape. These tribes are usually defined by sect and ethnicity but it's not uncommon to find a tribe with Sunni and Shiite members. Iraqis often introduce themselves according to their ancestral tribe, a good clue to a person's political leaning and social stature.

Iraqi tribes were historically nomadic peoples who came from the Arabian Peninsula and migrated north to settle near the Tigris and Euphrates. Saddam revitalized tribal identity and counted on tribal sheikhs for maintaining order and loyalty among their clans by handing out cash and subsidized agriculture material. When Saddam's regime collapsed, tribal leaders naturally replaced his patronage with that of Americans, hoping to secure financial support in ways of farm subsidies and involvement in reconstruction contracts. At first, according to the sheikh, the Americans made a lot of promises, such as guaranteeing him a lucrative contract for refurbishing a school. To date, none of these promises have materialized, and lately, skirmishes have broken out within his tribe about his friendliness toward Americans.

Last week, Sheikh Hassnawi discovered an assassination plot against him from tribal members who had joined the local resistance cells. At nightly sermons at the mosques, they passed around letters and leaflets with the sheikh's picture, and a list of his contacts with the Americans. The local imam called publicly for the sheikh to be deposed, saying the tribe "must find a brave new leader who would stand up against the invaders."

"The tribe is turning against me. They see that I meet with the Americans every week. I invite them here to lunch sometimes, but it doesn't add up to any benefits for them, so they think I'm selling out to the foreigners," the sheikh tells me.

He gestures for his son to bring his leather wallet. He flashes several VIP identification cards the local American commander has issued him for easy access to the base and speedy passage through checkpoints. He shakes his head. These privileges are about the only tangible advantages he has been granted from his friendship with the Americans so far. But without the Americans, he is afraid the mosques and insurgency will wipe out moderates like himself. For their part, Americans are pressuring the sheikh to inform on insurgent activities he detects within his tribe and to hand over suspects.

When he learned of his assassination plot, Sheikh Hassnawi summoned the implicated men and spent an hour lecturing them against the insurgency. Under Saddam, defection of a tribal member resulted in harsh public punishment that sent a strong message to other tribal members. But now tribal members openly challenge Hassnawi's authority. At the end, they reached a compromise: Sheikh Hassnawi promised not to turn the men over to the Americans or to punish their families if they quietly disappeared from the community.

"I told them if you want to resist a foreign army, it's not enough to just kill them, you have to have a political program. You have to have a leader with an agenda who can negotiate and dictate your demands. But my words are falling on deaf ears. The resistance is only focused on making life very difficult for the Americans. My men are no longer really afraid of me, and they are not afraid of the Americans. They do what they want. If I report on them or turn them in, it would be the end of me and my family," the sheikh says.

When our conversation turns to the future of Iraq and what type of government the sheikh envisions, I am surprised to hear him say he is in favor of "democracy and freedom."

His answer rings like a well-rehearsed line from a script. How, I wonder, does he think democracy would work within his tribe? If Iraq were to truly be democratic would he accept a vote from his people to select a new tribal leader? And would he step down if they chose someone else?

"Absolutely not," he roars. "That's nonsense. Iraqi society and tribal rules cannot and will not be changed. It is the way we have lived for thousands of years."

"But you say you want democracy, and that means people's choice. It means people are free to elect whomever they want, right?" I insist.

"This is not America, young lady. In Iraq people don't understand what is good for the country. Okay, people can vote for a government in Baghdad but we have to guide them on who they should choose. Let the central government be democratic, but we will keep our tribal ways," he says.

On our way back to Fallujah we hit rush-hour highway traffic. Haqqi is napping, and Munaf has his eyes glued to the road. I think of Sheikh Hassnawi. He was raised believing that his tribal patronage was an inherent God-given right, which his subordinates were raised to respect. Now the balance of power in Iraq's tribal society is shifting. I wonder if Sheikh Hassnawi's eagerness for the Americans to stay has more to do with securing his own position as the head of the tribe than with his affection for American democracy. How long will the alliance with the Americans serve such tribal leaders? Will the day come when their only chance of maintaining their helm will be by endorsing the insurgency? Increasingly, religious identity is replacing tribal loyalty. Clerics, rather than tribal sheikhs, have the last word at mosques. There is no leadership to unite the Sunnis in the way that the Shiite clerics mobilize the masses. For decades the Sunnis bonded under the umbrella of a Baathist identity that guaranteed them supremacy. With the dissolution of that guarantee, they are grappling for a common thread. Increasingly, it is an anti-Americanism that speaks to the masses. Before leaving the sheikh's quarters, he sums it up to me by saying, "The Sunnis are like sheep without a shepherd."

One day Haqqi arrives in the office and reports that his relatives in Tikrit are saying that the insurgency is spreading to Samarra, a city of about 200,000 people between Baghdad and Tikrit. Because Samarra has both a Shiite community and a shrine of a revered Shiite imam that draws flocks of pilgrims to the city, the news is especially surprising. Samarra was never a bastion of the Baath party, nor was its population fond of the regime.

Because he saw it as a direct rival to the prosperity of his hometown, Saddam neglected the city, cutting funds and relocating its university and government buildings to Tikrit. He expediently destroyed Samarra's infrastructure, executing local Baathist activists, and firing local officers from the ranks of the army. Samarra was one of the Iraqi cities Americans counted on for winning the hearts-and-minds campaign of the country. In Samarra, unlike other Sunni cities, there was deep resentment against Saddam to bank on. Why are the Americans losing ground to the insurgents?

On the highway north to Samarra traffic snarls. The American military convoy, a neat line of Humvees and supply trucks, stretches like an oversized caterpillar across several miles. After about an hour of being stuck in such close proximity to the military, we are apprehensive. I crane my neck out the window to see what is holding us back. Haqqi taps his fingers on the glove box and scratches the white patch of hair on his head. Munaf, looking hip in his dark sunglasses, uses his new American slang with a charming twist, "We are ducks sitting."

American soldiers have sealed off part of the road and set up checkpoints. Some of the soldiers are on foot, others are in bulldozers busy leveling the palm trees on the median separating the north side of the highway from the south so they cannot shelter attackers. On our left, another group of soldiers is flattening an orchard of orange and citrus trees. When we get close enough I ask one of the American soldiers what is going on. He replies in a polite, formal, soldierly voice, "We are clearing out the area, ma'am. Insurgents hide in these trees and attack us, ma'am." When I comment that clearing the fields seems like a radical measure that will create animosity among the locals, the soldier tells me that they have no choice. "We've asked the farmers to cooperate with us, but they don't."

Munaf and Haqqi are furious. Altering Iraq's natural landscape to quench uprisings was a method Saddam used in southern Iraq against the Shiites when he dried vast swaths of marshlands. On the long list of Saddam's crimes against humanity, these environmental crimes created collective punishment for the crimes of a few.

"See, there is no difference between America and Saddam. They all do the same thing when they feel threatened. I thought America was going to bring us justice," Haqqi mocks. It's hard to argue with him. The American military is adjusting its tactic to fight a counterinsurgency war for which they are unprepared. In the process farms are being razed and farmers are stripped of their livelihood.

The American military is systematically turning tree-lined roads in dicey areas into barren fields to deter insurgent attacks. In the town of Dhuluiya, north of Baghdad, five acres of thick farmland and orchards were recently cut down. Haqqi tracks down a petition addressed to the U.S. military from thirty-two families who are pleading for compensation for having lost their sources of income.

It's now November, and by all accounts the insurgency is evolving into sophisticated guerilla warfare. The number of attacks on the military has risen and the sporadic hit-and-runs have morphed into sustained firefights and sophisticated ambushes. Insurgents are planting explosives under the roads and in car engines, and are making remote-controlled bombs. Their target list has expanded to include high-profile Western organizations and embassies, and has already claimed dozens of lives and wreaked havoc across Iraq. Even humanitarian aid agencies like the International Red Cross have not been spared. The accumulating effect has had a chilling impact on the international community, forcing the UN and the Red Cross to pull out their foreign workers and to operate with reduced local staff. In addition, a string of reprisal attacks has been aimed against new police recruits, most of whom are Shiite, for cooperating with the American agenda.

The exact identity and goals of the insurgency still remain a mystery, but at least one common goal seems to be to create chaos and mayhem. From what we can gather from talking to people, local cells are operating independently in both Baghdad's Sunni neighborhoods and towns in the Sunni Triangle, a prominently Sunni area north and west of the capital. Recruits range from unemployed young men to former army officers and tribal militiamen. The goals of these operatives vary from avenging the death of a family member to rebuking a foreign occupation. There are reports of cooperation and funding from Islamist fundamentalists like al-Qaeda and even criminal gangs acting as fronts for the cells. In Fallujah, successfully ambushing an American soldier is rewarded with a hundred dollars cash. The salary of an Iraqi government employee is only a few hundred dollars, so the ransom is significant. In Samarra, the mayor tells me that the biggest threat facing the city is a Salafi Islamic movement that is spreading through mosques whose leaders preach the strictest, most fundamental form of Islam and call for true believers to take arms against the Americans. A year has not yet passed since the invasion of Iraq. In parts of the Arab world the Iraqi insurgency is being deemed as jihad, and the fighters killed, martyrs.

When we arrive in Samarra, we find a sadly neglected city. The landscape is flat and dry and the brick buildings look like they are about to crumble. The main market area comprises a narrow street lined with cramped shops. We stumble into one that sells tapes, CDs, and DVDs. At first we take it for a music and bootleg movie shop but it's stocked with religious teachings and propaganda videos about insurgencies. There is a poster of Chechen commander Khattab, a Saudi-born militant killed last year. A sign above a stack of DVDs reads, Jihadiyat, the plural of jihad. It's a collection of lectures by Osama bin Laden, footage from al-Qaeda training camps in Afghanistan and the attacks of September 11. There is even a *History of the Towers* DVD on the rack. The shopkeeper, who has a thick black beard, is twenty-eight-year-old Mohammad Hassan. When I ask him about his clients, he fixes his gaze on the counter to avoid eye contact with me.

"I sell these to all the brave people of Samarra who want to learn about other resistance groups around the world. We have our own jihad with the Americans, and so the subject is very interesting for people," he says.

His best seller is a recording of a militant Sunni preacher, Sheikh Ahmed Koubaisi, a radical cleric the Americans have banned from returning to Iraq. When I ask him what is making the residents here so angry at the Americans, his reply is brisk: "The way they treat us." I ask him for an example.

"There are many examples but I will give you one. We have only one soccer field in this province and it's a place for young people to play sports and have fun. But Americans don't let them. They are bombing the soccer field every night and warn people not to go to the youth club. They say the resistance is there. It's a sports club, not a military base; why are they attacking it? I tell you why, because they are evil."

What if the insurgents are really using the sports club as a shield, I wonder. The frontlines of this war are undefined and insurgents often do use civilian enclaves. Hassan's breathing gets heavy and his eyes dart about. When he finally speaks, he first corrects me by saying, "Stop calling them insurgents, they are resistance," and then settles the argument, as Iraqis often do, by launching a counter-blame strategy. He shoots off a list of mistakes by the American military, concluding that they are as bad as any insurgent group.

The Samarra Youth Club, less than half a mile away from Hassan's shop, is a shabby structure that looks more like a Soviet gymnasium than a place for youngsters to have fun. The pastel paint is peeling off the walls and the flimsy wooden doors are punctured with holes. The entrance leads into an empty hallway with small rooms used for body building and martial arts. Equipment is limited to a few basic weights and jump ropes. We climb a set of steep steps to get to the bleachers overlooking the soccer field behind the building. Samarra's soccer team is playing against a visiting team this afternoon. Players clad in shorts and numbered jerseys spread out across the field but they are not warming up as you'd expect. Instead, their backs are hunched, some are on their knees, and they are inspecting the grass closely, sifting through it with their fingers.

When I ask Jamal Jassem, the club's gregarious director, what the men are doing, he announces matter-of-factly that they are collecting bullets and shrapnel left from an early morning attack by American Apache helicopters. For the past month, the helicopters have opened fire on the field. The stadium light is blown out and the goalposts are riddled with bullets.

Machine guns have punctured holes in the water tank and damaged the pipes. Americans insist that insurgents are using the field and the empty swaths of surrounding land as a hiding place from which to launch mortars. Jassem vehemently denies this notion. To prove his point, he gives me a thorough tour of every nook and cranny of the stadium. As he opens and closes doors, he turns to me and says, "See, there are no guns here. We are not stashing weapons or giving refuge to any fighters."

As we walk the length of the field, Jassem cautions me not to step on any shrapnel. Pointing to a tall fence, he calls the guard to testify before us that he locks the gate and watches over the club at night. Last month, the Americans gave Jassem seventy-two hours' notice to evacuate the club. The Americans erected signs warning athletes not to show up for games. But dozens protested the club's closure and demanded that Jassem open the only entertainment center available to them. When Jassem was accused of allowing Americans to dictate the terms of the players' lives, he finally caved. In a comical tug of wills, Americans attack the field at night and athletes show up the next morning to carry on with their game. The cheering crowds that once packed the stadium have vanished. Aside from the coach and a handful of extras, the stadium is eerily empty.

"The players told me this is their club, not the Americans', and they are right. Why are they picking on us? What is their aim? To frighten people, to make them angry, or do they really think this way we will like them? Right now, I tell you, we have no such thing as resistance in the club, but if the Americans continue this way, these boys will not play sports anymore. They will go to the mosques and take guns to fight them."

The saga of the soccer field is a metaphor for the growing disconnect between Iraqis and Americans. The Americans attack and clear an area on the premise of security and in the process alienate locals, who view their presence as the core problem to insecurity. In Sunni areas, cries of "Let them leave!" sound out like a mantra. Americans are uninvited guests who are behaving with the mindset of owners. Let them leave, or we will force them out with our guns.

A week or so after our visit, the simmering tensions in Samarra boil over into the most brazen and highly synchronized attack staged on Americans since the invasion. In broad daylight, insurgents mount a sophisticated ambush of two American convoys en route to the city's banks with new Iraqi currency. According to the American military, the convoys carrying the cash were guarded by about a hundred soldiers in eight tanks, four Bradleys, and six Humvees. Sixty-odd Iraqi fighters scattered around the two banks, split into smaller cells, and with machine guns and rocket-propelled grenades and mortars fired on the convoys from several directions. The fight dragged on; the insurgents repositioned themselves behind concrete walls, on roofs, and in narrow alleyways. A network of drivers in taxis, beat-up BMWs, and Toyota pickup trucks provided them with transportation. Their faces wrapped in checkered Arabic *keffiyehs*, insurgents set up ambush points on routes in and out of the city and planted explosives on the roads. All told, the Americans reported they had killed 54 insurgents but locals in Samarra fiercely disputed this claim, accusing them of jacking up the numbers from nine dead civilians. By all accounts, the Americans were stunned.

A few days after the ambush, I return to Samarra to check up on the soccer team. We leave Baghdad at 7 AM but run into a monstrous military convoy blocking the highway for four hours. When Babak calls to see where I am, he tells me to turn around immediately. A friend of ours, freelance photojournalist Ashley Gilbertson, beat the convoy traffic and made it to Samarra earlier in the morning. He was talking on the phone in his car near the soccer stadium, where I was heading, when a car approached him and opened fire. Locals had spotted him as a foreigner.

And just like that, in a matter of a few weeks, Samarra erupts and a new frontline in the insurgency is born.

12

I Think, Yes,
It Will Get Better
in 2004

M*y reportage is* delayed by a three-day stretch because of the Muslim holiday, Eid al Fitr, which marks the end of a month-long tradition of fasting from dawn to dusk. In the Arabic calendar, each month begins and ends with the cycle of the moon. Shiite and Sunni religious scholars can never agree on what day the thin sliver of the new moon reappears. So there are two Eids, one day apart, one for each sect. All week our staff has been engaged with preparation for Eid by buying new clothes, boxes of fancy sweets, and gifts for the family. Because this year his salary allows him to splurge on lavish gifts for his mother and sister, Haqqi seems particularly pleased. He takes an afternoon off and drives them in his new black Mercedes-Benz to Arasat's fashionable shopping district, where he reports his mom picked out a fine crepe skirt suit and his sister bought a trendy pair of jeans and a sweater. We give the Iraqi staff the day off on the condition that they keep close to the satellite phone and monitor the news.

Baghdad's landscape is slowly changing. Twelve-foot-tall concrete barriers and layers of barbed wire surround government institutions, embassies, and the hotels in which foreigners stay. Many neighborhoods have been transformed into bunkerlike military fortresses with multiple checkpoints aimed at stopping car bombs, suicide attacks, gunfire, and grenades. At night our sleep is interrupted by the sound of American helicopters that fly low to avoid getting hit by mortars. The main bridge that arches over the Tigris and connects the two sides of the city is closed, and the redirection of traffic creates monstrous jams. Gasoline is in short supply, and lines at gas stations stretch for several miles. (We buy our supply for triple the price from the black market of young boys standing on the side of the road with jerry cans.) There are regular blackouts across the capital. A ration of two hours of electricity and four off has been instituted, but it's random and month after month the ratio decreases. For our purposes, we rely on a generator the size of a small truck that sits in the garden and hums loudly through the night.

On the night the Sunnis announce sighting the new moon, Babak and I drive from the Hamra Hotel to our new residence, at a pleasant villa in Mansur. On the way we make several stops at small vegetable stalls and grocery stores, until I have all the ingredients for a proper chicken salad except for the mayonnaise. For some reason, mayonnaise in Baghdad is a gourmet item, only found on the shelves of fancy supermarkets that cater to foreigners. We make a last stop near one such store in the main square in Mansur, and because it's already dark, Babak reluctantly gets out of the car with me. The mood in the street is unusually festive and cheerful, and feels strangely like the pre-Christmas holiday rush in the States. Random gunfire breaks out. Bright red tracers splash light into the sky. We are startled. Babak grabs my arm, and we both duck under an awning.

"Great, now we'll get a bullet in our leg because of your chicken salad," he says. I squeeze his arm, relieved, as always, that he is next to me.

We appear to be the only people taking cover. Around us, people are nonchalantly going about their business. Pausing to look, they point out the tracers to children as we do at Fourth of July firework celebrations. The shop owner, under whose awning we are hiding, comes out laughing.

"*Makoo shai, makoo jeish Ameriki. Eid,*" he says, reassuring us that the gunfire was not a battle between insurgents and American military but celebratory gunfire because the Sunni mosque just announced Eid will be tomorrow.

I have never understood the Arab custom of celebratory gunfire, on occasions marking religious holidays, a football victory, weddings, or birth of a son. Without fail, every time, the next day's newspaper carries tragic articles about people who were wounded or killed by stray bullets as they plunged back down to earth.

The shopkeeper, a fat, cheerful Iraqi man, wants to know what Americans do to celebrate. "Americans have guns; don't they shoot in the air when they are happy?"

"No, they drink champagne," I tell him.

He is surprised to hear that as Iranians, Babak and I didn't grow up celebrating Islamic holidays. Despite the regime's Islamic overtone, Iranians identify far more with their Persian heritage and the pagan traditions of the ancient Zoroastrian faith. The festive rituals Arabs practice for Eid al Fitr are carried out by Iranians on the first day of spring for Norouz. In Iran, religious holidays are a calendar day off, and for the devout, perhaps an occasion to telephone elderly relatives and congratulate them on the end of Ramadan.

Babak explains that as half American, half Iranian, he grew up celebrating both Christmas and Norouz. I admit that the holiday I like best is Thanksgiving. The shopkeeper smiles knowingly. He lifts the lid of the freezer, where he usually stores ice cream and popsicles, and puts a frozen American turkey in my arms.

"Where did you get this from?"

"From the American base in Kuwait; someone I know who works there brought me a few for my clients."

"There you go. I guess you're doing Thanksgiving dinner this year," Babak declares.

The shopkeeper walks down the two narrow cramped aisles and pulls off items he imagines that I will need: canned cranberry sauce, pumpkin pie filling, mashed potato mix, dry stuffing, and yams.

Our Thanksgiving dinner party excites our Iraqi housemates and office staff so much that they practically set aside all their other duties to help prepare for it. It's touching to see how they fuss to please us. I've always felt that my Iraqi staff feel very protective of me and believe that part of their job requires them to tenderly care for me like a sister. My driver, Abu

Munaf, who claims he is a chain smoker, takes great care in making sure no one smokes in our car and routinely sprays it with air freshener. Ever since I got sick from drinking contaminated water, he fills a cooler with ice and several liters of imported water, which he places in the trunk of his car each morning. Haqqi, the technology and pop culture lover, visits the bootleg DVD shop several times a week and returns with movies he thinks I will like. Munaf often brings me homemade cookies from his mother.

The holidays are no exception. When I can't find a proper oven pan for the turkey, Haqqi and Ayad, one of Babak's translators, knock on a dozen relatives' doors until Ayad's aunt lends a gigantic round pot she uses for cooking rice during Eid holidays. Munaf takes the pumpkin pie filling along with my instructions to a local bakery and convinces them to bake us a traditional piecrust. Our cleaning lady polishes china plates and sterling silver serving dishes. On Thanksgiving as my friend Annia Ciezadlo and I labor away at a meal for twenty guests, our Iraqi cook and the young houseboy refuse to leave the kitchen, hovering around, producing utensils and dishes as we need them.

When it's finally time to put the bird in the oven, our cook protests, "That's not how you make turkey."

"How do you know how to cook turkey?" we ask.

"Oh, I saw it on television many times, on Mr. Bean's show. He makes it differently."

We roar with laughter at his innocent remark. Often, Iraqi knowledge of American culture is distorted and polarized by unpleasant personal interactions with American soldiers or from superficial television shows. There is a perception that Americans are not religious, warmhearted, or family oriented. When Annia tells our cook that her ailing grandfather lives with her mother and that she takes care of him, his eyes widen. "I thought Americans left their families when they are eighteen and go their separate ways," he says.

Babak and I volunteer for the Baghdad holiday shift through Christmas and New Year's, partly because we'll get the house to ourselves for a week and partly because we think it's a good addition to our previous

New Year's Eves spent in Kabul and Tehran. We have fun shopping for a Christmas tree in an empty lot near a Christian neighborhood. We decorate our tree with blinking lights and glittery ornaments. We buy each other Iraqi Christmas gifts—an antique silver Arabic coffeepot for me and a brass cigarette holder with a hand-painted palm tree for Babak. His colleagues give us a DVD player, which we inaugurate by watching a mindlessly funny comedy. We are invited to more holiday parties than we can attend: a big bash at the restaurant of the Hamra Hotel, where the wait staff sport Santa hats and mix holiday punch behind a bar; an elegant Christmas Eve dinner at *The Washington Post* house; and our own Christmas night dinner party where American employees of CPA drive their SUVs from the Green Zone to our house.

On Christmas morning we wake up early to the sound of multiple explosions in the distance as rockets hit the Iranian, Turkish, and German embassies and the Interior Ministry. A rocket-propelled grenade hits the Sheraton Hotel, where many American contractors and some television network employees are staying. The rocket slashes the cable of the all-glass elevator, sending the machine free-falling twenty stories down. When I go to inspect the damage, the lobby is littered with debris and shattered glass that make a crunching sound under my feet.

I wonder if the early morning blasts will put a damper on church services. On the way home we stop at a small neighborhood church. I worry when I see a row of American military vehicles and Humvees parked outside, until I realize that the soldiers have come to attend mass. Dressed in full uniform, sitting in a back pew, they receive a sea of stares and turned heads. The church is half full, with a few dozen well-groomed Iraqi families. After reciting the Lord's Prayer in Arabic, the priest reminds his congregation that the traditional midnight mass is canceled because of security concerns before saying a special prayer for those killed in the past year. I hear muttered comments about how the soldiers feel safe enough to walk into an Iraqi church, sit among ordinary people, and pray.

We are invited to Sabah and Marie-Rose's house for Christmas lunch. In addition to the family, a Shiite Muslim couple that is close friends with the Nassers' sons attends. A fake Christmas tree adorned with an assortment of ornaments stands proudly in the living room. A few children dressed in party clothes rip open gifts as adults sip wine and whiskey and munch on *klaacha*, a traditional holiday pastry baked by Marie-Rose. For lunch, she serves a scrumptious dish of roast lamb with grilled vegetables and saffron rice. Winter in the desert is cold, and the Nassers warm their house with kerosene heaters. We huddle near the one in the salon and eventually Sabah moves all three heaters into the living room, closing the door to trap the heat. Late in the afternoon, the electricity cuts out and a dark gloom casts a shadow over what had been a cheerful party. Marie-Rose brings out oil-lit lanterns and candles. Saving precious fuel for darker hours of the night, they don't turn on their small generator.

Babak and I listen attentively to everyone's complaints about life in Iraq. The guests take turns sitting next to us and speaking, in broken English, about their problems. At the end they tilt their heads, stare into our eyes, and ask if we are going to "write a story about it?"

And then there is the standard question, "Do you like Iraq? Do you like living here?" What can I possibly say? Their worries are greater than mine, and I am embarrassed to complain. I nod my head. "Yes, yes, I really like it. The people are very nice."

Inevitably, the conversation turns to Americans. Between Thanksgiving and Christmas, American soldiers captured Saddam hiding in a grave-like hole in the farming village of ad-Dawr near Tikrit. The news and images of a disheveled and haggard Saddam being examined by an American medic electrified Iraqis. Shiites and Kurds were overjoyed while Sunnis were astounded at the hypocritical way he surrendered, hands swung up in the air, with no resistance.

"Why didn't he shoot himself? He had a gun. It would have been more dignified than this," Haqqi complained.

But more intriguing were rumors that began almost immediately after Saddam's arrest. Many of my Iraqi friends, including Sabah's family, speculate that the Americans have fabricated the arrest and had Saddam in custody long before their announcement. Above the hole where Saddam was hiding hung a branch of a palm tree bearing fresh yellow dates. Iraqis argued passionately that dates are not in season in December. The first time Sabah told me this, in a serious voice uncovering a deep secret, I laughed.

"No, no, no. It's true, I'm afraid. I went to that hole the very next morning and there were dates hanging above it," I tell him.

He won't believe me until I bring him the photographs of myself standing at the edge of the hole under the tree. Since then, the story of my visit to Saddam's hole has been an endless source of amusement for Sabah. Every time he has a visitor, he makes me repeat it like a proud parent forcing a child to recite poetry in front of a nonexpectant audience.

And again on Christmas Day, Sabah turns to his guests and announces, "Do you know Saddam was really captured by the Americans in the hole? Farnaz and Babak went there! I saw the pictures myself! She even went into the hole! She said it felt like a coffin! There were dates hanging from the branch! Imagine that! Tell them, tell them, Farnaz. What did you see there?"

The guests gasp.

"Well, we saw Saddam's belongings scattered everywhere. It was definitely very bizarre," I say.

"What did he have? Was it luxurious?"

"Definitely not. The farmhouse was primitive. It had one bedroom with a rickety single bed where we think Saddam slept and a kitchen and a bathroom further away in the garden," Babak says.

"There were a lot of his personal items all around. Sneakers, chocolate bars, a jar full of pistachios, a pair of black loafers, black socks hung to dry, and a lot of Arabic poetry books," I add.

"He had a few religious verses from the Quran hanging on the wall but the strangest thing was this poster of Noah's ark with all the paired-up animals," Babak says.

"Maybe he thought he is Noah and will save Iraq from the Americans by taking Iraqi couples and farm animals on his ship? Of course he will only take Sunnis and leave the rest of us here to die," jokes Ziad, Sabah's son, making everyone laugh.

I know the Americans are desperately hoping that Saddam is the true instigator behind the Sunni insurgency and that capturing him will lead to stability. But judging from the pathetic way Saddam was living at the end, shifting places, hiding like a terrified fugitive, I doubt that his arrest will lead to the fizzling of resistance cells.

New Year's Eve in Baghdad starts like any other with me standing in front of my closet, staring at my clothes and pestering Babak about what I should wear.

"Something red," he says, wrapping his arms around me. "I like red on you."

I take special care in dressing, combing my hair and applying makeup because I'm going to be on an end-of-the-year show on Iraq on CNN International. To do so, I have to go to the Palestine Hotel where the CNN bureau is stationed. Since cars can no longer drive up to the entrance, Munaf parks in a secured lot nearby. It's pitch dark, and we must negotiate our way through a maze of barbed wire and checkpoints. Munaf lights the way using a small flash. I caution him to be careful not to direct the light at the American military checkpoint ahead of us where a tank is parked. At the checkpoint, there are separate entrances for men and women. I get frisked by an Iraqi woman who empties my bag and amuses herself by opening up my wallet and checking out the color of my lipstick. We finally walk down a narrow corridor of cement barricades to reach the hotel's entrance.

"If you just explain on CNN how you got to the hotel it will give the Americans a very clear picture of Baghdad," Munaf says.

I am startled when a producer guides me to a room on the upper floors of the Palestine hotel that was recently hit by a rocket. The room has been badly damaged, bricks have fallen on the floor, the carpet is torn, and the furniture is mangled. A hole gapes in the wall. The cameraman has me stand on a creaky wooden plough, the damaged wall behind me.

"Why here?" I ask. I'm told that the hole offers a nice open view of the blue-domed mosque below us. Viewers apparently won't be able to detect the damage.

Jim Clancy moderates the interview, which includes me and veteran Iraq reporters Rod Nordland from *Newsweek* and CNN's Jane Arraf, who are, respectively, in London and Miami. We are each asked to offer our views on the biggest surprise of the invasion and occupation and how the process of democracy building is faring. To me the biggest surprise has been the deteriorating security in Iraq. I add that the United States has undermined the ethnic tensions between the Sunnis and Shiites and the emerging roles of the Shiite clerics, and how Sunnis are increasingly feeling marginalized in the political process.

Clancy wraps up the program by asking all of us a one-word-answer question: "Yes or no, is it going to get better in 2004?"

Jane says yes, Rod says no, and I say, "I think yes."

On the way back home, Munaf tells me he was very pleased about my comments, especially about the Sunnis. "Do you really think things will get better this year?" he asks. I tell him I think so. "Next New Year's Eve we will celebrate together and you will see I was right," I reply cheerfully.

"Inshallah, inshallah," he utters, the Arabic word for "God willing."

The interview has foiled our dinner plans for the evening. We have a quiet dinner at home, and at around 9:30, we get ready to attend a New Year's Eve bash at the BBC house.

I'm putting on my jacket when the frantic call for help comes on the walkie-talkie. A man is shrieking and screaming in Arabic for an ambulance. Babak grabs the walkie-talkie and starts yelling into it. "Who is hurt? Who are you? What's going on?" We don't know if our shared radio network, which print organizations set up for communicating with one another on security, has crossed waves with the Iraqi police, or if one of us is hurt.

In between the sentences we hear the words, "Explosion, Nabil restaurant, *L.A. Times*."

We pile into a car and rush to the restaurant where we were supposed to dine tonight. Here we're met with a chaotic scene of carnage and confusion. The restaurant's roof has collapsed, and flames shoot upward. Broken glass, debris, and blood coat the sidewalks for several blocks on Arasat Street. A suicide bomber rammed his car, packed with explosives, into the wall of the Nabil restaurant, killing eight and injuring over twenty people. Two American correspondents of *The Los Angeles Times* are badly injured. One of their Iraqi staff is fighting for his life in the emergency room of a Baghdad hospital and two others have suffered significant cuts and bruises. Black smoke streams out of the restaurant and emergency workers hurry to pull people out from under the rubble. Two waiters from the restaurant, their white shirts stained with blood, are standing on the sidewalk, their faces pale with shock. Neighbors wander up and down the street looking dazed, pausing to ask police questions. One woman sobs uncontrollably. American military helicopters buzz over our heads, while a cluster of tanks and Humvees occupies the ground. The smoldering remains of the car bomb sit on the curb. The street is draped in darkness. Without electricity, the only source of light is the bright blue and red lights of ambulances and fire trucks.

As we walk back to the car, Babak asks me if I'm still as optimistic about Iraq's future as I had been a few hours ago on CNN. "No," I reply. "I'm not." Suddenly 2004 doesn't seem so promising. We head to the BBC party, where only half the guests turn up. We get drunk on champagne, wear silly party hats, and dance until 5 AM, pretending we are not in Baghdad.

13

Look at
How Much
Freedom We Have

Winter settles in Iraq with clerics issuing religious edicts for democracy and militia competing to rule the streets. Though the occupation will formally end in June, a huge divide separates the Iraqi and American way forward. The Americans want an indirect election, in which caucuses representing Iraq's eighteen provinces appoint a new government, a scenario that would afford Americans great influence even after granting Iraq its sovereignty. This proposal has been forcefully shot down by Grand Ayatollah Sistani, who is demanding a general election, preferably before the handover of power. A United Nations committee, which Sistani approves, is now investigating whether countrywide elections are feasible by May or whether the solution is to have an immediate interim government and plan elections for later in the year.

In any case, the Iraqis like to say that the Ayatollah beat the Americans at their own game of democracy. Haqqi has pinned a cartoon from the *International Herald Tribune* on our office bulletin board, depicting President Bush rolling out a cart piled with jumbled wheels and wires with a sign proclaiming, The Handy Dandy Caucus Machine. Ayatollah Sistani, wearing his black robe and turban, stands defiantly before him holding a Ballot sign. Next to him a box reads, "One person, one vote," to which Bush replies, "No, no, no. That's much too simple, try this."

Sistani, a revered religious man who can transform political maneuvering into religious duty, has a significant advantage over Bush. As a Grand Ayatollah, Shiite Islam's highest rank for clergy, Sistani can back his words with a fatwa or religious edict, which Shiites take as the word of God. So it came as no surprise when he issued a fatwa calling for elections. The other three Grand Ayatollahs of Najaf, who are less influential, joined ranks with Sistani and issued similar edicts. Elections would most certainly grant leadership to Shiite politicians, simply because their political parties are organized with experienced leadership, sufficient funding, and a common vision for power. The Sunnis remain disenfranchised and lost.

Sistani's decree hit on the Americans harshly by declaring their plan "fundamentally unacceptable." His fatwa will ultimately serve as the blueprint for tackling the two most important issues for Iraq in terms of governance: A new constitution must be written by Iraqis and ratified in a national referendum. A national assembly must come to power through general elections.

At one of my weekly visits with the young Shiite clerics I've befriended, I find Sheikh Nassrawi and Seyed Hashem preoccupied with campaign planning. They are hosting Islamic educational conferences at mosques and community centers, and making voter-education pamphlets that spell out the importance of voting and its relationship to religious duty. They have been instrumental in organizing demonstrations in Baghdad, where tens of thousands of people have marched in the streets, holding up posters of Ayatollah Sistani and shouting for elections.

The clerics' new political mission began when Sistani beckoned them, along with a few dozen other young clerics committed to spreading his cause, to his house in Najaf. The Ayatollah sat next to his son and gave his marching orders: Our country is going through a very critical time. Your duty is to spread the word that Ayatollah Sistani insists that any new government be chosen through a direct election, not by the U.S. or U.S.-appointed Iraqi leaders. There would be funding available to host community initiative classes and educational conferences executed by the clerics in each neighborhood. The clerics could visit or call to report progress and ask for additional direction. They have, so far, had educational seminars that are gender segregated: a session for schoolteachers, nurses, engineers, war veterans and their widows, and the elderly.

At one such educational seminar, I hear a cleric advise a room of about a hundred schoolteachers, huddled on the carpeted floor of a mosque, that they must ensure that every school have a designated prayer room and that they must observe Islamic dress code. He encourages teachers to advance the secular curriculum by teaching the Quran and Islamic texts on the side. It is every teacher's duty to forbid "un-Islamic" student behavior, such as watching music channels on satellite television and wearing tight jeans. I am particularly jarred when the cleric announces a special message for Iraqi people from Iran's hard-line supreme leader, Ayatollah Ali Khamenei. An aide brings out an old cassette player. Khamenei's voice echoes through the prayer hall of the Qamar Bani-Hashem mosque in Sadr City, urging Iraqis to resist the Americans ruling their destiny.

Since our first meeting when they were junior clerics liberated from Saddam's tyranny, Seyed Hashem and Sheikh Nassrawi have transformed into social activists, and now, political campaign officers.

Sheikh Nassrawi tells me, "You can't have Bush and Blair promising us democracy, but eight months go by and we have yet to see a single ballot box. Iraqi people are not stupid; we will not be tricked."

Seyed Hashem, always a tad more political in his comments, adds, "We didn't expect the postinvasion phase would be this bad. At least we thought we would have security and freedom, start rebuilding our country. Instead it's turning into chaos and now we look to gain independence from the Americans, in the fastest time possible and in a democratic way. It's Seyed Sistani's orders."

"How influential is Ayatollah Sistani?" I ask.

Sheikh Nassrawi unfolds a cotton napkin and wipes his forehead. "Seyed Sistani is like God. You don't see him anywhere, but his presence is felt everywhere."

There are more pictures, posters, and murals of Ayatollah Sistani on display in Baghdad than of any other person dead or alive. Almost every item—from watch to lighter—that I remember once bearing the face of Saddam is now available with a picture of one cleric or another. While it's not fair to compare the brutality of Saddam to the religious clout of the Ayatollahs, the readiness to replace one authority with another is indicative of Iraqi society. Is a person's ability to think independently and critically slowly compromised by living under the iron rule of one man? Many Sunni friends have commented to me that Saddam was like a father, without whom Iraqis are lost. To an extent, Shiites seem disoriented with their freedom. Heralding the Grand Ayatollah as the nation's next father figure is one way to ground themselves in Saddam's absence.

Though his image is splashed with abandon through Baghdad, Sistani is himself an elusive figure. He has refused to meet with any Americans and has declined requests for interviews. I try to see him, disguised as a Shiite follower on a pilgrimage from Tehran. Munaf takes me to the guards manning the alleyway entrance to his house and introduces me as his cousin from Iran who has dreamed of meeting him in person. As always in holy cities, I am covered by a black abaya. The guard looks me over, adjusts the AK-47 on his shoulder, and says, "Impossible, the Seyed doesn't accept women visitors."

It's the first time that I've been denied access on the basis of my gender in Iraq. Until now, being a woman correspondent seemed an advantage. As a woman I am often invited into homes, where I am allowed to mingle freely with the women in the house. Frequently during interviews with men, I find them thrown by a female journalist and more genuinely candid because they take me less seriously than they would a male reporter. Having my gender thrown at me as an obstacle comes as a surprise and I demand an explanation. "But why?" The guard stares at me with a cold glare. "He just doesn't. For security reasons."

"What does security have to do with women? Most suicide bombers are men anyway and you are allowing the men inside," I protest, pointing to a group of men walking toward the Ayatollah's house.

"Look, this is not a woman's place. How many times do I have to tell you? He doesn't see women. Now go away." He shoos me like a pesky dog, and tells Munaf to take me to the shrine to pray and to the bazaar to shop.

Offended, I quote what I can remember about women in Islam, screening my memory for lines I've seen scribbled on murals in Tehran next to pictures of mothers holding the head of their martyr sons. "Islam says that paradise is under the feet of mothers. It respects women and now you are saying Ayatollah Sistani won't see me because I'm a woman? What kind of a *marjah* is he if he boycotts his women followers?"

My sharp answer bewilders the guard, who stares at me and figures out I'm not just a visiting pilgrim. He asks if I'm a journalist. I level with him, "Yes, but I'm still Iranian. I'm still Shiite. Does it make a difference?" He replies candidly, "No, because you are still a woman."

In the two weeks that we spend in the holy cities, my gender is a recurring theme in an increasingly Islamic environment. Holy cities, which are now booming with tourists and pilgrims from Iran, have always been conservative. But on my first visit under Saddam's rule and on numerous trips in the past year, I never had to tiptoe around my gender the way I do now. When we show up at offices of political parties or clerics, I am required to stand outside under the sweltering sun because the waiting room is designated for men. At the Yazdi seminary school, where I have spent hours interviewing male students and cleric instructors in the courtyard, the guard refuses me entrance, pointing to a sign that reads: No Women Allowed. "You have to bring a handwritten note from Seyed Moqtada himself if you want me to let you in," he tells me, slamming the door in my face.

On several occasions while we are walking or waiting outside an office, passersby criticize me sharply for letting my scarf slip a few inches above my forehead to expose a few strands of hair. The entrances to the holy shrines in Karbala and Najaf now have segregated entries with a female police officer checking the attire of visiting female pilgrims. At the entrance to Imam Hussein's tomb in Karbala, the female guard eyes me up and down, tugging my headscarf forward and lifting the hem of my abaya to inspect my clothes underneath. She is clearly trying to signal that she is in charge. When she notices I'm not wearing socks, though I'm wearing black flat shoes and long pants that conceal my ankles, she folds her hands across her chest and blocks my way. Pointing first to her thick nylon socks, she gestures to the door.

"Welcome to the Islamic Republic of Iraq. The New Iraq belongs to the Americans or the Iranians? Instead of having discos and fun we now have clerics and *hijab*," Haqqi declares, as we shove our way through the crowds in search of stockings.

Iraq *is* starting to remind me more and more of Iran. Unlike many of my Western female colleagues here, I find dressing up in *hijab* and navigating my way among Islam's restrictions are more aggravation than novelty. Every time someone gestures toward my headscarf or throws me a hurdle, I lose patience. I have flashbacks of similar oppressive behavior from Iranian authorities in school, university, workplace, and the street. As I have been programmed to do in Iran, I fight back with aggression. In Najaf, I get into a screaming match with a young cleric while we wait in a side street outside the offices of Moqtada Sadr. Haqqi nervously translates that I'm fed up with their demands. I don't normally wear the *hijab*. I don't like it. I don't know how to walk with it. I am hot and uncomfortable. I am respecting them by putting this on. They should respect me for trying and shut up. The man eventually backs off, shocked and unaccustomed to a woman talking back at him. He apologizes, thanking me for trying to be a good Muslim woman.

When we try to find a hotel room, the receptionists question why a foreign woman is traveling with two Iraqi men and require us to produce paperwork that proves we are related—preferably married or siblings. When we protest that we are journalists, they require letters of assignment and press cards. Most of the decent hotels have been taken over on one-year leases by Iranian tour agencies for the hordes of pilgrims arriving by busload every day, and there are even tents erected in the center of town to accommodate the crowd. Receptionists tell me my best bet is to find the Iranian man in charge of the hotels. It takes hopping from one hotel to the next until we track down a middle-aged Iranian man, who first scolds me for being in Iraq on my own and wonders aloud what kind of a family would allow such indecency, and then scribbles a note for a third-rate motel to give us two rooms. In the interest of having a roof above our heads, I hold my tongue. On the first night, I wake up at 4 AM when someone pounds on my door to alert me to morning prayer.

The only thing that makes the presence of Islamic religiosity bearable is that it's mixed with impending progress. The cities are showing signs of economic opportunity and growth, buzzing with activity and livelihood, especially in the evenings, when all the pilgrims are wandering about the city. Sistani has been elemental to the boom, funding megaprojects toward the holy twin cities' revivals. We visit an Islamic center and a local human rights office that are supervised by Sistani's clerics and geared at gathering evidence and documenting Saddam's crimes against the Shiites.

One morning, as I'm drinking coffee in the lobby of the hotel, I notice a glossy magazine called *Holy Najaf* with a picture of Ayatollah Sistani splashed on its cover. The magazine belongs to a new educational and publishing establishment called al-Murthdada, established by Sistani and senior clerics in Najaf. The offices of the magazine are contained in two small rooms with several desks, rigid chairs, and one computer.

The editor is the thirty-one-year-old cleric Seyed Moustafa Jabouri from Najaf. Over tea, he describes his work. The magazine is distributed throughout Iraq and has twenty-nine local branches, mostly in Shiite cities and towns. It is, as he puts it, an independent media outlet supervised by the clerics to spread "Shiite missionary education."

The magazine was founded in secret in the last days of Saddam's regime by five students from the *hawza* as a newsletter. With money and the freedom of the press, it is now published monthly, with three hundred students contributing. Seyed Jabouri picks up a few copies and flips the pages to showcase the content: a cultural article about religious texts and books, technology updates on the use of the Internet, religious teachings and political pages devoted to spreading Sistani's viewpoint.

"If you ask me, for the Shiites the situation has gotten better little by little. Look at how much freedom we have; I can say what I want and even publish it in a magazine," he says, shaking the glossy copy in the air to stress his point. Then a shadow of doubt casts over his perky comments, and he puts the magazine on the table. "But I am worried that this equation will not last very long. No one can forecast a realistic future for us, not even Seyed Sistani."

Seyed Jabouri's glumness evaporates as he cites recent signs of progress: To promote the *hawza*'s line of thinking, a satellite-television station is about to be launched as well. Sistani's associates show us blueprints of housing complexes for theological schools and tourism centers that will cater to the pilgrims. The shrines will be expanded and restored soon.

While I never get my wish to meet Ayatollah Sistani, I learn quite a bit about him by sipping tea in tiny rooms with his associates and other Grand Ayatollahs in Najaf.

The Ayatollah was born in a small town in Iran near the holy city of Mashad to a long line of prominent clerics. He shares my father's name—Ali—from his grandfather, a prominent cleric who had studied in Najaf. When his associates speak of Sistani, their voices rise and fall adoringly, recounting anecdotes as if they were fable. Let us tell you of Seyed Sistani's childhood achievements: He memorized the Quran by the age of five. He was enrolled in a religious seminary by the time he was eleven. He challenged religious interpretations of many senior clerics in Qom before he was even twenty.

Sistani's older disciples remember him as a young cleric in Najaf in the 1950s whose impressive knowledge inspired the then-preeminent Grand Ayatollah, Abul Qassim Khoei, to take him under his wing and groom him as a successor. Central to Mr. Khoei's teachings was the notion of "quietism"—that clerics should push for observance of Islamic principles in public life but stop short of grabbing the reins of political power—a motto Sistani appears to be following in today's political wrangling. When Sistani replaced Khoei as the senior *marjah* in Najaf, he inherited a huge flock of new followers and control over the millions of dollars they contribute as part of their religious obligation to donate 20 percent of their annual income. With tens of millions of followers worldwide, Sistani commands more than any other Ayatollah, a position that places him at the Shiite world's helm and gives him significant clout. The Baathist regime's wrath struck Sistani when he was placed under house arrest in 1994 and prohibited from teaching in seminaries, holding lectures, or spending a dime of his followers' money in Iraq. Instead Sistani diverted his attention and resources to the Iranian holy city of Qom, where the Islamic revolution was conceived.

No conversation about Sistani is complete without mention of his wealth and his willingness to spend for his cause. His foundation pours millions of dollars a month into Shiite religious establishments and charities. In the city of Qom alone, Sistani spends more than $5 million a month on student and teacher stipends, housing for clerical students in Iran, a digital library of Islamic texts, and clinics and publishing houses. Without Saddam, Sistani has grand visions for Iraqi Shiites. The donated religious money is so considerable that the Shiites now have their own department at the ministry of Awqaf.

"What does Sistani really want?" I ask one of his close associates, a cleric named Qasem Hashemi who heads the Committee of the Friday Prayer Imams in Najaf, another recent creation of the Ayatollah, which acts as a union for clerics boasting of 350 imam members who are self-described "links" between the public and Sistani.

"He wants to return Najaf to its former glory as the epicenter of Shiite faith."

"What do his followers want?"

"We want what he wants," he replies. "Ayatollah Sistani has the last word. He is above any president, and his words are above the law."

Also above the law are the contending Shiite militias ruling the streets. The militia is becoming a real problem for the Americans trying to dissolve the ones they don't like and absorb others into the newly trained Iraqi police or army. In Najaf and Karbala the militias that are more powerful than anticipated think nothing of challenging local cops or getting into scuffles with the American army. The militias don't wear a uniform but are often dressed in simple, dark-colored shirts and slacks. Some don black bands on their foreheads or arms, some of which are emblazoned with the words *"Allahu Akbar* [God is great]." Almost all carry AK-47s and set up checkpoints in roads and neighborhoods. Refusing orders from Iraqi police and the American military to disperse, they claim it their duty to safeguard Shiite sites and clerics.

There's a hodgepodge of armed movements shaping up in Iraq; Shiite militias and the Sunni insurgency are made up of an array of people with different goals. The Shiite militia is roughly made up of armed men, often with no formal training, who protect Sistani from area tribes loyal to *marjayat*; Mahdi army volunteers, mostly young untrained thugs and criminals, backed by Moqtada Sadr; the Badr Brigade Force, a group of mostly middle-aged but very well-trained men loyal to the rival faction and Iranian-backed Supreme Council for Islamic Revolution in Iraq; and semi-trained men loyal to the Shiite party Dawa.

For Sistani, arguably the most powerful Shiite leader, the biggest challenge isn't the Americans, who are meeting his demands, but keeping the militia in check and reining in other Shiite factions, particularly the one led by renegade Moqtada Sadr. The most disturbing factor about the simmering Shiite rivalry is the battle over militia control of and rivalries over prominent mosques and shrines and over control of money generated from cash donations. Moqtada took over the Kufa mosque, where Imam Ali lived, prayed, and was stabbed to death. Moqtada's move on Kufa is seen as provocative by the senior clerics in Najaf, who tell me that a power struggle between militias is inevitable and risks destroying the cities' newfound boom.

The rivalry runs so deep that even the question of who leads Friday prayers in the holy cities is politically loaded. For months Sistani and Sadr compromised, staging one communal prayer, for the sake of appearance on Shiite unity, and alternated weekly between whose appointee would lead the prayers and deliver the political speech. Now every city has two Friday prayers, one for each side. If America fails to make good on its promise of democracy and freedom, the voice of a moderate like Sistani will be trampled by fringe figures like Moqtada.

Bickering among Shiites feeds the Sunni belief that they will regain power. After each day of meeting with Shiite clerics, I have dinner with Haqqi and Munaf in the cafeteria of our hotel. We are served an Iranian dish of saffron rice with caramelized red berries and baked chicken. Although Haqqi has been on a strict diet to slim down, he devours the meal, commenting on how even restaurants in Najaf, limited to a handful before the war, are topping Baghdad's. Between our interviews, Haqqi, who has a taste for sweets, hunts the bazaar for Iranian imported sugar cookies and chocolate sponge cakes for dessert. Munaf, fit and slim, teases him about falling for Iranian-made goods. Haqqi reminisces about life before the war and his family's privileges as Sunni elite. He is deeply pessimistic about his country's future and its new leaders, whom he calls American stooges.

Like many Sunnis, Haqqi dismisses the demographic that suggests Shiites are a 60 percent majority, writing it off as a myth created by Americans to justify taking power away from Sunnis. He grumbles about the return of hundreds of thousands of Iraqi Shiite refugees from Iran, which he sees as a ploy by Iranians to rig the numbers in favor of their Shiite friends. Other Sunni friends accuse the Shiites of being uneducated, uncultured, and utterly unprepared for their governing. The current Sunni thinking is that if they ignore the Shiites long enough, they will go after each other, make a mess of things, and realize they can't rule without them.

Shiites are equally skeptical about Sunni motives. For months now, they've been facing attacks from the Sunni insurgency. Suicide bombers packed with explosive belts have targeted big crowds during Shiite rituals, killing and injuring scores of people. This sort of instability is damaging the little economic hub the Shiites are cultivating for themselves in the holy cities.

While the Shiite clerics are busy issuing fatwas about elections, the Sunni extremists linked to al-Qaeda and the ultraconservative Wahabi sect are posting religious edicts pronouncing Shiite Islam sacrilegious. When Haqqi comes across a website that declares the murder of Shiites is not a sin, he calls me to the office, and points to grisly pictures of men holding daggers and to links to videos of people being beheaded.

"I think we should avoid Sunni areas for a while or we should hide that you are a Shiite," he says.

I wonder if it's better for me to say I'm Christian.

"No, no, that's even worse," he protests. "At least being a Muslim you still have a chance. Do you know how to pray like a Sunni?"

He instructs me to fold my hands on my chest in submission, put my forehead on the ground, not on the compact prayer stone, remember to omit Imam Ali's name from the call to prayer. I memorize his instructions to cultivate two identities in order to survive.

YEAR 2004

If They See Me with You, They'll Kill Me

14

My Ambulance
Is Like Iraq;
It Is Cursed

hen I first see the man, I think he must be a patient stranded in the Ministry of Health's emergency-relief operation center. His body is scrawny and bent, carrying the weight of a small hunchback. His brownish yellow skin is the color of a malnourished person and his heavy-lidded, half-open eyes have a stony gaze. His cheekbones are hollow and a deep scar the size and shape of a fossil caterpillar runs across the right side of his face. He is Majid Bechai Leftah, an ambulance driver who, like many Iraqis battered by poverty and pressure, looks more than a decade older than his forty-two years.

Taking me to a window that overlooks a parking lot, Majid points to a brand new Mercedes-Benz ambulance sporting the emblem of the Red Crescent, Islam's equivalent of the Red Cross. "You see that car? It used to be blessed. No one ever died in it before the war. Now my ambulance is like Iraq, it is cursed. Every day people die in it. I have stopped counting the numbers."

Each day Majid is dispatched to scenes of carnage from suicide attacks, bomb explosions, firefights, and rocket attacks from which he rushes the dead and injured to the emergency rooms of Baghdad hospitals. Particularly violent incidents in Iraq, the attacks on the United Nations, the headquarters of the International Red Cross, and the shrine of Imam Ali in Najaf are sobering milestones of the war. In a voice that is boastful and sad, Majid tells me that he carried victims of all those attacks in his car.

We are at the recently opened relief center in a cold, damp room, where the paint on the walls is flaking off bit by bit. The center has been established to provide humanitarian responses, ambulances, medical supplies, and volunteer teams for daily outbreaks of violence. It's April of 2004, the one-year anniversary of Baghdad's fall to American troops and the end of Saddam's regime. I linger in front of a whiteboard on the wall noting the number of dead and injured from the past week in Fallujah. Wounded: 791; Children: 44; Women: 55. Killed: 264; Children: 28; Women: 24.

On Friday, April 9, the anniversary of the fall of Baghdad, Majid left the dispatch headquarters at 10 AM. CPA officials had finally granted permission for thirty-four ambulances to drive into Fallujah to bring out injured civilians. It took the convoy over three hours to make the half-hour run to Fallujah city center.

At four American checkpoints, the ambulances were stopped and searched. Papers were examined, drivers and doctors questioned. When the ambulance drivers finally reached the city, they found it abandoned. Houses were emptied and shops were closed. Gunfire cracked the silence, and several buildings were burning. At the clinic, Majid saw dozens of families taking shelter with the injured piled in the hallway. Food and clean water were scarce. Majid brought back a seventy-two-year-old man with shrapnel in his hips and a woman and a young man with shrapnel injuries to Yarmulk hospital in Baghdad.

"This isn't how I imagined I would be celebrating the anniversary of Saddam's fall," he admits. Yesterday the makeshift clinic was cloaked with the unbearable rotting stench of piles of dead bodies awaiting burial. When Majid walked into the hallway, he saw a sheikh performing prayers next to the corpses as hospital staff wrapped them in white cloths before hauling them across the road for burial in a mass grave. The road to the cemetery was blocked by American checkpoints, and the bodies were deposited in a hole dug in a former sports field.

"It's very difficult; we see everything. I want to remain neutral and do aid work. But at the end, I'm an Iraqi and it upsets me to see my countrymen getting hurt and killed every day."

Majid was born to a peasant family in a village near the southern Shiite city of Nassariyah. He received elementary-level education and worked on a farm to help his parents support their nine children. His youth was defined by Saddam's wars. He joined the army when he was eighteen for the security of a regular paycheck. When I ask about his scar, he brushes his fingers across it, and calls it his souvenir from Saddam's war with Iran. An army tank driver, during an intense ground fight with the Iranians in Basra in 1984, shrapnel pierced his face and slashed his leg. He spent nearly seven months recuperating in the hospital before reporting back to the field. When Saddam invaded Kuwait in 1991, Majid was called again to fight. Again, he was injured, this time from a sniper bullet that hit his shoulder and sent him back to the hospital. During his extensive hospital stays he concluded that he wanted to work as an ambulance driver.

After his injuries it took eleven years for the army to finally dismiss Majid on the basis of being physically unfit to fight. Two of his brothers had joined the Shiite opposition movement of Dawa: one had been executed by Saddam, and the other had fled to Iran. His brothers' brush with authority disqualified Majid for government jobs, so he drove his minivan as a taxi around the capital. In 1999, a friend finally helped him get hired as an ambulance driver for the Ministry of Health. A year later he got married. Now the father of three daughters, he is waiting for God to grant him a son. "Inshallah, if I live to see it." He points to a string of prayer beads hanging from his front mirror and tells me that every time he gets behind the wheel, before turning on the engine he rolls the beads in his fingers and says a prayer, asking God and the revered Shiite Imam Ali to protect him and keep him alive.

After a fellow ambulance driver was held at gunpoint for his keys, Majid has been forced to contemplate the need to carry a gun. For a mere $70-per-month salary, the risks of an ambulance driver are formidable.

129

"I expect everything when I sit behind the wheel. Maybe the Americans will think I'm carrying a car full of guns and attack me. Maybe insurgents will kill me to steal my car. Maybe criminals will take me for ransom. An ambulance driver used to go do his duty with no worries and come back home to his family at the end of the day. Now you come an hour late and everyone is worried about you."

Majid parks the ambulance in the ministry's lot overnight because insurgents are carjacking ambulances, packing them with explosives, and using them for attacks or as a means to transport guns. His minivan was stolen during the rounds of looting when the city fell. Driving near American convoys is risky and slow. Once, Majid was transporting a young man bleeding from a gunshot wound in his leg who was crying in pain. After twenty minutes behind an American convoy, Majid raced past traffic toward the convoy with the ambulance siren wailing loudly. When the tip of his ambulance reached the first Humvee, a soldier pointed a gun at him and shot in the air. He pulled the ambulance to the side of the road and let them pass. The dispatch center has recorded four incidents in the past few days where American soldiers opened fire on their ambulances entering Fallujah.

Stumbling upon insurgents is equally dicey. Yesterday on his way to Fallujah, the roads were blocked and a gang of men, their faces wrapped in *keffiyehs,* flagged him down. They inspected his car, checked his papers and instructed him on which road would lead him safely into town. When Majid pushed his luck and asked them for a written note to bypass other insurgent checkpoints, one of the men said, only if he would let a few fighters hide in his car and get to the center of town, cordoned off by the marines. Majid took out his Quran and said he had pledged to God to serve only the injured and the sick. The man backed off.

On the one-year anniversary of the invasion, the American military is entangled in what it has most dreaded since it marched into Iraq: a double-front war with Sunni insurgents and Shiite militia. In Fallujah, trouble began when locals attacked a car carrying contractors working for the America security company Blackwater. The four men were murdered and set on fire in broad daylight. Their burnt, mutilated corpses were dragged before cheering crowds and hanged from the town's bridge. In Sadr City, Mahdi army fighters retaliated when the Americans shut down Moqtada Sadr's newspaper and arrested one of his right-hand aids for an alleged role in killing a rival cleric. Moqtada ordered his followers to "terrorize your enemy," and uprisings erupted in four cities.

The Americans are responding by laying siege to both areas, but opinion is shifting against them. Iraqis know that militia and insurgents are fanning the flames of instability, but guerilla warfare is the natural order of humanitarian crisis. As the attacks get more brazen, the number of dead and injured civilians, mostly women, children, and elderly, shoots up to several hundred. Shell-shocked refugee families, their belongings packed in cars, arrive by the thousands in Baghdad whenever fighting permits civilian movement. Neighborhood mosques have once again stepped up, taking the displaced and finding them host families. When I visit the Sunni enclave of Ammariyeh, where residents are taking in Fallujah refugees, Haqqi won't go with me for fear of being spotted working for an American company. He could easily be recognized since he invested his savings in a modest electronics shop on Ammariyeh's main drag. Two neighborhoods before Ammariyeh, he tells Munaf to pull over and gets out of the car.

"I am really scared. There are fliers warning people not to work for the enemy. If they see me with you they will kill me," he says.

To celebrate the first anniversary of the U.S. invasion, Iraqis have gone on a three-day strike. Stores are shut, streets are vacant, and schools are closed. Even government employees have refrained from reporting to work. There is a prevailing sense of a real turning point for both Americans and Iraqis. In the first spring of the new Iraq, long days of overbearing heat and violence betray the sense of novelty. The most striking thing about the double uprising is that it took almost no time for Sunnis and Shiites to declare unity against their common enemy to mobilize the public. Clerics spoke and citizens responded, whether it was to stay home, protest in the streets, volunteer, or donate blood or cash to charities. Compared to the clerics, the voices of secular Iraqi officials who have aligned with the Americans are muffled and irrelevant. The official line from American officials who insist the uprising is without grassroots support is dangerously naive. Just like that, as if a ball of yarn were rolled down a steep hill, Baghdad unravels.

On the second day of the strikes, I finally convince the staff to leave our villa in Mansur for a drive around the abandoned city. When our car turns from the tree-lined quiet side streets to the main thoroughfare, we come upon anti-American graffiti on the walls and banners that calls for a united Shiite-Sunni front.

"Last year this time, people were dancing in the streets when Saddam's statue came down," Munaf says as he slows down the car. "We had a lot of hope. Now look at our city, everywhere empty, all the people angry and scared."

We stop at Malek supermarket, because I notice the shutters are half open, and the owner, a friendly, burly man named Salman Daoud, is inside. Haqqi sticks his hand into the iron shutters and knocks on the glass door. Salman, who appears mesmerized, doesn't hear us until we call out his name. He is sitting on a stool amid cramped isles of canned goods, candy bars, and boxes of cereal, staring up at a small television hanging from the ceiling.

"My shop is closed. If you want to buy anything, you have to wait until the strike is over," he tells me.

Salman is a Sunni moderate and a good businessman. He opened his shop in the mid-1990s, largely serving foreigners who worked for NGOs or the United Nations offices. After the war, his customers mushroomed to include journalists, military personnel, and contractors, who flock to him with requests for comfort foods like peanut butter and mango chutney. For Thanksgiving and Christmas he had provided us with a turkey and prided himself on his knowledge of our needs. I'm surprised to see Salman swept up by the uprising's fervor.

When I tell him I'm interested in his opinion on the strikes and uprisings, he sits down and lowers the television volume. The news channel

Al-Arabiya is showing devastating footage of ambulances and aid convoys returning from Fallujah with wounded civilians.

"You see? This is America's aggression against us," Salman says, evoking a phrase I hear more and more every day in casual chitchat with our staff and Iraqi friends when they want to describe situations where they feel some form of injustice is being inflicted upon them by Americans.

"The past few weeks have proved to me that Americans are occupiers and liars. They are killing innocent Iraqis, women and children. I am 100 percent with the resistance group now, both Sunnis and Shiites. They are giving their lives to free our country. Now I am resisting in my own way, by closing my shop."

It's the first time since his shop opened that Salman has closed his doors. "I didn't close during the invasion; I didn't close during the bombardments. I have always been here to do business, but not now. I am listening to the imams."

Salman went to Friday prayer last week for the first time in over a decade because, although he's not religious, he couldn't think of any other place to vent his anger and feel connected to his fellow Baghdadis. The sermon inspired Salman to donate a crisp hundred-dollar bill to a man collecting funds for the displaced. The next morning he took a truckload of canned goods to the volunteer food drive before stopping by a clinic to give blood for the injured.

"Has your feeling affected your business, Salman?" I ask.

"Yes, in the past two weeks my relationship with my customers has changed. I don't like it anymore when Americans come to my store. I think they are murdering my countrymen, and I'm selling them candy bars."

"The Americans say the insurgency has no popular support."

He lets out a big guffaw and a loud sarcastic laugh that shifts his large body on his stool. Stretching out his arm, he points to the window. "The street is our witness. You can see how empty it is, you can see how much support our mujahideen have among the public."

"It's the anniversary of the fall of Baghdad this weekend; how do you feel about that?"

"I feel very sad. When the American forces came here, they didn't know anything about the Iraqi people. They miscalculated everything and made one mistake after another. They didn't know how to deal with Iraqis. After one year, they still have no idea what they are doing in our country."

As we leave Salman's shop, a teenage boy selling cigarettes approaches us. He shoves a box of Marlboro Light cigarettes into Haqqi's hand and declares proudly that he is charging extra tax on each box and donating it to militia who are fighting the Americans.

"Which militia? Shiite or Sunni?" I want to know.

The boy smiles at me and says, *"La Sunni, la Shiites, wahda wahda Islamiya,"* reciting a slogan chanted at protests and mosque sermons these days that translates, "No Sunni, no Shiite, Islamic unity."

❈ ❈ ❈

We go to the sprawling Mother of All Battles Mosque. Um al-Qura in Baghdad doubles as a Sunni headquarters for senior clerics and volunteer drivers. A testimony to the egomaniac, warmongering mind of Saddam Hussein, its minarets are made in the shape of AK-47s. Scud missiles and a gigantic verse of the Quran, rumored to be written in Saddam's blood, hang in one of its rooms.

Ever since rhetoric has found a common enemy in the Americans, sectarian attacks against Shiites have dwindled but I wonder how long it can hold. The two sects are deeply mistrustful of one another, and it's hard to see how they can turn uprisings into zealous political alliance. The major Shiite political parties are vying for power on the coattails of the Americans. In the parking lot, we encounter a handful of Shiite volunteers who are driving their own vehicles to rescue Sunni Fallujah casualties.

The double battles the Americans are waging do not come as a surprise to those of us on the ground. Confrontations with Sunni insurgents and Shiite militia have been long in the making, fueled by a year's worth of decisions and mistakes about the Iraqi army and security, about the depth of popular tolerance for occupation, and about the role of the country's important Shiite leaders.

This is not how either side, Iraqi or American, imagined they would be commemorating the toppling of Saddam's dictatorship. In an ideal scenario America could have claimed some level of victory as it prepared to pull away its administrative occupation, and Iraqis could have been appeased by prosperity and progress. As it is, Americans are trapped in a quagmire. I ask dozens of officials and ordinary Iraqis to assemble the mistakes in sequence for a story on the war's anniversary.

At the top of any Iraqi's list of American mistakes is the breakdown of law and order after the invasion. The military's decision not to interfere and stop the mayhem and looting will forever translate, in Iraqi minds, as a sign that the foreigners did not care about the ordinary citizens. Subsequently, the United States' decision to dismantle the Iraqi army and border patrol contributed to the flow of cash and arms to militant cells and facilitated jihadis' crossing over into Iraq. Many technocrats, particularly the Sunni, criticize the exclusion of the Sunnis from the political process and high-level posts, largely due to the de-Baathification policy, because it automatically alienated a well-educated, experienced population and turned them into enemies of the new regime. Perhaps one of the hardest things for the Americans to grasp is how much the official declaration of their presence in Iraq as a "military occupation" legitimized the insurgency as a national resistance and how accommodating Shiite clerics has given rise to political Islam here. And, of course, no conversation about American mistakes with any Iraqi is devoid of complaints about the lack of basic infrastructure and the need to restore electricity and clean water supplies and fix sewage problems.

15

Is This Freedom?
Where Is Your Freedom,
Mr. Bush?

As *the pictures* of the tortured detainees in Abu Ghraib prison circulate throughout the world, outrage is mounting. In Iraq, the torture scandal has shattered America's image and its moral high ground for advocating human rights and justice in tyrannical countries. It has given new credibility to the rumors and conspiracy theories Iraqis have been reciting since the invasion. From the grocery store to visits with Iraqi friends and staff, every conversation I have is prefaced with the questions, Did you see the pictures? Now do you believe us?

Our office staff members are at once repulsed and mesmerized. They huddle behind the computer searching for the gruesome pictures that have overnight come to symbolize America's messy entanglement in Iraq. As news of the story unfolds, the American military tries to control the damage by inviting a dozen or so journalists to tour the prison to see how things have improved.

Visiting Abu Ghraib is like having a vivid nightmare that stays long after waking. The prison sits on a sprawling dusty stretch of land in the outskirts of Baghdad, between a busy highway and a shabby town. The high, thick walls surrounding it recall those of storybook dungeons.

When I first see the two levels of concrete, blast-protected, fifteen-foot-high walls, I'm sitting in a comfortable, air-conditioned bus. We snake through a winding road in a tunnel of double-decked barbed wire separating the tented detainee camps from the road. Outside, hordes of Iraqi men dressed in orange jumpsuits, T-shirts and pants, or the Arabic *dishdashah* are curiously following the movement of our bus. Some wave, and mindlessly, like tourists passing through the French countryside, we wave back. Within a few minutes the detainees figure out that we must be nonmilitary visitors. They call out to each other and run toward the edge of the wires. The momentum picks up; hundreds of men emerge from inside the brown tents. They twirl their shirts in the air, wave their arms, and shout for our attention in Arabic. They seem desperate. We are curious. Our military police guide, seemingly oblivious to the chaos outside the bus, directs our attention to portable toilets and iron tankers of water that supply showers, and to a large open prayer tent.

"Each camp has a mayor and we meet with them once a week to hear their concerns," he says, but his voice is hushed by the loud pleas of help from the detainees, who are mushrooming in number. The bus slows down and abruptly stops.

"What's going on out there?" we ask.

"Oh, they're just overexcited about having visitors; it's nothing. Please step out of the bus and see our clinic that treats detainees when we get mortared," he says, reminding us that Abu Ghraib is a troubled prison where mortars land from across the highway and prisoners frequently riot and scheme elaborate escapes. We step out to deafening cries of detainees who wave, screaming hysterically for our attention.

"We are innocent, we didn't do anything!" one man yells in Arabic.

"The Americans humiliate us here!" another screams.

"Help, help!" the crowd chants.

"Is this freedom? Where is your freedom, Mr. Bush?" screams another in English.

One detainee grabs a loudspeaker, provided to the camp's mayor for making public statements, and addresses us in perfect English. "We are stripped of our freedom and of our rights. We were arrested off the streets and from our homes. We are humiliated in the interrogations. The problem of the Iraqi prisoners isn't only what is written in the news. Iraqi prisoners need freedom, their dignity, and their rights."

The Americans are flabbergasted. The dog-and-pony show they had orchestrated as a damage-control publicity stunt is rapidly backfiring. They had not foreseen such interaction between the press and the detainees. These are not scenes they want journalists to record. When we head toward the barbed wire, the American military is shouting for us to get back in the car.

"Please follow the rules. Get back on the bus," orders Major General Geoffrey Miller, the new commander of Abu Ghraib prison.

One soldier yells at photographers to stop taking pictures or risk getting their press credentials revoked and thrown off the tour. The television camera crews are not allowed to film.

"But they're talking to us; they want us to be heard. This is important. Why did you bring us here if you won't let us do our job?" I protest stubbornly.

"Ma'am, don't argue. Get in the bus. *Now!*" orders the soldier.

As we begin climbing back into the bus, our necks crane to get a last glimpse of the commotion and the voice of the Iraqi man with the loudspeaker grows more desperate. "Where are you going? Where are you going?" he screams. "Wait! Wait! Listen! Listen!"

Our bus drives away. A few minutes later we are escorted into an empty medical facility set up to treat patients. The Americans can't figure out why we aren't interested in hearing about how many beds they have and what medicine they bring in from the United States. This is routine, we thought; you are supposed to treat inmates in a prison. When we ask about treating detainees who were tortured or beaten the nurse says she knows nothing of such behavior. She explains how there have been more mortar attacks on the prison than she can remember. Located on the highway to Fallujah, Abu Ghraib sits in a troubled spot where military convoys routinely come under attack by insurgents. RPGs, roadside bombs, and mortars are a daily event. The day we visit shortly after 8 AM, at the height of civilian traffic, a roadside bomb goes off about five minutes after we pass.

Our next stop is the indoor cell blocks, where Saddam kept prisoners and in which the now-infamous photographs of tortured detainees were taken. The narrow, dark hallway is painted institutional green. I peak into empty cells that contain a steel cot, a hole in the ground for a toilet, and a broken sink drilled into the wall. It's very dark. Five female detainees are in the upstairs cells. At first they are silent but when they spot us walking below, they violently shake the bars and wail out their stories.

"I have five children; they are home alone. I'm not part of the insurgency," one cries. A female guard walks over to her cell and orders her to "hush" and "be quiet." The loud screeching of the bars and the piercing screams of the women unnerve me.

An Iraqi female journalist with our group is shouting back questions at the inmates, "*Shoo Ismiak shoo ismak* [What's your name]?"

We hold our recorders toward the ceiling to record their voices, but our American guide is anxious. "It's time to leave. Come on, this way, this way," he says, ushering us out.

When I leave the cell, the daylight hurts my eyes. We walk to a cluster of wooden sheds perched atop the dusty ground that serve as interrogation rooms. Eight feet square, each booth contains one plastic round table and a few metal folding chairs. A steel loop is screwed to the ground. The American explains it is used to restrain detainees during interrogations. Each booth has a pane of one-way glass that allows supervisors to monitor interrogation techniques.

Despite its constant dealings with the media in two consecutive wars in Afghanistan and Iraq, the American military still hasn't figured out how journalists think. How could they have thought that by feeding us rhetoric and handing out chilled sodas and muffins on a tour of Abu Ghraib, we would be distracted from observing the mess, chaos, and utter despair of this hellhole?

The Abu Ghraib scandal radically discredited the American army with all Iraqis. It's a lasting image from which the army cannot recover. If the

American army had set out to set an example of a compassionate force, it has failed bitterly. Here was the army representative of a nation famed for its human rights, civil liberties, and compassion.

The scandal shames not just the army and the scores of soldiers who are trying to do good deeds here but every one of us who is in one way or another affiliated with America. It's no longer possible to look into an Iraqi eye and say with conviction that their lives are better now than they were under Saddam. The pessimistic anti-American Iraqis feel vindicated; the optimists have a healthy dose of fresh doubt. Sabah compares the scandal to the discovery of a romantic partner cheating. "How can we trust the Americans again?" Sabah asks me.

The expressions I see on people's faces when the subject of Abu Ghraib comes up are unsettling—eyes widening in shock, lips clenched in disgust, and voices rising in fury. Until now, I've doggedly pointed out the positive changes the war has brought—the ability of my staff to earn a living wage, speak their minds, dare to dream, and have contact with the larger world. But I don't dare to offer these examples after Abu Ghraib. In the Iraqi imagination, torture at the hands of Americans has been in play for a long time.

In an effort to exonerate any supervisors of responsibility, the American army is trying to blame the torture scandal on the small unit immediately responsible. We publish stories that challenge the army's stand that this was an isolated incident of a few low-ranking individuals who had taken justice into their own hands. I fly to Amman for two weeks to talk to Red Cross investigators who inspected the prisons and interviewed detainees. Over an Italian dinner at the Four Seasons Hotel in Amman, the ICRC regional director, Pierre Gassmann, reveals to me that the problem of detainee abuse by Americans was so widespread that the organization had considered whether it should go public with its findings of torture and abuse at the hands of Americans. The organization is not accustomed to visiting prisons operated by democratic regimes and, in this case, by the world's leading power.

From the outset, the detention operation of thousands of Iraqis was poorly planned. The Americans invaded Iraq believing that Iraqis would cheer them for toppling Saddam. Accordingly, they didn't expect detention facilities to swell with over ten thousand Iraqis whom the Americans suspected of involvement in sinister acts against them. Furthermore, abolishing Iraq's armed forces and justice system created an extra burden for the United States' already overstretched and understaffed military, which had to step in to run Iraq's prisons and courts. The detainees were divided into two categories: Those considered common criminals or harmful to other Iraqis are adjudicated under existing Iraqi law. Those suspected of presenting a threat to coalition soldiers are held and processed by the U.S. military. The charges against them can be as specific as throwing a grenade at troops or as vague as being a Saddam Hussein loyalist. The military hasn't made clear what legal rules apply in these cases, giving life to a limbo justice status.

International law regarding the responsibility of an occupying country is not ambiguous. I study every article of the Geneva Conventions carefully at night. I also consult *Crimes of War* as a reference for covering stories like Abu Ghraib. The Fourth Geneva Convention stipulates that the treatment of detainees requires prompt notification of family members, transparency about their whereabouts, separation of adults from juveniles, and communication and visitation with family members. The third article calls for humanly dignified treatment of detainees and noncombatant civilians.

Especially early on, in Iraq these tenets are never properly adhered to and detainees are swallowed up by a system that isn't prepared for them. Families are never notified of a person's imprisonment, and even when they actively search for relations, very little accurate information about detained relatives is available. Detentions can go on indefinitely. A small number of detainees are released from time to time after the military decides they have made a mistake. But the vast majority remain in custody pending further investigation. None have been charged and none are allowed legal representation thus far, in fall and winter of 2003.

I am shocked to find that many American soldiers I interview have very little information about their responsibilities as occupiers. Some say they have not been given a copy of the Geneva Conventions, nor were they required to study or read them. Almost every American soldier I speak to says he is overworked and complains that the environment is hostile; they have to worry about their own lives and try to stabilize the neighborhoods under their responsibility. In some areas, American soldiers serve as civil officers during the day, working closely with the community to establish neighborhood councils and volunteer task forces aimed at improving living conditions. At night these same soldiers could raid homes and arrest locals. Mistakes and mishandled detentions of true threats are commonplace in these sweeping house raids and neighborhood crackdowns. At a time when the Americans desperately need support from the Iraqi population, detentions are alienating extended Iraqi families and even whole communities, where layers of resentment and hatred slowly form a thick veil over people's hearts.

I first became interested in the detainee crisis in August of 2003, after hearing repeatedly how people, even children, went unaccounted for after being picked up by Americans. When I probed, I discovered the detention system the Americans had established was not capable of such simple tasks as registering detainees in a manner that could inform families of their fate or whereabouts. No list of names was available in Arabic, while transliterated names in English offered various spellings that added to the overall confusion.

When I interviewed Lieutenant Colonel Kirk Warner, the deputy staff judge advocate of the coalition forces, who oversees both the Iraqi and the coalition's justice system, we met in Saddam Hussein's palace. It was early September and Lieutenant Colonel Warner told me that none of the investigations for security detainees had been complete since the United States took over Iraq in early April. Human Rights Watch and the ICRC have begun sharply criticizing the Americans for their handling of the detainees. America's lack of resources is an insufficient excuse for failing to implement the Geneva Conventions.

"We had not anticipated the detainee problem. We prepared for prisoners of war from the Iraqi army, not security detainees. We did prepare for the worst, but we did not expect it to be this bad," says Lieutenant Colonel Warner candidly.

I ask Warner if he thought the Geneva Conventions were being appropriately implemented. His answer was vague. "We try to recognize to the extent we can all these international laws that apply by trying to balance them for the security of our people and of Iraq."

After a long pause he admits, "This creates a hearts-and-minds issue. I understand that well. The hearts and minds are not won."

It wasn't difficult to find families affected by the detentions. All one needed to do was stroll a neighborhood and ask old men playing backgammon at sidewalk cafés. Inevitably someone would point to a house and say the Americans came in the middle of the night and took the men away. This was how I found Najim Abdulhussein's family in September 2003.

At first the Abdulhusseins wouldn't talk to me. When Haqqi tells Mohammad, the fourteen-year-old son, that I'm an American journalist, his smile freezes. Mohammad, who is short and chubby with an innocent boyish face, looks younger than his age. He fidgets on the stool behind the grocery counter as Haqqi asks him about the detentions. I impress on him the fact that I'm not here on behalf of the military or the American government. I just want to hear what happened and how the family is coping. Mohammad runs inside to tell his mother and comes back with a firm refusal. When we insist, the family's sixteen-year-old daughter, Shahed, shows up at the door and listens carefully while Haqqi explains that speaking to me could help their case. A few minutes later, their mother emerges; I'm a little startled. She is a faceless, shapeless figure covered in black nylon from head to toe, an unusual choice of covering for an Iraqi woman. She and her husband are extremely devout Muslims who identify more with the ultraconservative Wahabi sect of Islam practiced in Saudi Arabia.

The wife, whose name is Jinan Ghattam, tells me in a shaky voice that she will talk only if her brother allows her to. We wait over an hour in the car for her brother to arrive. Over the week that I spend interviewing her, Jinan eventually gets comfortable, allowing me and Haqqi to sit with her for hours in the family's modest, scarcely furnished living room. Once I surprise her when I put my pen and notebook down to take her gloved hands in mine. I softly ask her to let me see her face if Haqqi leaves the room. How will we talk then? she protests.

"We don't have to talk, I just need to see your face and make eye contact in order to connect emotionally to the story," I reassure her.

She calls me a strange American girl unaccustomed to talking to masked faces. Haqqi leaves the house and her daughter locks the gate. We sit there in total silence for fifteen minutes as I stare. Her dark brown eyes are small and ringed with dark circles. Her round face is dotted with freckles and her uncombed brown hair is cut just beneath her chin. She nervously runs her fingers through her hair, stroking her cheeks, which are drained of color. She is acutely aware of another woman studying her face.

"*Shokran* [Thank you]," I say. She nods, shrugs, and quietly pulls the thick black scarf over her head. Haqqi is allowed back in the room and we continue talking.

Jinan tells me that the Americans came on a hot August night when temperatures soared past 125 degrees. Electricity was out and there was no relief from the oppressive heat. Her four-year-old twins, a boy and a girl, were crying. The older children sat in a corner on the floor, too hot to talk, play, or complain. Jinan, who is called Um Qutaibah by acquaintances, remembers how her clothes stuck to her body from sweat and how her head pounded with pain. She decided to roll out mattresses on the flat rooftop of their small one-story house and sleep outdoors with her kids. It was the only way to escape the heat. She had barely fallen asleep when at 2:30 AM, a loud churning sound woke her up. She sat up on her mattress, readjusted the bedsheet over her twins to protect them from mosquito bites, and peered down at the street. There were American Humvees parked outside. The Americans were banging on the door. She knew what it meant. There had been four raids on their street where Americans stormed the houses, searched for weapons, and arrested the men. Jinan grabbed her abaya, expecting the soldiers to storm the house at any moment. The kids had woken up and huddled next to her. She stroked their hair, reassured them that it must be a mistake, and begged them not to cry.

From below she heard her husband asking the soldiers to hold off entering the house until his wife and daughter were dressed. But they didn't listen. They kicked down the wooden front door and entered the living room. Jinan tumbled down the stairs with her kids behind her. A soldier shouted at her in a language she didn't understand. A translator explained that she must gather her children and step into the street while they searched the house and the tiny adjacent grocery stand that earns the family its livelihood.

The soldiers didn't find any weapons, nor did they take any money or jewelry. But they paused when they found a gas cylinder sitting in a corner of their courtyard and a plastic bag containing chemical powder and wax tucked away on a shelf. Her husband, Najim, explained that the material was for making the helium balloons he sold during Muslim holidays to neighborhood kids. The soldiers talked among themselves before handcuffing her husband and shoving him into the Humvee. Jinan's husband suffered from seizures and would need his medication; she ran into the house and grabbed his pills. When she returned she found her oldest son, Qutaibah, in handcuffs. He was still wearing his pajamas.

"Why, why?" she pleaded. "Why are you taking my husband and son?" She cried and screamed. Neighbors woke up from the commotion and poured into the street. Her other four children were crying. The Americans told her they were only taking Qutaibah for one week to question him, and that they would return him soon. The military translator told her to go to the local police station the next day for more information.

The next morning Jinan fed her children, asked her elder daughter to keep an eye on the little ones, and called her younger brother, Firas, for help. Together they walked down the palm-lined boulevard that leads to the Khadria police station, a block from their home, and told an Iraqi police officer their story. He listened patiently. He then said it was too soon to have any information about the pair. Sometimes it takes weeks or months before the names and place of detention are confirmed. Jinan sat down on a bench and cried. A crowd gathered around her, shouting angry sentiments at the Americans. A young American soldier took pity on Jinan and gave her a form to fill out with the detained relatives' names, address, ages, and profession. One day, a week or so after the arrests, Jinan and Firas drove up to a large U.S. military installation in the area known as FOB Red Falcon, which occupies an unfinished Iraqi army housing complex in a dusty field. When they approached the gate, an American soldier guarding the entrance listened through a translator. He radioed inside before informing them they had come to the wrong place; the base served as a way station from which detainees were quickly transferred elsewhere.

"Go to the police station," the soldier suggested.

"But we have just been there," the family protested.

"Go to the coalition information center; they are supposed to keep an electronic database of detainees."

For a brief moment the family felt a glimmer of hope. Jinan thought in simple terms. If she could track down her husband and her son, she could hire a lawyer. She could go to the prison and demand visitations. She could take them canned food and books and plead their innocence. For the first time in over a month, she was in a good mood. She went grocery shopping and cooked a nice lunch for her kids. That afternoon Shahed insisted on accompanying her uncle to the American information center.

When their father and brother had been picked up, Jinan's two older children's carefree childhood was replaced by adult responsibilities. Shahed had taken over household chores: she swept the house with a straw broom, dusted the few pieces of furniture, washed the dishes, and cooked lunch and dinner every day. She dressed, bathed, and fed her twin brother and sister. Her mother was too preoccupied and depressed to take care of her kids. The little energy Jinan could muster she saved for searching for her husband and son. When she got home from wandering around from police station to army base to prison gate, she fell apart. She either cried or prayed or just sat in silence with a blank look on her face.

Jinan had a hard time swallowing her pride and accepting charity from relatives, who often showed up with a basket of vegetables, a bag of rice, or dried beans. Her son, Mohammad, all of fourteen years old, declared himself the man of the house and took over his father's grocery store. He woke up before dawn and walked for miles or hitched a ride to the whole-sale vegetable market to stock up the store. All day, he manned the small grocery stand as his friends played. Jinan felt sorry for him.

"Go play with your friends. God is great; we will survive somehow. Go play," she would insist, but he wouldn't listen. "I want my father to be proud of me when he comes back," he would answer.

Neighbors stopped by almost every day, checking on Jinan and the kids, and lashing out at the Americans. Everyone was puzzled. Najim was the sort of Iraqi citizen that the Americans were supposed to nurture. He was nei-ther a Baathist nor a former member or supporter of Saddam's regime. The only thing that made the tall, well-built grocer stand out in the neighbor-hood was his extreme devotion to Islam. He wore his beard long and prayed five times a day at the local mosque. The family didn't have a television set or listen to music. Locally, Najim's devoutness offered him stature among neighbors, who often knocked on his door to ask for help in settling dis-putes. An active community member, he showed up at every neighborhood meeting led by an American civil affairs liaison named Captain Sean McWilliams. When Captain McWilliams asked for volunteers to distribute cooking-gas cylinders, Najim raised his hands. When the Americans began forming neighborhood councils, he was selected by his neighbors as one of the fifteen-member council.

When he was arrested, neighbors began telling Jinan, "Now we know the real face of Americans. They arrest even people who work with them. They are not here to give us freedom and democracy."

On the afternoon that Shahed and her uncle went to the coalition in-formation center, more than fifty other families were lined up behind the barbed-wire gate. The massive gray building had housed a government-run supermarket and department store during Saddam's time. After four hours of waiting in the oppressive Baghdad summer heat, they finally met with an American officer who patiently checked a laptop computer for several possible English spellings of Najim's and Qutaibah's names. Nothing came up. After several more weeks passed, the family began checking Baghdad's hospitals and the central morgue. Jinan called an Iraqi lawyer, who told her as long as the Americans had her husband and son, there was nothing he could do. He urged her to tell the military that her son was underage and should be separated from the adults.

It was around this time that I met the family, and followed them for a week as they hunted for Najim and Qutaibah. One morning we rush to the gate of Abu Ghraib with another one of Jinan's brothers, a young mild-mannered man named Nidal, after we hear news of a mortar hitting the camp and killing and injuring detainees. Jinan won't stop sobbing until she is reassured her husband and son weren't among them. But how to get that confirmed? After nearly two hours of standing at the gate, an American translator yells out, "No translator, no translator." A small crowd has formed outside the prison, but no one understands English. Nidal starts talking rapidly in Arabic to baffled soldiers.

"I just want to know if they are dead or alive. Imagine if it were your family in there. What would you do?"

The young soldier, who looks no older than eighteen, replies in English, "I don't know anything, sir. I asked for a translator several times to come to the gate and answer your questions, but they tell me all the translators are in a meeting." He walks over to the other side of the barbed wire and points to a piece of cardboard pinned to a sandbag, instructing families inquiring about detainees to go to the office of the International Committee of the Red Cross in Baghdad.

We get to the Red Cross office an hour before it closes, with over two hundred people lined up ahead of us in a packed courtyard. "You are too late," says the guard.

"It's been like this for one month. Wherever we go, they say no news, come back later, you are late, you are early. What am I going to say to my poor sister now? I can't bear to tell her 'no answer' again."

One afternoon I'm sitting with Jinan when one of the neighbors, Ahmad al-Naeem, stops by. He and Najim worked as volunteers at the local mosque during the war, escorting neighbors to the hospital, fixing electrical wires, and distributing food to widows and the elderly. He takes out a crumpled piece of paper from his pocket and shows me a letter he and Najim wrote to an American officer named "Captain McWilliams" shortly after the Americans arrived. Haqqi reads the letter, which says the two men are experienced at volunteer work and want to have good relations with the Americans to help make Iraq a better place now that Saddam is gone. Even Haqqi can't contain his rage. "So they pay you back by arresting him?" he says.

"You see? The Americans stabbed us in the back and arrested our friends. Now I don't even bother anymore. Why should I help the Americans? They treat us all the same, like we are their enemies. Then they wonder why people hate them and form resistance groups."

I spend the next few days retracing the family's footsteps and tracking down most of the Americans they encountered, from the local police station to the American military base, including Captain Sean McWilliams. As it turns out, McWilliams is in the precarious position of having worked with Najim on the neighborhood council and ordered his arrest in a house-to-house raid.

Captain McWillliams, thirty years old, is with the First Armored Division, Third Brigade, far from his home state of Florida. The FOB military base is a desolate, grim structure that looks like it mushroomed out of the barren brown earth it sits upon. To get there, you take a dirt road off an exit on a highway and drive up to a checkpoint and a watchtower. Munaf slows down as we approach the soldiers. They search our car, and radio inside for approval. When we are refused entry, Munaf parks outside and Haqqi and I are picked up in an open-sided, open-roofed military vehicle and whisked away. In the waiting room is an old mural of Saddam holding a shotgun and wearing a mafia-style fedora.

Captain McWilliams tells me that he sees Iraqis falling into three types: There is the friendly type, those who believe what we are talking about and are willing to move forward. There is the neutral element, those who are not sure about us. They kind of think we are "USA, the great Satan," but are not sure of it yet. And there are enemies, those out there who want to kill us.

"Do you think the detentions are turning the neutrals into enemies?" I ask.

"Maybe, but we have no choice. I have to take these kinds of threats very seriously."

Captain McWilliams's guiding rule is to act only on solid leads and tips from local informants and to cut down on random house sweeps and arrests, which have only served to anger the locals he relies on for cooperation. He received tips from two locals in the Khadria district, which he oversees, that Najim was acting suspiciously. Father and son were spotted driving around the neighborhood for no reason. The information struck him as odd. He knew Najim from the council meetings and had grown to like him. After a raid on his house turned up potential ingredients for explosives, combined with the informants' tips, he had little choice but to detain Najim and his oldest son.

"We thought the son was older. He looks like he is in his twenties, and I wanted to investigate him."

But once the father and son were transferred to a detention facility, they got swallowed up by the system and now, even Captain McWilliams can't for sure place them. The arrest of Abdulhusseins has caused his relations with the community to deteriorate rapidly, and at every council meeting, members accuse him of arresting their friends. When I ask him if he thinks father and son are guilty, he replies that he can't tell for sure. Army engineers determined that the explosive material found in the grocer's shop can be used for making bombs, but it could also be used to make helium balloons, as Najim had contended. I accompany Captain

McWilliams to one of his weekly community meetings in Khadria's elementary school. About two dozen neighborhood men are sitting in the courtyard on rigid iron chairs, forming a semicircle. Tension is boiling as outraged neighbors demand answers via a translator. Firas is also among the crowd.

"We used to consider you a friend!" one neighbor shouts at the captain. "But you are not our friend anymore. You arrest our friends and our children. If anything happens to them, you will be our enemy."

Captain McWilliams tries to explain: "You tell me your number-one concern is security, but when I arrest the people I think are dangerous, you shout at me. What am I supposed to do?"

Firas Ghattam raises his hand. "Where are Qutaibah and his father?" he asks.

"I was told they are at the Abu Ghraib prison, and I tried to get them out, but I don't think I can. They are under investigation for now."

"Do they know Qutaibah is seventeen?" the boy's uncle presses. "They cannot keep him with the adults."

"They didn't know at first. He looked older, and no one asked his age. I've informed the chain of command, and we'll see what happens."

After my story runs, I frequently visit Jinan for afternoon tea or send Haqqi to check if her husband and son are released. In January, Haqqi swings by the family's house and discovers Najim, the father, has been released from Abu Ghraib. I rush over to celebrate. The children hug me, Jinan cries in my arms, and Najim won't stop thanking us for writing a story about his family.

"At first I kept telling my son there has been a misunderstanding; we haven't done anything wrong; we will be released soon. But after we were taken to Abu Ghraib I thought I would never see my family again or be back inside my home."

On the first night of detention, Najim and Qutaibah huddled together on the floor of a dark room at the Ghazallieh military base near their neighborhood. In the morning, an American soldier pinned a sign to his *dishdashah* that read Bomb Maker and shoved the pair into a van and transported them to Abu Ghraib. They were separated upon arrival. Qutaibah was assigned to an adult camp for detainees considered to be a low-level risk. Najim was placed in Camp B, designated for high-risk detainees. It was filled mostly with former Fadayeen Saddam or Republican Guards—men suspected of being the hardest of the hard-core insurgency. The detainees were kept in tents with thin carpets on the floor; some had mattresses, and others did not. Each detainee was given a blanket and towel and issued a capture number and a tag, he says. Najim's new identity was No. 150185. In the 130-degree summer heat in August, the tents had no air-conditioning or fans. There was no heat during the chilly winter desert nights, and they were given winter coats, hats, gloves, and extra blankets to keep warm.

Najim's eyes fill with tears, and he looks down as he recalls the interrogation sessions. When I convince him to tell me all the details he can remember, he asks his wife to take their children to a neighbor's house because he doesn't want them to hear any of the torture tales.

Interrogations typically lasted for three hours every other day, sometimes taking place in the middle of the night when detainees were sleep deprived. Once, he was ordered to stand upright and not move. His hands were tied behind his back, and his face was covered by a hood, under the sweltering sun. After thirteen hours he collapsed, unconscious. His interrogators accused him of being a terrorist, of having been trained in Afghanistan, and of being a member of al-Qaeda. One interrogator was insistent that he saw Najim in Afghanistan during the war. Najim, who didn't even have a passport, had never left Iraq in his life. The Americans spit on him; they burned his arm with a cigarette; they knocked him to the ground and kicked him in the abdomen.

On the night he arrived, Najim was escorted into a circular outdoor area for his first interrogation. Three Americans and an Arabic translator sat on chairs before him as he was forced to kneel in the sand, his hands tightly bound with plastic cuffs. They asked his name, address, education, profession, and religion. They asked him if he was Sunni or Shiite. When he replied he was Sunni, they wanted to know the name of his mosque and whether he was a Wahabi. Then they asked him if he had links to Osama bin Laden. When he said no, he was told by his interrogators that he looked like an Afghan or an Iranian. They pulled on his beard and shouted questions at him. Sometimes he was forced to hold his arms above his head while he was being questioned in the summer heat. Once when an American interrogator asked if he was thirsty and he nodded yes, the man poured a bottle of water on his face without letting him drink.

This pattern became a routine of Najim's interrogation sessions. If he looked down, the interrogator would shove his fingers in his face and threaten to beat him to death if he didn't look him in the eye. Repeatedly his interrogators threatened to ship him to Guantánamo Bay, where al-Qaeda prisoners were being kept, if he didn't confess to insurgent activities against Americans. They promised him he would never see his wife or children again unless he admitted immediately to being a terrorist.

In a particularly emotionally taxing session, the interrogators smirked at Najim and said they were sending soldiers to his house to gang-rape his wife. Then the interrogator grabbed a female colleague and pretended to have forceful sex with her, as she screamed and called out Najim's name to save her. He broke down and cried, begging them to stop. Every time Najim answered a question, an interrogator would yell at him and accuse him of lying. When he replied that he was Muslim and didn't lie, his American interrogator would yell back that all Muslims are liars.

During his six-month imprisonment, Najim met with representatives of the ICRC twice and complained about his interrogator's abusive behavior. When I ask him if there were any Americans who treated him kindly, he nods his head yes. There was a nice nurse at the field hospital who spoke to him in a soft voice. There was a soldier who once let him sit on a chair and handed him bottled water as he waited to be checked by a doctor for his epilepsy. There was the guard who warned detainees against eating the army's readymade meals number 2 and number 22, because they contained pork, which was forbidden under a strict Muslim diet.

Najim's days in prison fell into a dull routine. He slept on a thin mattress in a big tent in which twenty other detainees were kept. He woke up before dawn every day to pray and pace the area outside of the tent for exercise. At the high-risk camp, he was allowed to shower once a week; at the lower-risk camp, every other day. The water was cold and the portable military shower cramped. He filtered the muddy, foul-tasting water through a pair of his socks before drinking it. He read the Quran and had religious discussions with his inmates, who eventually designated him as their imam, praying behind him five times a day.

Najim's fortunes suddenly reversed one day in October, shortly after his story ran on the front page of *The Wall Street Journal*. When he was summoned to interrogation, it wasn't the same gang who usually grilled him. They offered him a chair and smiled at him. They asked him about the article, whether he knew Captain McWilliams, and whether he had served as a council member in his neighborhood. They asked him about Qutaibah. They told him the military had almost finished investigating him; soon he would go home. The next week, Najim was transferred to Camp Six, an area designated for the low-risk detainees, where he was reunited with Qutaibah. When father and son hugged each other inside the tent, everyone around them cried. At the camp, he wrote a note to Jinan, and asked an Iraqi doctor to deliver it.

After the capture of Saddam in December, more and more detainees were released three times a week. One Saturday night, without any warning, they called out Najim's number and told him he was free. Qutaibah stayed, but the American guard promised he'd be out soon too.

A week later I accompany the family to Abu Ghraib. The Americans had announced they would release about five hundred prisoners. We think Qutaibah may be among them. We arrive at seven, when the morning light gently strokes the sky, and a chilly desert wind pierces through our bones. Hundreds of families have already gathered in the parking lot.

Najim's cell phone keeps ringing. His phone number seems to be stored on everyone's speed dial today. He clicks on the green receive button, takes a deep breath, and answers, *"Na'am,"* in a voice shaking with anticipation. "Is he out? Is he free?" the callers ask. Najim shakes his head, tugs at his long black beard, and replies, "*La, la*, not yet. Inshallah, we are waiting here outside the prison." Beside him, Jinan paces, kicking up the brown sand under her feet. I can't see her eyes to gauge her anxiety. In the absence of facial expressions, I focus on her feet. Her black leather shoes nervously tap the ground. Rocking back and forth, she presses her toes downward before pressing her thick heels into the sand.

By 11 AM, with no sign of Qutaibah, Jinan is getting restless.

"I'm afraid, I'm afraid. Allah, Allah, Allah. I'm afraid because he may not be released today," she utters under her breath. Najim notices a commotion by the gate as an army interpreter is making an announcement. He zips up the baggy black leather jacket he's thrown over a traditional gray Arabic *dishdashah* and runs to the gate. He returns breathless and orders everyone to pile into the car.

"The Americans have changed their mind. They are asking the families to go to Abu Ghraib town. They are releasing the detainees there."

In the main town square, near a mosque, trucks loaded with detainees pull in. The newly released, all men, step out of the truck beds into the arms of tearful spouses, parents, children, and siblings. Although I can't see her face, I can tell that Jinan is crying. She gulps for air, and from the corner of my eye I notice how she tucks her gloved hands under her face covering to wipe away tears.

"My son is not here. He is still a prisoner. Every day he is in that prison, he is losing his innocence and his education," she tells me between her sobs.

"I'm sorry; I'm sure he'll be out with the next group," I say, somewhat at a loss for words.

A middle-aged man, who has just been released, approaches us from the crowd and takes Najim into his arms. "We were kept in the same tent," the man tells me. His name is Mahdi Abdulaziz; he is forty-three years old and was in detention for sixty-one days. He rolls up the sleeves of his checkered shirt and holds out his wrists toward my face. I notice a red bruise; he explains it's from the plastic handcuffs the Americans tied around his wrists.

"How did the Americans treat you in there?" I want to know. Najim's tales of torture are unnerving, and I've been trying to find other prisoners who can corroborate some of the abuses inside the prison.

"They used to hit me with the end of the gun on my head and on my face. They would put me on the floor and spit on me and step on me and kick me in my stomach. They always said 'fuck, fuck'," he says, imitating their swearing in English with a heavy droll. Jinan's sobs get louder.

"Why were you arrested?"

"I was in the street in my car in Yousefiyah; they stopped me at a checkpoint, searched my car, and didn't find anything. They arrested me and said they would investigate."

"Did you see my son?" Najim asks.

As far as Abdulaziz could tell, their son was not among the released. He spotted him in the tent a few days back and noticed he had shaved his beard and head to clean up in case he got out. Jinan won't go home. She stands for another hour until every truck has unloaded every detainee and the town square has emptied out. I lean against the white Toyota they have borrowed from a relative for the trip and think about how one family's life has been transformed because of a mistaken detention. I wonder about the emotional impact of Najim's detention on Jinan and her children, the enduring scars of imprisonment on their teenage son, and the hatred brewing in the family's hearts for the Americans. It is easy to extend that animosity to neighbors, relatives, and friends and to multiply that by the tens of thousands of detainees.

When Qutaibah is finally released a year and a half later, I can't visit to do a follow-up story about him. The family's neighborhood is a bastion of insurgency and too dangerous for even our Iraqi staff to go to inquire on behalf of an American newspaper.

16

My Name
Is Moonlover,
So Romantic, So Free

In June we attend two celebrations, each displaying significantly less fanfare and flash than is customary, where planning revolves entirely around security. The organizers are intent on passing the day relatively uneventfully by avoiding any spectacular bloodshed. Sabah throws a low-key wedding lunch for his younger son, Ziad, in sweltering afternoon heat so that guests can make it home before the streets are dark and dangerously impassable. At first Ziad and Rana consider bypassing a wedding party altogether to elope in a safer location like Jordan or Syria. But Ziad vetoes the idea, pointing out that a wedding is a once-in-a-lifetime event; traveling can be done anytime.

"If we gave up our dream, it would equal defeat," Ziad says.

In his young macho way Ziad is determined to create a memorable day of their union, one that is filled with laughter, dancing, and adoring family. Twice their wedding was postponed because of the invasion and the subsequent uncertainty. When the Americans announce the formal end of the occupation, Ziad settles on a date two weeks before the handover of power.

Sabah tries to persuade him otherwise by offering to pay a lump sum of cash he was planning to spend on their party so the couple can travel. He wants them to escape Iraq for a little while, and to alleviate for him and Marie-Rose the stress of hosting a big party. Sabah seems a little ashamed that his anxiety overshadows his dream of witnessing his younger son wed. We are talking about the wedding after a typical weekly lunch at their house. Marie-Rose and Theresa are clearing the table, and I'm left sitting with Sabah. He pushes his empty plate aside and places his hand under his chin and sighs. "Can you believe a father asking his son to take his joy and happiness somewhere else? Do you think I'm a bad father for saying this?"

I can appreciate Ziad's desire to defeat conventional wisdom and march ahead with his wedding plans. Clinging to plans in wartime, even if they seem insane, provides a sort of relief. I tell Sabah that in Iran, during days of war, my family tried to normalize our lives by having fun. My parents took us to the countryside with a troop of cousins and orchestrated sing-along sessions, dance competitions, excavation walks along the river, and group storytelling around a fire at night. The adults entertained themselves by hosting parties over the weekend to play cards, drink, and dance. At the time, I thought my family frivolous, or in denial. But I know now that it wasn't denial that compelled them to behave as they did. It was their understanding of war. They knew that in extreme circumstances each minute is laced with uncertainty and a chance to flirt with normalcy is an occasion to cherish.

Sabah chuckles at my story. Marie-Rose emerges with a tray of tiny cups filled with rich Arabic coffee and instructs me to leave a thick lining of the liquid at the bottom. I'm then to turn my cup upside down on the saucer and make a wish. When the coffee stains have dried, Theresa holds my saucer to the light and carefully decodes each image: a bird with its wings spread is good news, a narrow passage is a new travel opportunity. Theresa reads Marie-Rose's fortune next, interpreting each coffee stain as it relates to the wedding. When she spots a fish, a sign of life, we are motioned to see for ourselves and Marie-Rose clasps her hands and gives out a delighted yelp. For weeks she has been kneeling before a framed poster of the Virgin Mary saying a silent prayer for God, Lord Jesus Christ, and Mother Mary to keep explosions, car bombs, kidnappings, and guns away from her son's wedding. Even Rana is more preoccupied with security worries than with the usual bridal anxiety over the gown, hair, and makeup. She tells me that she goes to bed every night clutching rosaries, rolling each bead until her fingers go numb, while she whispers a prayer for a wedding day on which no one is killed.

"We don't want electricity, we don't want food. We just want our normal life back. I want to go to my son's wedding and not be afraid of someone dying on the way," Marie-Rose tells me.

She invites me to see the bride and groom's new home: a bedroom upstairs in the Nassers' house directly across the hallway from where their older son, wife, and baby reside. Marie-Rose takes pride in pointing out every item in the bedroom as testament to Ziad's good taste and his desire to make Rana happy despite their limited financial means. The bedroom set consists of a queen-size bed, chest of drawers, armoire, and wardrobe of matching dark brown wood. A pink satin spread with flower appliqués and heart-shaped cushions covers the bed. A mini refrigerator packed with soda cans, candy bars, and bottled fruit juice sits in the corner next to a small television and a DVD player. Opening one of the drawers, Marie-Rose proudly displays a neatly folded pile of sexy bridal lingerie. "Ziad has been buying these for Rana as a surprise to give her on their wedding night. You see how much in love my son is? May God grant him a safe and nice wedding day," she says. "For Ayad's wedding, it was a different story, everything was different. I had zero worry."

When their older son Ayad was married two years ago, before the American invasion and the war, the Nassers threw a huge party. Four hundred guests attended, and the best band in town played for a night of dancing and drinking at the posh Alawiya club. Waiters in black tuxedos carried trays of whiskey and wine in crystal glasses. A sit-down dinner of stuffed grilled lamb and fish was served at elegant tables decorated with candles and fresh flowers. The party lasted until dawn, when family members went for a customary drive around town, on which they clapped, honked their horns, and sang before dropping off the newlyweds at the city's best hotel.

"Compare the happiness we had before to now," Marie-Rose says as she wipes tears off her cheeks. "Saddam was a dictator, yes, but what is this we have now? You call it life? We are always afraid."

A few days earlier, Ziad and Marie-Rose had a close call while they were driving around town delivering wedding invitations. They were in Baghdad Jadid neighborhood around five in the afternoon, when the car in front of them suddenly stopped and a man emerged from a nearby house and jumped in the front seat. Immediately, another car pulled alongside the vehicle and three masked men bearing machine guns opened fire. Ziad shoved his mother's head down and kept pressing his palm on her head. "Mom, keep your head down! Keep your head down!" he screamed.

"Be quiet, be quiet. Don't scream." Marie-Rose was terrified that the gunmen would kill them next for witnessing the crime. The assassins killed the driver, abducted the passenger, and drove away with their car. The man's body was thrown into the street, staining the pavement with blood. His hands shaking and his heart pounding fast, Ziad drove away. A few miles down the road he pulled over on a bridge, put his head on the wheel, and sobbed uncontrollably. With a pile of elegant wedding invitations still on her lap, Marie-Rose cried softly beside him. She reached over and caressed her son's short black hair. "It's okay. It's okay; we are safe," she said.

Ziad and Rana are married on a hot sunny day in a small church of Karadah. Far from the Nassers' neighborhood and their regular church, it is, however, near the reception hall and will save guests from having to drive long distances around Baghdad. The bride and groom enter the church before noon. The pews have been decorated with white satin ribbons and white plastic roses. A small group of close family members joins them. Rana wears a beautiful white dress embroidered with little flowers. Her hair is swept up in a stylish chignon and set with tiny, bejeweled flowers. When their bridal car, decorated with flowers and ribbons, arrives at the church, Marie-Rose gets inside with a red velvet box filled with gold and diamond jewelry to be worn by the bride. To minimize the risk of attracting criminals and hijackers on the way to the church, Rana traveled unadorned.

Aseel looks elegant in a long, strapless black dress. Marie-Rose wears a stylish black suit with Italian lace sleeves. The maid of honor is clad in a floor-sweeping, sleeveless gown the color of pomegranate. During the ceremony, it's so hot that the guests press napkins to their foreheads to mop up sweat. The generator can only give enough juice for the bright flash of lights for the camera crew filming the ceremony and for a slow-moving ceiling fan. Turning on the air-conditioning could pop the fuse and disrupt the service.

The Nassers' is the first wedding I've attended in Iraq, but I feel more melancholic than joyful. Although everyone is happy, anxiety is still written across their faces. Sabah keeps looking toward the door as the priest reads the wedding vows. He has hired two armed guards to stand by the door in case of a kidnapping or insurgent attack. Before coming inside, he whispers in the guards' ears to keep an eye out for strangers and not let anyone park on the street.

The ceremony feels much like an American marriage union, except that the prayers are recited in Arabic and the bride and groom linger for photographs. Afterward we line up to squeeze Ziad's hands and kiss the bride. Most guests hand the couple white envelopes stuffed with cash as wedding gifts.

The wedding reception is held in the drab banquet hall of a mediocre hotel. Ziad's criterion for choosing a suitable location was that it should not be surrounded by cement walls and barbed wire, guarded by armed men, packed with foreigners, or frequented by American soldiers. Every nice hotel in Baghdad has by now been turned into a fortress by foreign journalists and contractors.

"Ninety percent of our planning was focused on security and safety. It was like I was preparing for a military operation instead of my own wedding," Ziad told me before the big day.

Guests heading from church to reception must leave in fifteen-minute intervals to avoid a long procession of wedding cars attracting attention. The banquet hall has ornate molding and heavy, red velvet curtains that block the afternoon light. There is a little pavilion for the bride and groom on a mini stage, with two satin-covered chairs beneath a canopy of gauze. Big baskets of fake plastic flowers and plants are set around them. Fresh flowers are hard to find in any season in Baghdad but almost impossible in June, when temperatures reach 120 degrees on any given day. One hundred guests are seated at tables and chairs that sport heart-shaped red and white balloons. In the large open area in the middle of the room an Iraqi pop band plays Arabic tunes.

Despite it being early afternoon, everyone is eager to dance. Before the first round of drinks is served the dance floor fills up with women shimmying their hips and men shaking their shoulders up and down to the rhythmic beat of an electric keyboard. Babak and I join them for a dance after Sabah comes over to our table and pulls my hand. When we are dancing near the bride and groom, Ziad turns to me and says, "I am having a great time. I want to forget I'm in Baghdad tonight."

When we sit down, guests make polite conversation, asking how we know the family, before peppering us with questions about politics. Do we think Iraq will stabilize after the handover? Will there be a strong government or a weak one that bows to the Americans? Will the insurgency fade? Will "the situation" get better or worse? Neither I nor Babak want to engage in political debates, and our answers sound strained. We mostly just nod and say, "Inshallah better," until we are left alone. When a chair at our table opens up, Zahra, the wife of Ziad's best friend, slips next to me. She is in her mid-twenties and is wearing a stylish beige pantsuit and a semisheer headscarf wrapped elegantly around her head, the tails of the scarf bunched up on one side and pinned with a diamond brooch near her ear. I can barely hear Zahra's voice over the loud music, as she goes on about discovering the Internet and spending hours each day in chat rooms.

"Do you ever chat with strangers?" she murmurs in my ear.

"Not really. I don't even chat with my friends. I find it disruptive," I reply.

"Oh, I love it. I want to quickly finish up housework and cooking every day, just so I can chat. I'm addicted," she says.

"Who do you chat with? Friends in Iraq or outside?" I ask.

"Oh, no. I like to chat with people from other countries. Sometimes I chat with men and women. It's very interesting. I have several online friends now from Canada and America. They ask me about my life in Iraq, about my family, and about the situation. It's very nice, because I've never had foreign friends before or any men friends. I don't use my real name. My chat name is Moonlover. I chose this name because it's so romantic and so free."

She interrupts the conversation as abruptly as she started and tugs at my arm, the way teenage girlfriends do in school. "Come on, they are about to cut the cake. Let's go and watch."

Standing in their pavilion, Ziad and Rana look happy and beautiful. A big white cake, set atop a table with wheels, is rolled toward them. Marie-Rose hovers by the pair, handing them cold drinks of sherbet—sugary sweet with rose water—served in silver champagne glasses. She fixes Ziad's tie and adjusts the flower he has pinned to his jacket. With the same motherly attention, she attends to Rana, fixing the crease in her veil, applying a dash of glitter to her cheeks, and straightening the back of her dress. The guests cheer at the cutting of the cake.

"Look, Rana looks so happy. They love her so much," Zahra whispers. Rana is an orphan, so to speak, and the Nassers encouraged the match in part because they loved her and wanted to protect her. The two families were neighbors when Ziad and Rana were children. Rana's father abandoned them when she was a little girl and her mother died of cancer when she was sixteen. Zahra tells me "She is very lucky. They have rescued her from uncertainty and given her shelter in their family and a safe home."

⊠ ⊠ ⊠

Two weeks later I'm reminded of Zahra's words during the swearing-in ceremony of Iraq's new government. I wonder if Iraq will be as lucky as Rana, rescued with love and care from the claws of uncertainty and despair. The newly appointed ministers have a look of almost disbelief on their faces. They are also dressed up in their best clothes; the men wear shiny new suits with bright-colored ties and leather shoes so new they still look stiff. The women ministers poised in heels and well-tailored skirt suits are the picture of elegance. Until not so long ago, many of them were just ordinary people living quiet lives and dreaming of such a day, and others were well-known figures in the opposition diasporas that encouraged America to topple Saddam. Sitting on velvet chairs under giant Iraqi flags, they look proud. As each is called to swear on the Quran to serve their country, it's impossible not to feel sympathy. While their political agendas may differ, each individual here desperately wants the new government to succeed. The interim prime minister, Ayad Allawi, points to the day as a turning point. "This is a big day for us and the Iraqi people. The first thing is to really ensure the safety of our people and our country."

Adel Abdul Mehdi, the new finance minister who is also a Shiite, compares occupation to slavery and says about today, "It's the difference between a slave and a free man. Occupation is slavery."

It took Paul Bremer less than ten minutes to dissolve the Coalition Provisional Authority but it will take years, if not decades, for the Iraqi government to restore the messy legacy the Americans leave behind. The success of this new government hinges on its ability to convince skeptical Iraqis that they are nationalist caretakers of Iraq and not merely puppets controlled by Washington. In order to take part in the ceremony, we had to rush over to the Green Zone with a thirty-minute advance warning. For the first time, I notice a massive Iraqi flag fluttering above the compound against the backdrop of a clear blue sky. An American Apache war helicopter circles and swoops above the flag, and the gunner's machine gun pokes out from the helicopter's slightly open door. It's the perfect metaphor for the day, Iraq may be sovereign but its armed American guardians are still hovering right over its head.

17

A Place of
No Dreams

W*elcome to the* new Iraq.

These were Munaf's words to me this morning, followed by news that our night driver Nahid, who is Munaf's cousin, has been kidnapped. When he reports the news, his voice is sort of flat in the way that Iraqis speak of unspeakable things, almost as though he is telling me Nahid will be late to work today. I stare at Munaf for a second, nicely dressed, as always, in jeans and fitted shirt and clean-shaven, before involuntarily squeezing my eyes shut. When I open my eyes Munaf is still slouched in front of me in the office lounge chair. I can hear the *click-clack* of the guard's footsteps on the pavement outside my window. Munaf is looking down at his hands and twirling his fingers nervously. He recognizes the need for reinforcement and repeats his news, pausing after every phrase.

"Farnaz, this is very bad news, I know. Nahid was kidnapped with my uncle yesterday afternoon. I don't know where they are. I don't know who has them. You understand?"

"Yes," I reply. "Is it because he works for us?"

"I don't know yet. But we think the kidnappers are after money. If they find out he works for *The Wall Street Journal,* it will get very complicated. They could kill him for being a traitor or ask for millions of dollars because the *Journal* is a rich American company."

Nahid, a single man, moved from Mosul to Baghdad to be our night driver after it became too dangerous for us to take taxis. He lives with his uncle, a famous surgeon at a reputable hospital in Baghdad, and has a charming simplicity about him. Nahid offers an endless source of humor for the rest of the staff, who tease him lovingly about his accent and slang. Although he speaks only a few words of English, his constant laughter and smile have made driving with him a rather pleasant experience. In the kidnappers' hands, he may be carrying incriminating evidence that could easily link him to us and cost him his life. He has a photo identification card from Dow Jones and one from the Coalition Provisional Authority; a statement of employment on *WSJ* letterhead, which he kept in his car's glove box to get past American army checkpoints; and a cell phone in which he has saved all of our obviously foreign names and numbers along with those of the entire Iraqi house and office staff. It would be very easy for his kidnappers to trace him back to us. Even if they didn't figure it out on their own, Nahid could confess under torture. I begin to breathe deeply, inhaling big gulps of air and exhaling with a loud puff to calm myself down. This is my first encounter with a serious security threat in Iraq involving someone else's life.

"Tell me everything you know. Slowly, so I can write it all down," I instruct Munaf.

At around noon the previous day, Nahid and his uncle, Dr. Kaisar Abdullah, drove to Kaisar Clinic, his uncle's small private hospital in Baghdad Jadid. Baghdad Jadid is a formerly middle-class enclave at the edge of the city that is slowly being turned into a haven for criminal gangs and insurgents. (It's also where Marie-Rose and Ziad witnessed the murder while delivering wedding invitations.) Nahid and Dr. Abdullah ran into trouble about a block away from the hospital when three cars surrounded them on a busy road. Masked men toting AK-47 machine guns ordered Nahid to stop. They grabbed the doctor and Nahid at gunpoint and shoved them into the back of their car and drove off. When Dr. Abdullah and Nahid failed to show up at home in time for lunch, the family began to worry.

They kept calling the pair's mobile phones, but they were turned off. They sent instant messages, but no replies came back. The local police station had no record of an accident or an explosion on their route.

Hitham, Dr. Abdullah's son, went through the now-routine list of calls Iraqis make after someone has vanished: police, hospital emergency rooms, and the city morgue. Still no news emerged until late at night when Hitham's phone rang and Dr. Abdullah's number appeared on the caller ID. Instead of his father, Hitham heard a stranger in a muffled voice. He did not identify himself other than to confirm that he had custody of Dr. Abdullah and Nahid and that they were alive. He demanded half a million dollars ransom within twenty-four hours. Before hanging up, he warned that the family was under surveillance and one wrong move, like notifying the police, would prompt them to deliver Dr. Abdullah and Nahid's dead bodies.

"From where will we get half a million dollars?" Munaf asks me. "If all of my relatives sold their houses, their cars and gold, and we put down all our savings, it is still not half a million dollars."

"How much could your family pay?"

"If we put all our money together, maybe we can get $20,000."

I decide that we should consult with a professional security expert and find out what measures we can take to help Nahid and to protect the rest of our Iraqi staff. The *Journal*'s villa in Mansur is managed by a security company named ISI, which keeps a small office in our house staffed with at least one foreign staff member. The resident security guy is a New Zealander named Ken with an extensive military background and some experience in hostage negotiations. Ken recently advised a rich Iraqi businessman on freeing his son.

Ken tells Munaf that his family must negotiate the price down to an amount they can actually pay, and they should not be intimidated by the threats. Often gangs want whatever money they can extract and will settle for significantly lower ransoms. The family should keep a log of the calls and the times and an eye out for strangers peeping around their house.

Ken recommends that Munaf and his father Abu Munaf, who is also our driver, stay away from Dr. Abdullah's house, in case it's really under surveillance. We don't want to risk anyone being identified and followed back to our office.

For the time being, Munaf and Abu Munaf will take a taxi to work, exiting several blocks away from the office. Every day, they must use an alternative route. None of us should answer any unrecognized numbers. I can no longer answer my phone with my customary "Hello." Instead I say the Arabic *"Na'aam"* or *"Aloo."* If the caller is speaking Arabic, I should hang up or hand the phone to one of our Iraqi staff. We should play it safe and halt all outings and reporting trips in case our cars or staff have already been identified. Ken tells me that I should prepare for the possibility that the kidnappers will cut a deal with Nahid, under duress, torture, or threat of murder, and free him in exchange for access to us. I don't want to believe him, but I also can't take a chance. We may have to temporarily relocate so they lose track of our movement.

I barely sleep that night. A few times I doze off but then my body suddenly jerks, and I'm awake, gasping for air. I lie in the dark imagining ghastly scenarios of Nahid's kidnapping. Even with Babak's arms wrapped around me, I can't calm my mind. He wakes up through the night from my fidgeting and softly asks me if I'm still up thinking. "What if they kill him?" I ask. "What if they come after the rest of my guys? How am I going to face their families and live with myself if anyone is killed on our account?" Our Iraq assignment is turning into a nightmare. I am chronically sad and angry from the constant despair around me. I am mindful of death in a way that I have never been before. Death has become an intruder in our lives, lurking behind every corner, ready to grab us by the neck.

Our nerves are already shaken because we have just been through a kidnapping nightmare that involved Babak's colleagues and our housemates from *Newsweek*. We were forced to evacuate our house for three weeks, and have barely returned home. The *Newsweek* team was abducted in the Jolan district of Fallujah, the epicenter of insurgents' battles with the Americans when a local guide led them to the area with reassurance that the newly deployed Iraqi forces of Fallujah Brigade were in full control. The kidnappers seized reporter Josh Hammer and photographer Robert King along with their Iraqi driver and translator. Immediately separated and detained in different houses, Iraqis and journalists were kept for eight hours. They were interrogated, searched, and accused of working for the CIA. They fed Josh and Robert a lunch of kebab and rice while a man wearing a thick suicide belt packed with explosives sat next to them, occasionally pulling his shirt up to reveal his intentions. During their interrogation, the Iraqi team was told that their foreign colleagues had been killed. They were then led to a bathroom and ordered to wash and perform their last prayer in preparation for being slaughtered for jihad. The kidnappers extracted some information out of *Newsweek*'s Iraqi staff about our security setup from their captives, including the location of our house in Mansur. They seized the team's identification cards that allow Iraqis passage through checkpoints around our house. They were warned that they would only be released if they cooperated with their Baghdad cell to kidnap more foreigners and raid our house.

Their release is finally negotiated by the commander of the Fallujah Brigade and by a local imam whom the kidnappers happen to respect. Recently an American civilian contractor named Nick Berg was abducted and beheaded by a militant group affiliated with al-Qaeda, which claimed in a video that the murder was a response to the abuse of prisoners at Abu Ghraib.

Because we share a house and office with *Newsweek*, the kidnapping inevitably compromises our security. After a day or two we evacuate the house while trying through intermediaries in Fallujah to gauge the threat and convince the jihadis that they are dealing with real journalists, not spies. In the interim, we move across town to a fortified Sheraton Hotel, where the rooms smell like mold, the wobbly mattresses barely cushion the box springs, and the bathtub is permanently stained. This relocation strains our sanity and disrupts our work. We can't set up high-speed Internet, phone lines, or an office. In a foreign setting, we encounter some truly bizarre moments, including running into the two Iraqi prostitutes who reside in a big suite and keep a white poodle. Rumor has it that the women service American contractors in the hotel. They pace the lobby and hallways in stilettos, stretched low-cut tank tops that accent their big busts, and micro miniskirts. Their faces are painted like cabaret dancers' in bright red, blue, and black. The most annoying thing about them is their pet dog, which they allow to relieve itself in the hallway. Given these grim surroundings, we are ecstatic to return to our villa in Mansur, where we have assembled a routine that resembles normal life, until Nahid is kidnapped, and we are thrown for a loop again.

On the second day of Nahid's capture, his abductors again make contact with Hitham. This time Hitham negotiates the ransom down to $50,000, then to $25,000. The captors tell him to keep the money for funeral fees before hanging up. Several conversations of this nature take place before they finally agree to release Dr. Abdullah. Nihad they will keep. The whole family pitches in to raise the money. Munaf takes his cousin's car and speeds to his home in Dora to fetch every penny he has saved working for us over the past year and a half. His dream was to use his $5,000 savings to buy a car and take his first trip abroad. Hitham stuffs the cash in a plastic bag and drives to a side street in Mansur about two blocks away from our house to meet the kidnappers. While they are counting the money, Hitham pleads with them, "This is all the money we have. All of my relatives have pitched in. Now we are at your mercy, please return everyone to us alive."

The next morning Dr. Abdullah is released. The kidnappers are holding out for more money for the release of Nahid. So far there has been no mention of Nahid's American employers, so we stay put. Dr. Abdullah thinks that the kidnappers are a criminal gang, most probably Shiites rather than Sunni insurgents, because the pair was jailed in a house in Rusafa district, which is predominantly Shiite. In order to secure his freedom, Dr. Abdullah had promised the kidnappers more money, up to half a million dollars, despite his family's separate negotiation to reduce the ransom.

"I will sell my house; I will sell my hospital. I will sell everything I own; just don't kill me," he begged.

"We'll let you go but your nephew stays until you get us the money," they told him. The kidnappers discover that the best way to make Dr. Abdullah react is to torture his nephew in front of him. They hang Nahid upside down from a ceiling fan and beat him with a wooden stick, kick him in the stomach, and slap him hard on the face. They beat him so hard that his body convulses and twirls like a rope.

But once Dr. Abdullah gets out, he realizes delivering half a million dollars is next to impossible. Again, they threaten to kill Nahid. Another week of negotiations ensues. The morale of the rest of the Iraqi staff in our household dips low. Nahid was the life of the crowd, cracking jokes and telling funny stories to lighten the mood. Our Iraqi employees used to hold ping-pong tournaments in their downtime. Now the ping-pong table is collecting dust. One afternoon, I walk out to the garden and see them huddled together, intensely going through numbers in their mobiles and whispering. Their anxious expressions alarm me.

"Is something going on?" I ask.

"No," replies Mohanad, Newsweek's office manager. "We are just changing all your names and giving you Arabic code names in our phones. This is in case we get kidnapped like Nahid. I am telling everyone to do this from now on. It's better for you and better for us."

I'm named Farah. Babak is Basem. Rod is Ra'ad. Yochi is Yousef. And so on.

When his family pays another $5,000, Nahid is finally released. He is blindfolded, shoved in the trunk of a car, and thrown on the side of a highway. A car passing by notices him and stops to help. Nahid conveys instructions to his uncle's house, where he collapses on the sidewalk. His relatives rush out, carry him inside, splash water on his face, and massage his badly bruised body. "You are safe, you are safe, it's over," they keep repeating.

Nahid tells us later that his kidnappers searched the list of names saved in his phone and asked him one by one about each person, what they did, and whom they worked for. Randomly, they dialed some of the numbers to see if he was telling the truth. When they couldn't figure out how to unlock the phone, they handed it back to Nahid to fix. Immediately he erased our names. Nahid's loyalty and his attempt to protect us may have saved both himself and us from a worse outcome. But he is now a marked man, because some criminal gang somewhere with God-knows-what kind of ties to which insurgent cell now knows Nahid's name, his address, his relatives' names and numbers. There is no way of telling whether the gang will come after Nahid again, looking for more money. We can't take that risk. We agonize over whether we should keep Nahid employed with us, despite being a marked man, or let him go. In the end, we ask him to leave in order to ensure safety for all of us. In the cruel circumstances of Iraq, an innocent man not only endured a tormenting kidnapping experience, but he also lost his job. It could compromise our security, our foreign housemates, *Newsweek*'s, and all our Iraqi staff combined. Our fate and security are invisibly linked.

In Iraq anarchy shatters the lives of ordinary folks like Nahid. With the Americans so preoccupied with fighting attacks on them and Iraqi task forces largely ill-equipped and poorly trained, criminal gangs thrive. Kidnapping for ransom is quite a lucrative endeavor and relatively risk-free, as so few are ever arrested and brought to justice. Kidnapping incidents, particularly those that target professionals, skyrocket. In many instances victims are released after a sum is paid. But many others are murdered or ordered to leave Iraq upon release. Iraqi officials tell us that crippling the country's health-care and justice systems is the latest tactic by insurgents to destabilize Iraq's social welfare.

I suspect, though, that the financial motive of criminals is stronger than the political one. How else could a bunch of thugs score between $20,000 and $200,000 (the average rate of ransoms) in one go and get away with it?

Baghdad now outranks Bogotá, Colombia, a city notorious for its drug crimes and abductions by twofold in the number of kidnappings and homicides. The head of the kidnapping squad at the city's crime division claims kidnapping accounts for over 50 percent of all crimes. Under Saddam that number was 2 percent. More disturbingly, with most abductions, someone close to the victim is cooperating, either out of fear or for a fee.

Now that we have experienced our own kidnapping episode, Iraqis are forthcoming with their tales. Everyone seems to know someone who has a relative or friend kidnapped recently. On an afternoon tea visit at the Shiite office of Ayatollah Sistani, my cleric friend Sheikh Haydar tells me that the son of one of Sistani's senior aides has been abducted in Najaf for a hefty ransom. At the Um al-Qura mosque, the Sunni Association of Islamic Clerics is now doubling as a hostage negotiator team as their phones buzz with requests from constituents, government officials, and foreign companies who plead with the clerics to use their influence. The group is particularly influential if the abductors claim to belong to an Islamic militant group.

The Association of Physicians holds a press conference to inform us that at least one hundred doctors have been taken from their homes and clinics since early spring and that now, almost all physicians have hired bodyguards. Hospital rounds and patient examinations are conducted in the presence of an armed guard. The head of the association blames the problem on coalition forces and Iraqi security and police for failing to stop the abductions. In Iraq, we are fairly accustomed to waking up in the morning to the deep *boom* of a car bomb or artillery shell. On the morning of my thirty-third birthday I awake to a loud explosion that shakes our bed and rattles the windows. I carry out the day's reporting before dining with friends at a party Babak throws me at the Hamra Hotel. Like Iraqis, I have become fatalistic. Iraqis believe strongly in fate and predetermined destiny.

Some Iraqis go to great lengths to decrease the possibility of abduction. Amal finally packs a suitcase and moves in with her niece because she is terrified that someone will break into her house in the middle of the night to kidnap her. Amal possesses a deep sense of defiance, viewing the war America has unleashed on her country as yet another storm to weather. Thus far, her approach has been very matter-of-fact. She insisted on moving back to her huge villa after it was badly damaged by bombardments after the invasion. When her neighborhood became a bastion for insurgents, she was too fearful to sleep in her own bedroom so she turned a small studio next to her study into a safe room—barricaded with padlocks. If intruders came, she would open a street-facing window and scream for dear life. Two burglaries of her home occurred while she was away, despite the presence of her Shiite guard. When kidnappings surge and rumor spreads that they are inside jobs, Amal finally decides to move. Civil war eventually closes off her neighborhood, and she is blocked from returning to her beloved home and gallery.

I visit Amal at her niece Annam's house, not far from our villa in Mansur. Despite the low walls that allow us to be seen from the street, we sit in the garden, because Amal determines that I can pass as a local guest to curious passersby. Speaking in English, we keep our voices down.

"Have you thought of leaving Iraq for a while until things get better?" I ask.

"Everyone is asking me why I'm still staying," she says, looking me in the eye. "But how can I leave? If you have a sick relative, do you throw them out on the street, or do you stay and nurse them back to recovery? Iraq is my sick relative. I cannot abandon it under any circumstances."

"Do you believe things will get better, Amal?"

"I don't know what will happen anymore, but I know that it's important to fight it. I want to feel like I am doing something, that I'm not just sitting and letting Americans ruin my country. How much longer can this situation continue? Americans let us rule ourselves and maybe then Iraqis can find a way to restore what is left of our national identity."

At seventy-one, Amal is one of the rare Iraqis I've met with the ability to harbor deep anger and at the same time take positive measures toward improving situations. She has recently formed two nongovernmental organizations to restore Iraqi art and archeology, Friends of Antiquity and Heritage and Friends of the Iraqi Museums. Enlisting the help of many of her old acquaintances from the art world, she has formed a board of directors, orchestrated meetings, and written to embassies and foreign organizations for funding. She has even managed to organize a modern dance performance at the National Theater about the Abu Ghraib tortures, performed by an Iraqi performer who returns to Baghdad from Europe at Amal's invitation. At the performance, which is held in the morning rather than the customary evening theater hour, I sit next to Amal.

The choreography makes dramatic use of light, sound, and video clips of the American military parading through Iraq. Throughout the performance, the dancer's hands are chained, his head is wrapped with a hood, and his body is locked in a cage. The theater comes to life with an outpouring of emotion as people cry, clap, and call out praise. I notice Amal wiping tears off her face. Beside me, Munaf holds his hand over his mouth as if to withhold his surprise. In a question and answer session after the show, the dancer lashes out against the American handling of Iraq. Amal looks more content than at any time I've seen her since the war. "It feels like the old days," she whispers to me. "I feel alive again."

But at her niece's house, Amal's mood plunges. Her voice rattles as she speaks, repeating words I have heard from her many times before. "We have to preserve what is left of our culture and art after all these lootings and destruction. Sometimes I don't recognize the country we have now. In the name of democracy they turned my country into a battlefield. Everyone is resisting in their own way; my way is to stay and to do what I can for our art and culture."

Amal has just returned from a tour of the United States with her friend, the Iraqi journalist Nermin Al-Mufti, as part of a national Iraqi women's tour sponsored by the Fellowship of Reconciliation. They spoke at several prominent universities and attended round-table and town-hall-type meetings from Washington D.C. to San Francisco. Despite her deep resentment of the United States, Amal went so her voice could be heard by Americans who are so far removed from the war their country has inflicted on Iraq. Sometimes during the lectures she was so overcome with rage she had to stare at the wall or the ceiling to prevent herself from breaking down in sobs. During her visit to Boston where she stayed with an Iraqi friend, Amal insisted on walking everywhere. Sometimes she spent an entire day wandering in the streets, just because she could.

"Iraq is now an open-air jail. You forget what you are missing until you visit another country and see people walking freely, laughing, and eating at restaurants. I didn't know that Americans were so careless and joyful. I was envious and angry. My friend said, 'Why do you want to walk in this weather?' I told her it's because in Iraq we are like animals in the zoo; we dash from one house to the next, always afraid that someone will harm us while we are traveling in between." She shows me pictures of the trip and newspaper articles from local papers all across the States that reported on the Iraqi women's visit.

"Are you happy you went?" I ask.

"Of course. I went to beg the Americans to end their occupation of Iraq. I went to tell Americans that Iraq is not a barbaric nation. We are not terrorists, and we are not a village for Americans to come and teach us how to rule ourselves. Even if I succeeded in changing one person's mind about Iraq, then I am happy I went."

"Look at me," she continues. "I have lost everything I worked for all my life. I have lost my art gallery; I have lost my home. I cannot even sleep in my own bed without fear that someone will come and rob me or kidnap me. The Americans have stripped us of our dignity. At this age, I am a refugee at my niece's house; all my life's worth is now just one suitcase."

Amal's niece, Annam, a woman in her forties, comes out to the garden to call us in for lunch. Amal falls silent, reluctant to grumble in her presence, as Annam puts her hands on her shoulders and softly caresses her aunt's back. "Are you getting angry again?"

"We are just talking about the situation, same story," she replies, waving her hands in the air. As we enter the house, we step into a foyer with floor-to-ceiling windows cluttered with objects. A small television set sits in the corner. Several plants grace the room, Iraqi paintings hang on the walls, and an inviting wooden bench covered with colorful cushions beckons from the middle of the room. Heaps of folders, letters, and newspaper clippings are scattered on the sofa. A small wooden table covered with boxes of beads, silver ornaments, chains, and semiprecious stones sits beside it. Annam tells me she makes jewelry, a hobby she picked up after the war as a way of stilling her mind.

"This is our workroom," she says semicheerfully. Looking around, I imagine the women's evening ritual. An aunt and a niece brought together by war's circumstances each taking mental refuge in the other's company and in art. I can imagine Amal poring over her papers and drafting correspondence to secure funding, while nearby, Annam bends over the table, diligently stringing necklaces no one will wear.

The legacy of Iraq is one of trauma. It has fought three wars in three decades, was ruled by one of the century's most brutal dictators, and survived a decade of cruel international sanctions. At the beginning of my time here, right after the invasion, there was a gleam of possibility about the new world. That sensation has long since died. Here, suffering is a solitary practice. For all its openness, warmth, and hospitality, the Middle East is not known for its honesty or its soul-searching practices. It's common for people to hide their true intentions in favor of politeness or to mask their true feelings in fear of association. Iraqis think nothing of inviting me into their homes moments after we've met, only to vent their anger and lash out at "the others" (often political leaders), whom they blame for the war. But they are far less likely to confide about the personal toll of tragedy. Admitting psychological trauma and seeking professional help outside of prescriptions is the equivalent of declaring insanity. To cope with the madness of daily life, many Iraqis pop antidepressant, anti-anxiety, and sleeping pills like candy.

Dr. Hashim Zainy, a psychiatrist at the Ibn Roshd psychiatric hospital, describes the Iraqi psyche for me: "Anything can happen at any moment. You can't plan for the next day or the next hour. You are always afraid, in every waking hour and in your sleep. This chronic stress gives you a deep sense of helplessness, an inability to take charge of your life and make decisions. There is an internal weakening inside every Iraqi personality. Do you know that most of my drug-user patients are not hooked on cocaine or LSD or any major narcotics? They're all on tranquilizers and can't live

without them. In today's conditions, who can blame them? I have had patients come in here with a gun and threaten me to get valium."

One afternoon, the middle-aged woman who cleans our house asks
me, through an involved act of pantomime, if I have any sleeping pills I
can give her. She takes a bottle of Advil from my bathroom and shakes it
with force.

"For sleep? For sleep?" she asks in Arabic, rattling the bottle.

"No, no, for head pain," I say pointing to my forehead.

"Please, please," she says in English. "I no sleep," she repeats.

When I tell this story to Munaf and Haqqi, they admit that they too
are having trouble sleeping. Lack of electricity makes sleeping indoors in-
sufferably hot, and bullets from random firefights rule out sleeping on the
balcony or the roof.

Haqqi shyly pulls up his trousers to show me his legs. They have
swollen twice their size; his feet resemble cushions crammed into tight
shoes. He is developing a kidney malfunction that the doctor says is being
exacerbated by stress and anxiety. In one month, I have witnessed Munaf
and Haqqi, among the dearest Iraqis to me, lose all of the hard-won capital they saved from working for us, money earned by risking their lives.
Munaf's dreams are simple: save enough money to buy a car, marry a
good woman, and flourish in a prosperous career. He comes from an educated middle-class family with strong values and as the oldest son feels
responsible for sharing the financial burden of running the household.
Despite his taste for fashionable clothes, Munaf saved every penny until
he put aside $5,000, with which he had planned to buy his first car. His
money disappeared as part of the ransom for our night driver, his cousin
Nihad.

Haqqi is shrewd with money, plotting how to invest his salary in a
shop and dreaming of becoming an entrepreneur. He always has some
side gig in addition to our work—managing the guards at the Chinese
embassy or helping his aunt run a shop. Outside of work, his passion is
electronic gadgets, and he invests most of his salary in the latest phones
and cameras available. He has managed to save about $10,000, every

penny of which he has put toward the lease of a shop for mobiles and gadgetry. He took such pride in the shop, painting the walls different colors, ordering glass display cabinets and countertops. One afternoon this month a group of armed men raided the shop clean of all cash and goods.

Munaf asks me if life is supposed to be this hard. I don't know, I say. I hope not. Maybe we are just unlucky because we are born in Iraq, he suggests. "In this new Iraq, we have no more dreams," he concludes.

18

Imagine If
New York
Were Baghdad

It is almost impossible to imagine what a city under siege looks like. The presence of a foreign army, an occupying force, combined with the utter lack of security, is palpable. War forces a city to redefine its boundaries. Gradually war robs the city of its character. And in time, it becomes a strange place, unrecognizable to even its own inhabitants. In the fall of 2004, Baghdad feels almost comically absurd. My friend Borzou Daragahi, from *The Los Angeles Times*, accurately calls it science fiction reporting. When I receive stony looks of incomprehension from friends and family back home, I try to equate Baghdad with New York.

Imagine that a foreign army invades New York City and cordons off a chunk of midtown. Around the area it erects two-story blast walls that seal it off from the rest of the city. People whose homes fall within this zone are issued special identification cards. When they return from work they must sit for several hours at military checkpoints where they are frisked, searched, and sniffed by dogs. Checkpoints are erected on the east side, west side, uptown, and downtown and are the common targets of bombs. Residents can only invite and escort one adult guest per day to their homes.

Some of the city's key transportation routes, the Lincoln, Queens-Midtown, and Holland Tunnels and the bridges, are shut to civilian traffic. If you want to get from downtown to uptown or enter the city from other boroughs, you must skirt the barriers and blast walls of midtown to find alternate bridges and tunnels. This adds several hours to your commute each day. Well-known city monuments are occupied by the foreign force. Famous hotels, like the Waldorf and the Hilton, are encircled with barbed wire and closed to the public, and their banquet halls and ballrooms are now military cafeterias. The windows of the hotels are boarded up. There is a military checkpoint at every subway stop. The foreign soldiers guarding them point guns at your car when you approach, and may shoot if you approach too slowly or too quickly. Tanks roll down Second Avenue, while convoys alert other vehicles to keep their distance.

Most of the shops on Fifth Avenue are empty and the restaurants have shut down. Macy's is open, but you have to enter through a metal detector and risk getting bombed, robbed, or assassinated while looking for clothes. The Metropolitan Museum, the Museum of Modern Art, and the Public Library have been looted. Police precincts are targeted daily by suicide bombers. The airports are shut down. JFK is now part of a giant military base. If you can afford to fly the expensive chartered planes, the road from the airport into the city is incredibly dangerous and littered with landmines. Leaving the city in your car requires taking your life in your hands as bandits and insurgents lie in every direction until you cross the state line.

Central Park is barren. The invading army has chopped down all its trees to clear a potential insurgent hiding spot. The park's football field and meadows are riddled with bullets every night by military helicopters eager to discourage loiterers.

Mortars are launched from the west side to the east side, from Soho to Wall Street. Electricity is only available for a few hours a day. You can't turn the AC on in the summer, you can't watch television at night, and you can't store food in your refrigerator. Sewage gushes into the streets of formerly posh neighborhoods. Garbage pickup and other civil services are indefinitely suspended. Each of the city's famous churches has at least been bombed once. Only a few of the city's gas stations are operational and the line to get gas stretches for twenty to thirty blocks. Because gas lines are common targets for car bombs, it's not uncommon to die or lose limbs while waiting to fill up your tank.

The city's hospitals are overwhelmed with patients, and the city morgue has reached maximum capacity.

During attacks, ordinary citizens are terrorized and barricaded indoors. They can't go out, and no one can visit. Looking to curb the insurgency, the foreign army hunts down guerilla cells, raiding apartments and knocking down doors in Chelsea or Harlem. Often they drag men to detention. La Guardia Airport has been turned into a gigantic detention facility in which uncharged detainees are tortured. Each time you step outside onto the streets of New York could be your last day on earth.

While chaos reigns, the occupying army reassures you that they have come to bring you democracy and freedom.

If you can imagine living like this, you can imagine Baghdad in the fall of 2004.

19

No Informal
Guests Are
Invited Here

It's not surprising that no commercial carriers dare fly to Iraq, aside from Royal Jordanian, which ensures its passengers' safety by painting the small aircraft a chalky white color, without any identifying logos, and commissioning a crew of former South African military personnel who are better versed at flying into war zones than an average civilian crew. A round-trip ticket to Baghdad from Amman costs about $2,000, roughly the same as the transatlantic flight from New York to the Middle East. It's quite common to see high-level Iraqi officials, like the foreign minister or prime minister, seated with their entourage in the first few business-class seats. In August 2004, there is no alternative safe way to enter Iraq other than on this flight.

Landing in Baghdad aboard the chartered Royal Jordanian airplane always feels like a prolonged crash. The plane doesn't gradually descend from its high altitude above the clouds. Instead, it hovers for a few minutes before it nosedives toward the runway in spiraling corkscrew turns. The dusty horizon is lined with palm trees and dotted with brown buildings that look as though they have grown out of earth. Gravity pulls me forward as I clutch the seat and the plane rocks to forty-five-degree angles right and left. These evasive maneuvers save us from mortars. The airport's old runway and decaying terminal look like a mismatched patch in the large quilt of Camp Victory, a sprawling gigantic U.S. military base located some six miles away from Baghdad. Safe routes for arriving in Iraq are elusive and ever shifting. The highway from Jordan to Baghdad, which we used until a few months ago, is now ruled by bandits and insurgents. The airport, despite the risk of crash or attack, is safer.

A young Iraqi man in the immigration booth stamps my passport, checks my press card, and snaps a quick photograph of me with a digital camera. "Necessary for security," he informs me, and I nod my head. I claim my bag and drag it to a minivan that treks between the arrival terminals to the first American military checkpoint at the airport's entrance gate. Cars without special permission or an appropriate badge are not allowed to pass. Munaf and Haqqi wait in our newly purchased BMW full-armored car, which cost the paper $100,000. I dive in, pulling my headscarf down and slouching down in the backseat. Munaf throws my suitcase in the trunk. Haqqi tests our walkie-talkie, telling our office that I'm in the car and we are heading home. My flak jacket rests sideways next to the door, providing an extra shield in case we are shot.

The road from the airport to the city is a wide three-lane highway. Open fields of date farmland stretch endlessly along either side. It is an area commonly used as a hiding place for attackers. My heart always pounds faster when we approach the overpass, where snipers fire at cars carrying foreign passengers. I remind Munaf to stay in the center of the road, where there is less risk of driving straight over a landmine. A few minutes later, we are driving directly behind a convoy of American Humvees and tanks. If Americans are attacked, we will get caught in the crossfire. Munaf can't slow down the car or speed up to pass the convoy because the soldiers could get suspicious and shoot us.

In my one-month absence Mansur has become more fortified. Security has been beefed up; we have more guards at the gate and one on the roof. Now our house is a luxurious prison.

Iraq has become the stage for a war of superlatives. Insurgents compete for the most spectacular attack, the biggest carnage, and the largest casualties, while Americans and Iraqi officials constantly examine the safer, better, quieter alternative for running the country. It's an endless competition to show who is gaining the upper hand. Is America succeeding in establishing security? Is the Iraqi government asserting itself? Or is the cocktail mix of havoc makers, known to all as "insurgents," stealing the show from under everyone's feet?

The main roads and bridges connecting the city are shut down as a security precaution this week. It's becoming routine for Iraqis to wake up to discover large swaths of the city cordoned off and major transport arteries shut to traffic. These extreme measures are always somehow justified for the sake of security, and people are used to adapting. The important event now is the Iraqi National Conference held at the Convention Center inside the heavily fortified Green Zone. This conference has already been postponed twice as officials held off for security improvement. When it became clear that security was worsening, they went ahead with the four-day event anyway. Now the city is being punished for a conference billed by Americans as a breakthrough for democracy. But this democratic exercise can only breathe behind heavily fortified walls and barricades. Out in the open, it would surely wither and die.

The conference is a four-day marathon of meetings, dealings, and debates for Iraq's various ethnic and religious sects to hash out the selection of a hundred-seat national assembly. The assembly will serve until elections for a permanent government are held in January. The Iraqis must comply with strict requirements established to ensure that every sect, ethnic group, and minority is represented. There is even a quota for female candidates.

So far the Shiites are leading the show while the major Sunni parties have boycotted the assembly, resulting in zero representation in the next government. After negotiations and horse-trading, at the end of the meetings, two lists are submitted: the Democratic Forum list, a hodgepodge of smaller and lesser-known parties, and the National Unity list, the collective triumph for the major political parties—namely the Islamist Shiites and the Kurds, all close allies of the Americans. During a tea break everyone gathers in the hallway. Shiite clerics clad in sweeping robes and turbans stand next to women in skirt suits and high heels. Shiite women wearing head-to-toe *hijab* mingle with Kurds dressed in traditional baggy pants and fringy head wraps, while Western-educated technocrats wander about in suits and ties.

I have tea with Samir Sumaida, former interior minister, who sees the conference as corrupt. Yet he admits that, for Iraqis, it's still noteworthy. No one has a point of reference for getting under one roof to hash out political demands freely and to listen to varying points of view. Samir says, "We have a body far more representative than ever before. This is what democracy is all about; these are the first steps and we are learning."

"Do you think this kind of cooperation will translate into better security for Iraq? The entire city is besieged so you can have a conference; is this how it's supposed to be?" I ask.

Before Samir has had a chance to answer my question, a loud *boom* shakes the building. We jump from our seats. Samir disappears instantly. Everyone is suddenly running to take cover while an American soldier screams, "Mortars! Get away from the windows!" Several mortars land in the Green Zone and after a little commotion, participants of the conference return to business unfazed.

The fourteen thousand Iraqis trapped in the Green Zone are subject to all manner of weird restrictions as they are increasingly forced to conform to the security needs of frightened foreigners. They can't invite more than one guest at a time, they can't enter or leave without American-issued photo identification cards, and they can only enter through designated checkpoints where they are searched and interrogated.

The Green Zone occupies about six square miles of prime real estate in Baghdad. Before the war, it was an elite, affluent district in the shadow of Saddam Hussein's palace. Among Saddam's affiliates were ordinary families and professionals who had bought their land prior to Saddam's rise to power. After the invasion, the Americans cut the area off from the rest of Iraq, labeling it Green to imply a safe zone. The rest of Iraq is labeled Red, a color now synonymous with the enemy. The Green Zone houses the U.S. and British embassies and their staffs of thousands, key U.S. military command centers, a U.S. army hospital, scores of Western companies, and the Iraqi government officials.

Americans have transformed the neighborhood in unimaginable ways. SUVs cruise the tree-lined boulevards. Bars, cafés, and Chinese restaurants have opened. A supermarket now sells imported American goods. American fast food chains like Burger King and Subway have set up stalls; they sell only to foreigners. Inside the Rasheed Hotel is Baghdad's sole disco. New, air-conditioned buses crisscross the area. These spots are off-limits to those not employed by, or in contract with, the coalition.

Iraqi residents have pleaded with the United States to open more entrances to the Green Zone, speed up searches, and allow a few more guests to be brought in. But so far to no avail.

Even American journalists can't wander around freely unless escorted by a public affairs officer of the army or embassy. When my formal request to write a story about Iraqis living in the Green Zone is rejected by the American embassy's public affairs and media office, I try to sneak in on my own. Haqqi and I meet a resident named Omar Jumah at the checkpoint near 14 July Bridge and hop in his car at the end of the day. After about two and a half hours of sitting in a long line of cars that snakes for several blocks, we stop at one of the many checkpoints. A young American soldier asks for our identification cards and scolds Omar for bringing in two outside guests. "You are only allowed one adult guest at a time, don't you know that?" he says. He examines my press card, points back at the gate, and orders me out.

An American friend with a special escort badge eventually smuggles me into the Green Zone, and the checkpoint soldier, seeing foreigners, waves us in without further inspection.

We find Omar's house, a spacious villa tucked away on a quiet street flanked by the office headquarters of foreign security firms. Omar's mother comments that bodyguards have replaced her chatty neighbors, whom she used to exchange greetings and gossip with before they all moved away. The Jumah family has so far resisted the temptation to rent out their house to foreigners, as many of their friends have, largely on account of Omar's mother, a talkative, opinionated woman. She says leaving her home, even if it's for $20,000-a-month rent, would be the equivalent of an exile sentence. But Omar thinks it's just a matter of time before tight security measures on Iraqis drive them out.

"We can't go on living like second-class citizens in our own country," he says.

Omar is a twenty-six-year-old clothes salesman, but his manner and speech are as stern as a banker's. He lives in the Green Zone by virtue of the location of his family home, and muses over his neighborhood's transformation from posh residential enclave to bizarre American security zone with wonder and frustration. Like many, he misses the old Baghdad.

Every time Omar leaves the Green Zone, whether for work every day or to visit friends and relatives, he faces up to six hours of checkpoint traffic each way and risks getting blown up. The constant threat of being identified as an American collaborator looms large. Omar leaves for work at 6 AM even though his shop doesn't open until 9, and returns home around 10 PM, when the lines at the checkpoints are shortest. He keeps a bicycle in the trunk of his car in case lines are particularly bad. To the extent that he can help it, Omar never leaves the Green Zone unless for work. This has become a point of contention between him and his young wife, who moved to the Green Zone to live in his family's house and who now feels that she is too cut off from her family. Months go by between her visits home to her family, a few miles outside the concrete barriers that separate Baghdad proper from the Green Zone.

The fate of the Green Zone and its perimeters is a contentious issue between the Americans and Iraqis. The mayor of Baghdad, Alaa al-Tamimi, has made noise by claiming that he will tear down blast walls around hotels and reopen the bridges, highways, and tunnels that the Americans have closed to traffic. For some time now he has been wrestling with the Americans over the Green Zone. He wants to shrink the area they control and limit it to the palace and surrounding blocks.

Al-Tamimi lives in a roomy villa a few doors down from our house with a small troop of guards and house staff. His wife and children refused to follow him to Baghdad, preferring their anonymous existence abroad to assuming the high-profile and risk-magnet status of the first family of Baghdad. Mayor Tamimi greets me formally, insisting that we sit in the fancy living room, where the coffee table is covered with silver trays piled with sugar and jam cookies, a basket of fruit, and a crystal bowl of salty nuts. When I protest, saying I expected a neighborly visit for a cup of tea and some political gossip, he laughs, telling me that there is no such thing as an informal guest in Iraq. All guests are formal visitors, even "our American brothers," he adds with a laugh. "Informal guests can get too comfortable and never leave!"

When I ask him what his experience as mayor of Baghdad has been, he doesn't mince words. "Very tough." He tells me, "My main goal is to restore the basic services to before the war status. Forget about going above and beyond the services offered under Saddam's rule. If I can restore electricity and clean water, then I can say I succeeded."

When he speaks, Tamimi refers to the coalition forces as "occupation forces" who are "occupying" Iraq.

"I thought you are an ally of the Americans, so how come you call them occupiers?" I ask.

"Americans have to agree that Iraq belongs to us. We cannot go on this way forever. We cannot convince our people that there is a transfer of sovereignty when Iraqis see checkpoints and walls and American soldiers and tanks. We can understand their safety concerns, but visually and psychologically Baghdad looks like it's still under occupation.

"I am the mayor of Baghdad, and I cannot enter the Green Zone unless I have a privilege badge or an escort. Is it possible that our embassy in the United States or Germany, for example, would put barricades around the neighborhood, close entire streets in a country? They do this all without even asking our permission."

20

He Sits
All Day Waiting
for Someone to Die

ecurity has become a full-time occupation. We now get full security reports e-mailed every day that detail the number, time, and place of various attacks. Coalition forces are being attacked approximately eighty times
a day. Foreigners are nabbed left and right. I read through these reports as
diligently as I read the headlines, before I meet with the staff to map out a
strategy for safe reporting. Instead of worrying about filing a great story, I
fret about keeping everyone alive. The constant anxiety over death extends
beyond the usual risks of war reportage. There is no telling what can happen to us anymore. Babak and I have established a "check-after-the-boom-
call" to one another.

To the extent that we can, we try to coordinate our interviews to minimize our anxiety about the other. I worry more about Babak's safety than
I do about my own. Maybe it's a mind game I play because I can't come to
terms with the risks I'm taking. If I don't hear from Babak for a few hours
when he is out reporting on an embed with the military, I pace the room
and clutch my phone, checking every few minutes for a missed call or a
text message. I think I can handle anything myself, but if something happens to Babak, I don't know how I will handle the heartache. Babak and I
have survived a handful of near-death encounters. Gunmen have shot at
us in a highway chase, angry mobs have threatened to kill us with AK-47s,
and we've been trapped in crossfire.

Iraq has made me superstitious. Maybe because I can't explain the randomness of the violence and the way everything is slipping out of control. I'm praying less and putting more stock into lucky charms and superstitious rituals that offer me a sense of comfort and control. My most prized charm is a silver Tiffany's necklace in the shape of a circle, from my mom. I treat it like a voodoo spell capable of shielding me from evil, and I practically never leave the house without it dangling from my neck. I have lucky boots for military embeds, a lucky scarf for road trips, a lucky handbag, and lucky days of the week. I tap into my gut for "right" or "wrong" feelings about such simple things as whether I should go grocery shopping. On several occasions I've backed away from interviews at the last minute, once at the doorstep of the source's house, because my gut suddenly turned against it. I try to stay away from reckless reporters or reporters who seem to attract trouble in the field. Now I only consider teaming up on road trips and interviews if Babak or a select number of my close friends are involved.

At first, my family treated my Iraq assignment as a source of pride and bragging, until it became their worst nightmare. My mother and sister struggle with my decision to work here despite the growing risk. At the same time, they try their best to be supportive. But I can tell that it's taking an emotional toll on them. My sister, Tannaz, says she has so much anger about Iraq that she can't read the papers anymore and switches the channel as soon as Iraq footage appears on television. Part of this anger stems from worrying sick about me.

For her part, my mom drowns herself in news, reading every wire report, and memorizes the precise location of every attack and the number of casualties by 8 AM every morning. When the stress becomes unbearable, her tactic is to grill me about when I will settle down into a suburban house and give her grandchildren. "Living out of a suitcase like a nomad is no way of life. I don't understand what you find so appealing about these godforsaken countries when you can have such a nice, comfortable life back in New York," she says.

I do my part by calling or e-mailing diligently after every major explosion.

One day my cousin Afrouz calls from Tehran. She is the closest to me among our big troop of cousins, and I am overjoyed to hear her voice. Before we've completed our exchange of greetings, Afrouz is shouting at me. She tells me that the entire family is freaking out because they haven't heard from me in a week. The Iranian television channels broadcast nonstop scenes of carnage and bloodshed from Baghdad. My grandmother, Etty, is at the verge of an emotional meltdown.

"What the hell are you doing there? Is your mother Iraqi? Is your father Iraqi? You have no obligation to that country. Leave! Why do you have to risk your life, put the whole family through hell, for the sake of Iraq? If you wanted adventure, you have had enough; if you were after recognition and career advancement, you have achieved your goal. Why are you still there? Do you have a deathwish? You know that everyone is proud of you, and they have always supported you, but this is going too far. What's worse, you have found a boyfriend just like yourself, a culprit for your craziness. Can't you see that you are both becoming war junkies? You are feeding off each other's addiction to this insane lifestyle."

It's true that our reporting and romantic adventures have slowly morphed into a grueling, soul-crushing, and life-threatening commitment. People constantly ask why we are still here. It's hard to articulate other than to say that most war correspondents have a sense of mission. War reportage is driven by something far deeper than a thirst for adventure and high ambition. At best you want your stories to make a difference, contribute to the public's knowledge and understanding of war, particularly when your own country is involved. Iraq is arguably the biggest story of my generation and a historical turning point in the Middle East and American foreign policy. I have been here from the beginning, before the bombs even fell and the soldiers invaded. I am too invested in the story, my eyes have seen too much, and my mind is too intertwined to be able to pull the plug and walk away from Iraq. I could die. I could lose a limb or go through a harrowing kidnapping experience. But for now at least I am too deep in the vortex of Iraq to be able to detach. I know that I can't emotionally let go of this story yet, even if my mind willed it. But it's very hard for my family to come to terms with this reality.

I have to offer new ideas about how to conduct reporting here. We are relying on Iraqi staff and calling stringers to piece together stories. The staff's reporting skills are improving; they are paying attention to details. I have taught Haqqi to keep a separate page for conversations he overhears, and to jot everything down. He has a knack for charming people and putting them at ease, skills that come in handy when he is reporting. He can walk into a crowd, a mosque, or a government building, and within minutes he has made acquaintances who seem eager to please. Munaf's English is improving rapidly and he's started filling in as a translator and reporter. As a method of practice, I print out all the stories I write and have my staff read them carefully, paying particular attention to the material and quotes that make it into the story.

Haqqi is yelling into the phone, "We are at the main square in Sadr City, there was an American tank in front of us, and this young guy ran toward it with an RPG on his shoulder and attacked it," he goes on panting. "The tank blew up in front of us, it's on fire, the body of the soldier flew in the air, and then the other soldiers started shooting into the crowd and at our cars."

Haqqi and Munaf went to Sadr City this morning to secure an interview with Moqtada's representative before returning for me. Sadr City, home to 10 percent of Iraq's population, is quickly being added to our list of "no-go zones"—off-limits to the Iraqi government and the American military, and out of the reach of journalists. The truce between Moqtada and the Americans is holding in Najaf but fighting has picked up again in Sadr City. Young men are overtly placing improvised explosive devices into the ground, and marking them with old tires or plastic cans to tip off locals. On the main roads of Sadr City, every ten yards are a dozen landmines. Behind city walls sit angry Iraqis ready to detonate them as soon as American convoys come near.

I instruct Haqqi to come back to the office immediately.

I miss my mobility. I miss being able to strike up conversations with strangers and wander the streets, poking my head into shops and restaurants. It's hard to believe that only six months ago I could take a trip to Najaf, Samarra, or Tikrit on a moment's notice. It seems ludicrous that last December I was making daily trips to Samarra to report on its local soccer team. I ate kebabs in downtown Fallujah last October before visiting a tribal sheikh deep in the groves of Anbar province. I'd be decapitated were I to attempt that trip today.

The freelance crowd is thinning out, and there are only a handful of Western shooters left in Baghdad. It's impossible to work here without the infrastructure and backing of a media organization to provide you the basics: a secure location, guards, trustworthy local staff, satellite phones, flak jackets, and so on. Our social lives as reporters pale from what we once enjoyed as security hobbles everyone's moves. A few nights ago, we went to the Chinese restaurant with a group of journalist friends. On our way home, still tipsy and singing "California Dreaming," we were warned by my night driver Mohammad that he doesn't think it's a good idea to come here anymore.

"Why not?" I asked.

"Because while you were having dinner, the guard told me that the restaurant received a threat letter from the mujahideen yesterday. They said if you don't close and stop serving the infidels, we will bomb you."

That night was the last time I ate at a restaurant in Baghdad.

▨ ▨ ▨

I watch Mazen al-Tomazi, an Arab colleague with the Al-Arabiya news channel, gunned down by an American helicopter as he conducted live coverage on Haifa Street. He died on television as I sat curled up on a chair, sipping my morning coffee. For days, I can't shake the image of Mazen crying for help. I ask Babak if he thinks we will need therapy once we are done with Iraq. He shakes his head. "Probably," he admits. For the past four days, Haifa Street, a strip of old houses and Soviet-style apartment blocks, is a battleground between Americans and rebel insurgents. Last week, Babak and I visited Haqqi's parents, who live in one of the apartment blocks, for lunch. We stayed late into the afternoon looking at old photographs of Haqqi's family from their diplomatic postings around the world. He showed us pictures of his father and Saddam while his mother described the difficulty of being confined to the house all day, and how hard it was to keep Haqqi's teenage siblings entertained at home. When I asked how the kids spend their days, his mother shrugged and confessed that they watch soap operas.

This week, the entire neighborhood is under a dusk-to-dawn curfew. Haqqi can't visit his family, and they can't leave. Street fighting is raging outside their door.

"I can't concentrate on work. I am too worried about them," Haqqi tells me. He is dragging his feet, which have again swelled enormously because of stress. Ringing his mother every hour or so, he hears the sound of gunfire. He wants to get his family, but his mother begs him to stay away. When the Ministry of Health releases the count of casualties in the past four days, the numbers are astounding: 110 dead and more than 300 injured in Baghdad alone.

Everyone is having a hard time coping these days, even friends who were previously resilient. When I walk in through the door of the Nassers' house, Marie-Rose takes me in her arms and bursts into tears. "I was hoping you had left. What are you doing here still? It's too dangerous now," she says. Two Italian women were kidnapped recently by gunmen who broke into their house in central Baghdad and dragged them out at gunpoint. Employees of a humanitarian organization, their kidnapping sent shock waves through the foreign crowd.

Sabah looks pale. His skin is yellow, and he's thinner than before. Without his vibrant energy, he seems like a broken man. He complains about having developed a heart condition from stress and tension. He is now taking medicine. Marie-Rose whispers to me in the kitchen that Sabah has had several episodes of anxiety attacks in which he collapsed to the floor, his chest spasmed, and his breathing was labored. Each attack occurred after a major bomb or explosion rocked their neighborhood in Adhamiya.

"Every day he says to me, 'Marie-Rose, prepare yourself.' It's like he is sitting and waiting for someone to die," she says quietly. "I don't know what to do. I think he is depressed."

Sabah, who doesn't crack jokes or pepper me with stories in his usual fashion, is strangely laconic. "The doctor says it's from anxiety. When they can't figure out what is wrong with you, they just say it's stress."

He tells me he is happy. He still hasn't lost the house to insurgents and militia, and everyone in the family is alive. In Iraq, the barometer for assessing happiness is often determined by whether any immediate family members have died. But Sabah's business is dead. "Who wants to paint their home?" he asks me. "Who wants to build anything anymore?"

Like any man forced into early retirement, Sabah is bored and frustrated by sitting at home. He bums around the house in his pajamas, nagging Marie-Rose, and cursing "the situation." He can't watch television because there isn't enough electricity. He loves reading the American newsmagazines that I bring him. Stacks of *Newsweek* and *Time* are usually piled in a prominent spot in the living room, like a prized antique collection. This time I notice the magazines are missing. When I ask him about them, he tells me matter-of-factly that he's hidden them under his bed. He doesn't want to give the wrong impression—that he is sympathetic to the American cause—if a stranger were to enter the house.

For the first time in their lives, the Nassers are missing church service after a suicide car bomb recently targeted their church. Even family gatherings, one of the remaining backbones of normal life, are few. Both of their sons are plotting how to leave Iraq for good. Ayad has taken his wife and baby to Amman to check out work opportunities. Ziad is researching asylum applications to Canada and Sweden. "If they go, what is left for us here except a big empty house?" Marie-Rose asks. The family is suffering financially because the shops are generating so little revenue. Sometimes an entire week goes by without a single customer. They are now tapping into their savings but they have little money. Sabah says he has convinced Marie-Rose to sell a few of the antiques she inherited from her parents. I have always admired a gorgeous Persian rug that hangs on their living room wall. A geometric design in earthy colors from Tabriz, it is a cherished gift from Marie-Rose's father.

Sabah announces that they have decided to sell the carpet. "Do you still love it? I want to sell it. It's the only thing I have that could bring me quick money. Do you think I can sell it for $5,000? Can you please ask your friends? You can take pictures to show around, and I will bring it anywhere you want."

An hour or two later, I sense that it's time for me to leave. "You don't want anyone to see you here and follow your car," Marie-Rose says, holding my hand. They seem a little apologetic and embarrassed for not insisting I stay for dinner or that I come back for lunch next week. For the first time since I've known them, they seem relieved to see me go, for my safety as much as their own.

21

This Is a Holy City;
I Have to Respect
All the Laws of Islam

Sheikh Kashef al-Ghatta, a middle-aged progressive Shiite cleric, sketches me a diagram explaining how the political machine works here. While I ask questions, Sheikh Kashef answers me in impeccable English with the patience of a mild-mannered, soft-spoken clergyman. When he puts down his pen, he asks if I've ever seen the Godfather trilogy. "Of course I have," I reply. "My father was a huge fan."

"Excellent. I tell you something: Iraq's five political parties are like the five families in *The Godfather.* All the people around them are getting jobs, money, government posts, influence, and everything you can imagine. They have old rivalries within them; they take revenge on each other, they make secret deals behind closed doors. Just like the mafia. I studied the *Godfather* movies very closely and found it very similar to our situation in Iraq."

I've come to see Sheikh Ghatta because Najaf, one of the few cities that flourished after the war, is disintegrating. Several weeks ago, Moqtada Sadr moved his Mahdi army militia into Najaf, where he took shelter inside the holy Shrine of Imam Ali. The American military and Iraqi forces are trying to force him out with fierce street-to-street, house-to-house urban warfare. Americans perceive two Shiite movements in Iraq with contradictory goals. Believing that Sistani favors separation between state and mosque, they see him as a friend, while they brand Moqtada, who, seeking a direct clerical influence on the government, is an enemy.

Sheikh Ghatta is close to Sadr's circle, and the Americans are relying on him to negotiate a way out of this mess. While I'm sitting in his office, with its floor-to-ceiling library of books, he takes phone calls on his mobile from the American embassy, the UN, the Iraqi government, journalists, and Sadr's associates.

I hear him tell an American diplomat, "You are like the horse Allawi is riding. He is using your military to clean up his act. Have you thought of what happens after Najaf? You think Moqtada will disappear?"

When Sheikh Ghatta hangs up, he tells me he was speaking to Chris Ross, one of the embassy's experts on Shiites and southern Iraq. He sighs. "They tell me, 'We want out, but at the same time we want to get rid of Moqtada, his Islamic movement, and Jish Mahdi.' I say that you can't have it both ways. Moqtada is not stupid; he won't agree to a truce unless it's a face-saving deal."

For the moment, it appears that all sides are cornered. The Americans are pounding Najaf's old city and the surrounding area of the shrine with artillery and the Mahdi army is ferociously fighting back. There is a quiet understanding that the soldiers, be they American or Iraqi, can't raid the shrine. People are comparing the actions of the Americans and Iraqi coalition government to Saddam's. Saddam once shelled the shrines of Najaf and Karbala in 1991 when he wanted to squash the Shiite uprising.

Since Moqtada's April uprising in Sadr City against the Americans, he has failed to build up a proper political, religious constituency. As a resource, he has focused all his attention on recruiting unemployed, angry young Shiites from the slums, tapping their already existing anti-American sentiments and handing them arms. Sadr has cleverly mapped out his strategy, knowing full well that Americans would never break into a shrine for fear of public Shiite outrage.

Ordinary Shiites are divided over what should be done with Najaf. On the one hand, they want to see Moqtada rooted out, but on the other, they can't come to terms with the holiest of their shrines under siege by American military forces. Although Ayatollah Sistani is on a medical trip to London, he has been asked to intervene. He is waiting to see if the Americans can make the Moqtada problem go away.

Sheikh Ghatta doesn't think that the problem can be solved without Sistani. "You see, nothing gets done without his permission and approval. Now Moqtada is upsetting the balance of Shiite hierarchy; he is trying to insert himself and his movement into the establishment by force. Everyone is wondering how to deal with him without making the situation worse, and everyone is waiting for Sistani to comment so they can plan their next move."

Even as early as the summer of 2003, American embassy officials would often tell us at background briefings that they were gravely concerned about inter-Shiite rivalries. One of the embassy's advisers once warned that Shiites have a great tendency for anti-American feelings and the imams are able to spread those sentiments very quickly through the mosques. Such scenarios, like the one playing out in Najaf, undermine the coalition's efforts.

Most of the senior clerics I've met point out that Moqtada lacks credentials and is capitalizing on those of his father, a revered Grand Ayatollah with status as a Shiite martyr. During one visit to Seyed Ali al-Waezi, the custodian of the Kadhimiya shrine and a close ally of Ayatollah Sistani, he switches to fluent Farsi in the middle of our interview. I am puzzled, but, as he explains, he wants to talk freely without Haqqi understanding.

"Seyed Moqtada, Seyed Moqtada," he mocks, as he repeats Moqtada's title. "Since when did this kid become so important? We are fed up with him. Moqtada must first finish his studies, gain a certain amount of respect among people, and then he can interfere in political matters. For now it's best if he focuses on his studies and leaves Shiite leadership to the more experienced clerics."

Moqtada's appeal to the masses, however, is based not on religious credentials but on his willingness to publicly challenge the Americans, a strategy he has carried out cleverly since Saddam's regime toppled.

Clad in a scarf and long robe, I head to the two main Sunni and Shiite neighborhoods. In Kadhimiya, the main Shiite enclave, I discuss the situation with passersby. There is widespread anger at everyone: the government, the Americans, Sadr, Shiite senior clerics who failed to stop the fight.

"Until now, the builders of our so-called new democracy have Saddam disease. They want to fight and kill; no one cares for the people," says a forty-two-year-old shopkeeper named Abu Hassan.

In Adhamiya, a Sunni, largely anti-American neighborhood, I am forced to be more discreet. We drive around for some time until we find a crowded bookshop. The bookseller praises the brave mujahideen of Fallujah and calls it "a nationalistic resistance," dismissing the Sadr militia as politically motivated opportunists. Standing close to the counter, practically whispering in English to Haqqi, I take notes as discreetly as possible.

When the Najaf crisis escalates, I'm determined to go, but everyone, including my Shiite cleric sources and our staff, judges such a trip to be suicidal. "They'll kidnap you and kill us," Munaf warns. Today's newspaper reported the kidnapping of an Italian journalist in Najaf. The dead body of his driver was discovered in his car. Two French reporters have disappeared on the road from Baghdad to Najaf.

When Babak and I finally persuade our Iraqi staff to accompany us to Najaf, it's almost the end of the siege. The drive from Baghdad is only three hours, but it takes us a day because we have to spend the night in Karbala. Babak and I leave Baghdad early in the morning. Despite the 130-degree heat and blazing sun, I wear two thick layers of black head-to-toe *hijab*. Never once during the drive do I look out the window. I stare ahead or down at my feet, like a proper conservative Muslim woman. We are driving in a beat-up, secondhand BMW instead of our fancy armored car. We leave behind U.S. passports, press cards, driver's licenses, and any other documents that could identify us as Americans. We take our Iranian passports, a small Quran, and a picture of my friend's baby girl to pass as our own child if we are nabbed. Maybe they'll have mercy on us if they think we have left a small child behind. We instruct our nervous driver and translator that if we are stopped on the way, they must vouch that we are an Iranian couple visiting from Tehran on a pilgrimage to Karbala. As we are about to leave Baghdad's city border, Babak finds a floppy disc in his pocket that he quickly breaks in half and throws out the window. Even in Baghdad, journalists are now careful about the documents they carry around. Most everyone I know has printed fake press cards with vague names of imaginary news organizations. My fake press card says *International Journal Newspaper*, with a picture of me in a scarf. It's common for an Iraqi to ask, "Which country is the newspaper from?" to which Haqqi always replies, "*Jaridah Alamiya* [international newspaper]," and starts naming our bureaus: Asia and Europe first, and then sometimes an off-hand mention of New York.

On the way to Najaf the Iraqi police wave us through the checkpoints. We are in touch by satellite phone with our colleagues in Baghdad and our journalist friends in Najaf. They tell us to avoid the usual road that cuts through the city of Koufa because of ongoing clashes. We detour toward Karbala. Ten miles before we reach the center of Najaf, the road is blocked and the Iraqi police are going nuts, firing openly into traffic. We don't know if it is a real police checkpoint or insurgents dressed as cops. A unit of the Iraqi National Guard is scattered around the empty fields alongside the highway. With guns out they seem to be looking for someone. When gunfire breaks out around us, we duck. We must quickly decide whether to return to Baghdad or take the desolate back roads that pass through dense farmlands to Najaf. Neither is a safe option, it's getting too late in the afternoon to drive safely to Baghdad, and the dirt roads seem unfriendly territory. We opt for spending the night in Karbala.

Karbala is quiet and empty and most of its hotels are shut. When, after hours of trying to find a place to sleep, we finally convince the manager of a small hotel to open up his damp rooms, he balks. He looks at our Iranian passports, figures we are Muslims, and asks for a marriage certificate. When we protest, he says, "Business is business and we like good business very much. But this is a holy city; I have to respect all the laws of Islam." Ayad, our Iraqi translator, thinks quickly on his feet, telling the virtuous manager that because our wedding certificate was issued in America, it would be a liability on a road trip. This answer seems to satisfy him. He shakes hands with Babak, smiles at me, and gives us each a set of keys before disappearing into the back room to turn on the generator.

When we arrive in Najaf early the next morning the fighting is over but surviving members of the Mahdi army are lingering in the shrine. Sistani returned from London yesterday and successfully brokered a truce. Until a few weeks ago, Najaf was a success story in the new Iraq. Now whole areas of the city lie in ruins. The main road that separates the old city from the modern outskirts is littered with ordnance, glass, shrapnel, and unexploded devices. We trudge carefully until we reach an intersection where yesterday the Iraqi forces opened fire onto a marching crowd of hundreds. A sea of plastic slippers and mismatched shoes, some stained in blood, lies before us. We hear the *thump* and *bang* of machine gunfire in the distance. When the sound approaches, we take cover beneath the half-collapsed ceiling of a building until the shooting subsides. Until yesterday, snipers from the Mahdi army lined the rooftops of the buildings around us. I have stuffed a white napkin in my bag, in case there is a need to wave it. As an extra measure of protection, I leave open the front of my abaya so the big bold white letters, PRESS, printed on the front of my flak jacket, are visible. I can barely walk. My flak jacket is crushing my chest and the two layers of black nylon, head-to-toe abaya are weighing me down in 125-degree heat. When an old man passes with his donkey and cart, we hitch a ride to the shrine.

Nearer to the shrine, the scope of destruction worsens. Deserted streets are carpeted with ammunition and debris. We pass corpses of dogs swarming with flies. Heaps of garbage line the streets, and the air assumes the stomach-turning odor of trash mixed with blood and smoke. Around the shrine, several storefronts are completely blackened by smoke. The remains of dozens of shot-out cars are smoldering quietly. Electricity lines stretch from one end of the road to the other, tangled in knots. Sewage oozes out of pipes, plastic water bottles have melted into the ground, entire buildings have collapsed into piles of rubble.

A lump wells in my throat as I recall all the places I've been in Najaf—here is the hotel where I've stayed numerous times; here is the textile shop with the two Farsi-speaking brothers; here is the small vendor that sold us sweets dripping in syrup; here is where Munaf parked our car; here is that kebab restaurant that was always packed with pilgrims. Everything looks familiar and yet alien. A ghost of rubble has replaced the vivid landscape I remember.

"It feels like we are in one of those 'day after' movies, after a nuclear attack or something," I say to Babak.

"Yeah, or being in an episode of *Twilight Zone*," he says.

War is a ghastly experience of collective punishment, no matter how you put it.

22

Do We Stay
or
Do We Leave?

A*t the precise* moment of the attack, I am sitting in my bedroom on a chair, clutching my satellite phone to my ear and talking to Babak. The force of the explosion throws me violently to the floor. I scream, expecting the house to collapse on my head. Windows smash, doors buckle, and bricks fall out of the wall. My books slide off the shelves to the floor. I drop the phone but the line doesn't cut off; I hear Babak's voice shouting my name from thousands of miles away.

Shreds of glass fly like tiny crystal confetti, covering the black marble floors of the living room, blanketing our desks and computers. The Iraqi staff hurries inside the house from the garden, screaming and shouting at each other in Arabic to take cover and instructing us to stay put. Thick black smoke and orange flames as tall as a ten-story building billow into the sky. Pieces of flesh and twisted pieces of metal from the suicide bomber's car and the American Humvee it targeted rain down in our garden. My stomach churns, and I fight a wave of nausea from the smell of burning flesh and smoke.

My housemates, *Newsweek* journalists Rod Nordland and Joe Contreras, rush down the stairs in their flak jackets and helmets.

"Go put on your body armor; there may be another attack coming," Rod, a veteran war correspondent, advises.

I stuff an emergency pouch with cash, my passport, and satellite phone. The first hours after the attack are horrid. It's difficult to determine what exactly has happened to gauge the risks we face by staying put versus leaving the house. If we stay, the house could get mortared or raided. If we leave, we could get ambushed or kidnapped on the way.

Our Iraqi staff—translators, drivers, and house staff—are also trapped. They fear being targeted or followed home if they are seen leaving our compound. As we ponder what to do, my editor, Bill Spindle, calls from New York to tell me my story is running on the front page and I need to check my e-mail immediately for a readback.

Unable to form a proper sentence, I quickly say, "Uh, I can't right now. . . . There was a car bomb outside the house; we are all okay. I will call you later," before hanging up in haste.

It is remarkable that no one is injured in our house. The children of an Iraqi family living next door have cuts and bruises from broken glass. The suicide car bomb that targeted the Humvee killed a young American soldier and badly wounded three others. The flames caught a passing vehicle, burning and mangling the bodies of two Iraqi passengers. A testament to how rapidly security is deteriorating, the incident hardly makes news. It's mentioned in a fleeting paragraph of a wire story.

Babak calls every half hour to check up on us. It's rare that we leave Iraq separately. "Remind me from now on to make sure you've cleared out of that hellhole before me or drag you out with me," he says.

I don't sleep at all that night. Fully dressed, with my shoes next to the bed, I place my emergency bag on the pillow next to me in case we have to escape in the middle of the night. I stare at the ceiling and listen to distant cracks of gunfire. Strangely, I don't really feel anything.

The next day we evacuate the house. I pack a small bag of clothes and the equipment I need for filing stories and move back to the Hamra Hotel, where we lived before Mansur. Mansur, where we have lived for a year, was once the Beverly Hills of Baghdad. Wide, well-paved boulevards lined with palm trees, mansions with marble columns, oval swimming pools, and rose gardens shaded by orange and lemon trees lent to its lustrous, privileged atmosphere.

Here, young couples and fashionable women sipped coffee in cafés, pastry shops baked apple pie and chocolate éclairs, and boutiques imported European sandals and rhinestone-studded evening bags. Well-to-do Iraqis and Iraqi officials lived here. The mayor of Baghdad and the German and Spanish ambassadors lived on our street. With more checkpoints than other areas, embassy guards, snipers, and private security for Iraqi officials manned Mansur's roads. Nonetheless, in September of 2004, insurgents began to infiltrate the seemingly secure enclave like an epidemic. By the time everyone realized what was going on, it was too late.

In a matter of weeks, foreigners, journalists, aid workers, and contractors were nabbed from their homes in Baghdad in broad daylight. Sometimes their terrified faces turned up in jihadi videos as they pled for their lives. Other times, their mutilated bodies were discovered in dumps.

In our neighborhood, within the space of a week, two incidents shattered our nerves. A drive-by shooting targeted a Russian embassy convoy, and three contractors (two British and one American) were abducted from their home a mile away from us. After beheading them, the captors threw the contractors' limp bodies back into the neighborhood's streets.

My relocation to the Hamra Hotel marks my sixth move in Baghdad in the past sixteen months. The hotel is not 100 percent safe, but I feel safer here, perhaps because I think the odds still work in my favor in a place packed with journalists. All my friends, with whom I've bonded in various war zones over the past three years, are staying here. Every night after filing we get together to have dinner, a drink, or a talk. It's a relief to be among friends, away from the hostile outside world of Iraq.

In addition to the stress of Baghdad, I am dealing with the public brouhaha over my leaked e-mail and my editor's concerns that I am being attacked (for having a critical opinion about Iraq) and praised (for speaking the truth) by a polarized American society on the eve of presidential elections.

I have long conversations every night with my editor, Bill Spindle, and the *Journal*'s managing editor, Paul Steiger. They are extremely supportive and caring, taking long hours from their busy days to reassure me that this media frenzy will pass. Initially we discuss whether the e-mail should be printed in the *Journal*, now that it's so widely distributed, but senior editors decide that because I openly call Iraq "a disaster" and President Bush's foreign policy "a failure," publishing the e-mail would validate those critics who say I am too opinionated to cover Iraq objectively. The editors argue that as long as we hang on to our claim that this was a private correspondence, not intended for publication, we are in safe territory. I can understand my editor's concerns about the perception of the newspaper's objectivity on the hottest topic of the presidential elections, but I make it clear that if they pull me out of Iraq I will resign. They reassure me that I will not be reassigned, but I detect a sense of relief that my long-scheduled rotation for a break is coming up shortly. I am more than eager to take a break since our house has been bombed and these past few months have been particularly taxing. In my support, Steiger releases a statement that says, "Ms. Fassihi's private opinions have in no way distorted her coverage, which has been a model of intelligent and courageous reporting, and scrupulous accuracy and fairness."

And then, a few days after the move, in one of the grimmest days I've lived through in Iraq, a car bomb aimed at an American military convoy kills thirty-four children. The children had gathered around the American soldiers, who were passing out colorful candies when the suicide car bomber rammed into them. I rush to Yarmulk Hospital, where most of the injured children are taken. The scene in the emergency room is chaotic and desperate. Doctors are shouting orders; nurses are running with bags of IVs and white bandages in their hands. The kids are wailing and screaming as emergency workers and parents carry their bloody bodies inside. There aren't enough beds in the emergency room for all of them. Some are stretched out on benches, others are lying on the bare ground. A few are slouched in wheelchairs. The floor is slick with blood. Every time a doctor pronounces one of the children dead, a parent drops to the floor and wails. The mothers beat their chests and slap their faces, while the fathers openly sob, asking, "Why? Why? Why?"

We drive back from the hospital in silence. My shoes and the hem of my abaya are stained with blood. Back in my room, when I soak my abaya in the bathroom sink, the water turns pink. I scrub at the bloodstains with soap. The lather turns pink too, and my fingers go numb. My stomach feels like a stone. I sit on the bathroom floor and break into uncontrollable sobs. The sink overflows, and the stained water streams down on the white floor tiles.

23

You Go into a
City Like This Already Dead,
and You Fight Your Way Out

The Sunni Triangle, a vast area of farmland and thick groves, is embroiled in insurgencies. Its epicenter, Fallujah, has a near-mythic stature in Arab minds for its openly anti-American stance. As far as rebellion goes, Fallujah is regarded as the head of the lion and Americans see a vital link between reclaiming Fallujah and crushing the insurgency. But this American strategy is more rooted in idealism than in fact. They argue that if they carpet-bomb Fallujah and spend $82 million rebuilding what they have destroyed, the residents and tribal leaders will come to their senses. They will realize that the insurgents are their enemy, and America is their friend. The path to a bright future is actively to participate in the political game in the upcoming January elections. In line with this course of logic, the Sunnis will come to accept their subordinate role in Iraq's next government and learn to live, peacefully, with a Shiite and Kurdish majority in power. If only this were true.

In this careful calculation, Americans forget that the intractable problem of the terrorism that plagues Iraq is a postoccupation hazard. The United States and the Bush administration made the case for war with Iraq based on two points—that Saddam had a link with al-Qaeda and an Iraq invasion would be an extension of the war on terror, and that Saddam possessed weapons of mass destruction.

Independent studies conducted in Washington have since proven both reasons false. Iraqis are keeping track. It's increasingly difficult for American troops to sell them sugarcoated stories about freedom and democracy by rolling forcefully into yet another city.

Sheikh Khamis al-Hassnawi, the tribal chief I visited in Fallujah last year, is the chieftain of the Bu-Issa tribe, one of Anbar province's largest and most influential Sunni tribes. He is not optimistic about the American plan to invade Fallujah, although he hopes for success. He complains that his worst predictions have come true, as his influence on tribal members has diminished, and more have joined the ranks of the insurgency. Sheikh Hassnawi, who used to sit on the city council, no longer dares visit an American base, and the Americans don't visit him. He blames the trend of tribal members' rooting for the insurgency on the Americans, who have lacked a clear plan for how to install law and order or create prosperous employment opportunities. The insurgency reward for killing an Iraqi affiliated with Americans has risen to $500. Hassnawi has received several more death threats since we last saw him and warns Haqqi sternly over the phone not to bring me to him, as if I could contemplate a drive onto Fallujah's lethal ground.

Fearing an imminent invasion of American forces, most of Fallujah's residents have fled. City authorities are either on the run or in hiding. Shops have closed and fresh graffiti pops up on buildings every morning. In bold Arabic letters, such phrases as "Long live the heroic Mujahideen of Fallujah," "Jolan is the neighborhood of heroes," and "Resistance is alive here" speak to the active spirit of opposition very much alive here.

Hassnawi is staying put for now and assessing the situation day by day, scouting options that vary from temporarily leaving for Amman to staying with friends in Baghdad. The city is slowly slipping away from the central political dialogue of the rest of the country, despite the best efforts of a handful of moderate tribal sheikhs like Hassnawi. The city boycotted the national conference in August when Iraqi politicians gathered to compose lists of candidates for a national assembly. There is talk of sitting out the upcoming January elections altogether.

"The Americans have to be very careful because if Sunni anger spreads, then the moderates will side with the extremists and all hope will be lost," he says.

When Haqqi reports on his conversation with Sheikh Hassnawi, he throws his own spice into the mix: "By the way, Farnaz, every Sunni is now supporting the mujahideen. The situation is very bad. Don't come back for now."

When Operation Phantom Fury, one of the big assaults since the invasion, begins, I am in Ramallah, West Bank, awaiting Yasser Arafat's impending death. Babak is in Fallujah. The marine unit he is embedded with is one of the first to enter the battlefield, in Jolan, the most dangerous district. On the eve before going in, Babak relays a word of advice the unit commander offered his troops, "You go into a city like this already dead, and you fight your way out."

The scenes of the battlefield mirror the ones we have seen in other cities, except, as Babak says, multiplied by a thousand. Almost all of Fallujah's civilians have fled. War planes drop massive bombs that shake the earth and kick off gigantic balls of fire. Low-flying gunships rain bullets. American and Iraqi forces sweep ahead, taking shelter in people's bombed-out homes, sleeping in half-collapsed buildings, eating ready-made military meals in courtyards that stink of rotting flesh, scribbling memorabilia on bedroom walls. They endure hours of intense gun battle, pass dogs eating human corpses, fire their machine guns at shadows lurking behind walls. They duck and run and hide; they attack and get hit; they kill and are killed.

Babak is on my mind all the time. I watch the news and check for wire updates obsessively, barely able to concentrate on my own reporting. Anxiety and restlessness course through my body constantly. I rest my phone on my lap when I'm writing, in case it rings. I take it to bed and hold it at night. On the day Arafat dies, Babak calls to report that his unit has suffered several casualties. I try to digest that information by asking him how often he feels his life is in danger over there. He says all the time, every day. I hear machine guns in the background and a soldier yelling at him to get off the phone. "Gotta go, gotta go," he says, before the line goes dead.

When he doesn't call for thirty-six hours, I wander the streets aimlessly with mobs of grieving Palestinians, unable to formulate questions for interviews. I walk up to a satellite truck parked at the square and ask a wire news photographer, who is urgently filing his photos, if he can check for updates on Fallujah. I am crying. He asks me who is there and hands me his laptop, shaking his head. I weep at the side of the road, in the car on my way to interviews, my Palestinian fixer at my side. I am enraged when we get lost in a perfectly safe neighborhood. When I return to my hotel room, I want to scream but I can't because security guards for Palestinian officials are down the hall. I fling my notebook and all the contents of my purse violently across the room. I bang the remote control against the wall. I curse at everyone responsible for making such a mess of Iraq and destroying so many lives. I have strange flashbacks that catch me off-guard: The sight of a pair of boots sitting outside a mosque reminds me of a maimed foot. I often see glass smashing when I look out a window or have flashbacks of missing limbs—arms, legs—when I look at people. I jump at the sound of a door slamming. I have nightmares about being trapped in an explosion. I shed ten pounds in two weeks. I have trouble filing my stories and keeping my deadlines. I don't recognize yet that I'm experiencing the first symptoms of post-traumatic stress disorder. The intensity of Iraq is finally hitting me. And I'm not even there.

When Babak returns from the battlefield to the base, he calls to say he is out of the line of fire. The line has static and his voice sounds far away. I hear loud booms.

"What's that sound?"

"Rockets. They're firing them at the base. I can't stand out here for too long," and then, "Hey, I love you."

"I love you too. Stay alive, will you?" I say.

A few weeks later, Babak flies straight from Fallujah to Amman by way of Baghdad. I meet him at the Four Seasons Hotel. When I open the door to greet him, he drops his backpack and flak jacket to the floor and scoops me up in his arms. We kiss. "I haven't showered for three days," he warns. The stench of sand, sweat, and blood drifts from his skin. But I don't care. He is alive.

24

A Place of
Mortars
and Bullets

"**Y**ou want a room on the mortar side of the building or the bullet side?" Lieutenant Colonel Ed Strosky, the current American military manager of the Rasheed Hotel inside the Green Zone, asks. I can't tell if he is trying to scare me away because he doesn't want to deal with journalists in residence or if he's unfazed by attacks by this point. Is the hotel that unsafe? "Oh, you bet," he says, hurrying me down the dark corridors of the hotel to show off the evidence.

"This side faces the garden and the Baghdad zoo and takes all the incoming mortar. Come here and look; see this crack in the window and the big hole in the glass? It's shrapnel from a mortar that hit the room right below this one."

In a room facing in the opposite direction, he continues, "This side faces the street in the Red Zone and gets hit with bullets all the time. See those holes in the wall below the window? They're bullets. It's from a few days ago. If someone was sitting behind this desk or lying in the bed, chances are they'd get hit by one of these things."

Strosky, a stocky man with an intense demeanor and a loud, high-pitched voice, tops off the tour with his personal advice: "If I were you, I'd take the mortar side. It's less risky. Of course, if you are unlucky and a mortar hits your room, you probably won't survive. But this week, it seems mortars are less frequent than random gunfire. That could quickly change, and you could change your room."

I am assigned a room on the seventh floor, the only commercial floor in the hotel now reserved for journalists. Strosky barks his orders at me. "One violation and I'll kick you out of here. Got it?" I nod.

I have moved yet again to the Rasheed Hotel along with Babak and the rest of our *Newsweek* housemates because after evacuating our Mansur villa, we have no place to stay. We pondered about where to go next and concluded that we would take the ultimate security decision and set up a house in the Green Zone. We don't want to go through the motion and expense of another dwelling only to be forced out again because of security or an attack. Babak and I have gone back to our house in Mansur only once, for half an hour, to pack and move our belongings. Houses, unless foreigners rent a cluster of them and turn an area into a security zone, are largely a thing of the past.

Being the first journalists to move into the Green Zone, we are required to wrestle with endless paperwork and bureaucracy. The American authorities are wary of allowing us in. They know that once we live here, they can't control our movements the way they do now. We sign a consent form agreeing not to report or write about things we see in the Green Zone unless approved by the proper public affairs channels. We have no choice but to agree. Our most convincing argument for living in the Green Zone is that we feel threatened and unsafe outside it. Although we head outside to conduct reporting in order to get the Americans to agree, we pretend never to leave the compound. I escape frequently, spending a few days at a time with friends at the Hamra for a decent meal, a hot shower, and regular electricity.

The check-in procedure at the Rasheed strips you of your identity and assigns you a number. I am no longer Farnaz Fassihi, a journalist for *The Wall Street Journal*. I am number 315. Like a prisoner in a maximum-security detention center. As long as I stay at the Rasheed, I am ordered to conduct all my hotel business by referring to my number. Under no circumstances should I reveal to anyone, particularly the Iraqi employees of the hotel, my name, profession, or affiliation. I must remove my photo identification cards from around my neck and hide them. And I'm forbidden from striking up a conversation with any of the Iraqi hotel staff.

In the privacy of my room, I should never leave any paper trail or documents that reveal my identity such as an article with my byline. No outside visitors, foreign or Iraqi, are allowed in the rooms. Iraqi hotel employees cannot accompany me upstairs or enter my room without the supervision of an American or Nepalese Gurka security staff. The hotel cleaning staff can only make up the beds and change the towels under a foreigner's supervision.

I can't use my satellite phone, which has to be set outdoors facing south, to connect to the Internet or make phone calls, because it would attract attention to the window. The first three floors of the hotel are completely off-limits to us, and wandering the halls is strictly forbidden. I am not allowed to eat in any of the hotel dining halls that serve the military and contractors. I am relegated to the service elevator, which can take ten to forty-five minutes to arrive. Despite charging $250 a night, the hotel lacks hot water, regular electricity, and hot food.

My room's thick black curtains must always be drawn to hide my presence. Any sign of life increases the chance of being targeted. Strosky makes it sound like insurgents are taking positions around the hotel, with binoculars monitoring our every move. While this might be true, I can't help but be reminded of the paranoid atmosphere of the hotel when I stayed here under Saddam's rule. Then too, we were forbidden from speaking freely in our rooms, which were tapped, and we had to be mindful of the paper trail left behind.

It's ironic that the Republican Palace and its surrounding monuments, once symbols of Saddam's tyranny, have survived the war only to be turned into the symbol of American occupation of Iraq. Now about five thousand foreigners are pent up here, protected from a security nightmare of their own making. It's quite common for an American to ask us, "So what's it like out there? What are people saying? What's the word on the street?" This self-admission of ignorance never ceases to amaze me. These people are in charge of this country and yet nearly two years into their nation-building enterprise, Iraq and its people may as well be from Mars.

To say that the Americans are obsessed with security of the Green Zone is an understatement. In October, the Green Zone had its first serious security breach when a pair of suicide bombers detonated themselves in the area's café and bazaar, killing three Americans and wounding twenty. Civilian contractors and embassy employees are also required to wear their flak jackets at all times. The ballroom of the hotel, where Bremer once hosted a formal dinner for journalists in summer of 2003, is abandoned. What's left of the Rasheed Hotel is a grim skeleton that bears little resemblance to its glory days under Saddam.

The glass windows of the lobby were smashed by a rocket attack and have been boarded up with thick wooden planks. The gloom is made more eerie by dim fluorescent lights. The fine leather sofas in the lobby are scratched from shrapnel and glass, and without heat, the hotel is permanently cold. Its restaurants are practically abandoned because most visitors now dine in the canteen. At the Scheherazade restaurant where in my prewar stay a lavish buffet of Eastern dishes was presented for lunch and dinner every day, the only foods now available are chicken sandwiches of stale bread and boiled chicken with a thin layer of mayonnaise and, occasionally, a watery lentil soup. Away from the watchful gaze of Strosky and his staff, I have befriended a waiter at the Scheherazade named Ali, who speaks fluent Farsi and has the deprived, hollow-cheeked face of a broken man. His service uniform hangs on his thin frame like a loose tent. A prisoner of the Iran-Iraq war, Ali was held in captivity for twelve years in Iran. His family, without any information about his whereabouts, declared him dead. When Ali was released a year before the American invasion, he returned to find that his wife had married his older brother and had two children with him. She had taken her and Ali's three children and moved to Najaf with her new family.

"My heart is broken. There is nothing left here anymore. My life is now just coming to work at the hotel and going to my mother's house to sleep. That's it. I am lucky if I don't die on the way."

When Ali asks me my name, I stumble. He has just told me his heart-wrenching life story, and I am forbidden from telling him who I am. I whisper, "Farah," and tell him that I'm a journalist but that he can't tell anyone. He nods in understanding. "I thought you worked for the Americans," he says.

Ali's remark makes me worry that all this mystery surrounding our identity is leaving the wrong impression on the hotel staff. I feel much safer saying I'm a journalist than having an ambiguous identity that can be mistaken for being a spy or working for the American government.

As the madness around us escalates, so, too, does the desire to create something resembling a domestic life. Babak and I have become experts in turning the dingiest rooms into livable space. At the Rasheed, Babak and I take adjacent rooms and open the middle door to turn it into a big suite. Aside from a few taken by our colleagues, the rest of the rooms on our floor are empty and the doors are open. Wandering from room to room, we select the furniture and push what we need into our quarters. No one seems to mind that we are amassing quite a collection. I light vanilla candles to mask the foul scent of mildew. Babak hooks up our television and DVD player, and an iPod for music. He mounts a Kevlar bulletproof blanket over the window to give us an extra layer of protection in case of shrapnel.

Our living conditions in the Rasheed are by far the most miserable and depressing of my Iraq stays so far. The hotel provides constant reminders of the Americans' ineptitude in fixing the crisis they've created. When the hotel's boiler breaks, it takes weeks for Strosky to find someone to fix it. A day after the job is done, a major attack on a water main cuts off the water supply entirely for weeks. No one can figure out how to turn on the central heating system, despite the freezing desert cold, and when, mistakenly, central air conditioning starts to circulate cold air in the rooms, no one knows how to stop it. Elevators don't work, the internal phone system is down, and electricity and generator service is sporadic. From our window, Babak and I sometimes peek out at the city, sliding aside the blast blanket to catch a glimpse of Baghdad. We like to identify famous monuments. If there is electricity, lights twinkle in the distance. But on most nights, the city is shrouded by absolute dark.

YEAR 2005

Our House May Never Be Safe for Us

25

When They Say,
Pick This Person,
We Obey

Everyone who has anything to do with elections, from poll workers to candidates, seems to operate in disguise. Voting triggers a good dose of paranoia. Munaf reports that when he went to his neighborhood's local grocery to inquire about his family's voter registration papers, which are distributed on the basis of previous government food-ration sheets, the old grocer told him he had received a death threat for carrying the forms. He warns Munaf against pursuing the registration sheets, which he returned to the electoral commission, whispering over the counter that neighborhood insurgents are watching everyone's moves. Along with the rest of our Sunni staff, Munaf has declared that he will boycott the election. The Sunnis' dominant political party, the Iraqi Islamic Party, and the Council of Muslim Clerics have announced their withdrawal of support for the election and have called on all Sunnis to abstain from participation.

Apprehension percolates as people wonder if the country will ripple with multiple explosions and attacks on election day. Even the Iraqi government has drastic security measures in place for the day, including a three-day ban on vehicular traffic throughout the country, and closing Iraq's borders and Baghdad International Airport. American and Iraqi forces will be deployed to form security rings around polling stations across the country.

Candidates themselves are refraining from publicly announcing their candidacy for fear of being killed. Television campaign ads run for a scant two minutes, enough time for a quick mention of the name of each list and its affiliation with political parties. Voters are encouraged to vote for a number or a symbol that corresponds to a political party's list rather than a particular candidate. If you are voting for the Shiite political list, you have no idea whom you are voting into office, other than that they are a person blessed by Ayatollah Sistani and affiliated with the Shiite political parties. Candidates rarely appear on television for debates or discussions about their plans for the major issues and none of them seem to have set an agenda aside from getting a parliamentary seat and securing representation within the political sphere.

Through a wide, influential clerical network, the Shiites are campaigning for voters as if their lives depended on it, while the Sunnis are discouraging the vote with conviction.

Driving through a Shiite neighborhood in Baghdad, we see a colorful maze of posters and banners that cover entire blocks like layers of wallpaper. The main slate for Shiite political parties is list 169. Their logo depicts a candle, a metaphor for the Islamic parties illuminating the path ahead. Ayatollah Sistani's portrait is everywhere alongside the election slate he prefers—that of the Shiite Islamist parties. Banners reiterate Sistani's message about the absolute need to vote: "Your vote is as precious as gold, don't waste it"; "Election will prove that we are the majority"; "Voting is a holy duty."

In Sunni areas, it's nearly impossible to know that an election is approaching. There is no campaign literature or voter registration handouts. After fliers were distributed warning people away from the polls, no one dares speak publicly about the election. Graffiti splashed on walls warns, "Fallujah resistance is here," and "Voting is for infidels."

In such a polarized climate, it's hard to find a middle ground but I manage to locate a small but notable group of technocrats, seculars, and moderates who are trying to emerge as a third option by building a grudging camaraderie among Iraqi tribal chiefs. At the helm of this effort is Ghassan Attiyah, a political science scholar who stands out among a crowd of Iraqis with his neatly trimmed beard and affinity for tweed jackets and brown wool pants. Ghassan returned from two decades of exile in London in April 2003 with dreams of creating the country's first modern think tank. In London he published the *Iraq File*, an opposition periodical, and he banked on his experience and extensive network to found the Iraq Foundation for Development and Democracy in Baghdad. Most of his efforts have been directed at establishing a secular political movement capable of bridging the divide between the established political parties' ethnic and sectarian lines. He has been lobbying his American contacts to postpone the elections until they can reach an agreement with the Sunnis. He believes that a polarized election will pull Iraq further apart, a sure recipe for civil war. The first task of the elected 275-member national assembly is to ratify a new constitution and then prepare for another round of elections, in approximately a year's time, that would elect a permanent government. Ghassan can't see how all that can happen without the Sunnis on board.

"The vision of Iraq now is every fraction is digging more trenches around itself instead of cooperating. The whole society is being divided; each community looks at its own grievances. Iraq without Sunnis will not be Iraq. They'll be continued bloodshed of Shiites and Kurds and eventually they will start to retaliate," he forecasts one afternoon when I meet him at his house shortly before his weekly election gatherings.

"I'm very concerned. Is this the liberal secular society America wanted to see in Iraq? We are holding moderates hostage because rebellious areas will be too dangerous for voting to take place. I left because of dictatorship. We may be forced out of this country as a result of chaos if this election goes through and the government is completely polarized. Chaos is just as frightening as dictatorship."

By early afternoon dozens of tribal leaders clad in traditional Arabic clothes, as well as professors and former technocrats, begin to fill Ghassan's living room. The living and dining rooms have been merged by pushing three couches against the wall and placing a semicircle of chairs opposite to allow participants to see one another. Although there is no official seating chart, the prominent tribal sheikhs sit on the more comfortable sofas and at the head of the room, near the windows. People shuffle in their chairs, and offer up the house's best seats to the elderly chieftains.

The tribal chieftains have an air of faded glory about them. When they speak, they push their chests forward, tucking back their shoulders and raising their voices a notch or two below a shout. It sounds more like a king issuing an edict to his subordinates than a group discussion among members of equal rank. These men are unaccustomed to the free debate, open criticism, and tolerance of ideas that Ghassan promotes in weekly sessions. Quickly the chieftains are insulted and an argument breaks out. Occasionally a man moves to leave the session dramatically, at which point someone else steps in to calm him, apologize, and insist that he stay. Although Ghassan's political slate includes women, it is rare for any to attend these meetings, and I can sense that my presence both amuses and annoys the chieftains. When they discuss the insurgency, the American timetable for troop withdrawal, and Sunnis, emotions run high.

"The Americans could not bring stability and security to Iraq. They haven't fulfilled their promises and neither has the Iraqi government. The Sunnis are in a big trap. They are not including us in their circle. The Shiite Islamists and Kurds are getting together and the Americans are nodding yes. We need to get organized and create a third force. The people who get elected should have very strong roots and have ruled from grandfather to father. We are educated people who love our country. I don't see why America wouldn't support the tribes," says Sheikh Rabia Mohammad al-Habib, whom every one refers to as "prince" of the Rabaei tribe.

Ghassan intervenes, "If we don't act, then moderate Arab voices will be crushed. We need to make it clear that we are a neutral force here."

Before Ghassan finishes, Sheikh Mazen Obaid Khalaf raises his voice to make an impassioned speech: "Let's first establish that Americans are our enemy and they invaded us and then let's talk. If we label ourselves neutral, then people will label us as close to the Americans. We should make it clear that we are against them. If you don't want to take a stand against Americans, then I won't be with you."

"You want to throw out the occupiers with weapons or policy?" Ghassan asks. "Who do you want to depend on to throw out the Americans? The Sunni insurgency? The Kurds or the extremist Shiites? The path ahead of us right now is of armed resistance and a divided nation at civil war. The time of emotions is over; now we must pick the middle road and act."

The room falls silent for a few minutes, as his audience digests Ghassan's candid words. Someone coughs. Another tribal leader shifts in his chair. One raises his hand and motions for the waiter to serve coffee.

Sheikh Abu Sabah speaks first. "What is our official position on armed resistance? If someone asks us this question today, what do we answer? Do we support it?"

Ghassan doesn't reply. He turns his face to the tribal leader from Fallujah.

"If Iraqi people ask, we will say yes, we support the Iraqi nationalist resistance but not terrorists. Resistance, my brothers, is a fact of life. Any country that is occupied will have resistance," says Sheikh Saad Dulaimi of Fallujah. He continues, "Tribal tradition says an equal number of Americans should die for every member of our tribe that they kill. For every sheikh, then the blood of four of their leaders must be spilled."

When I gasp, Haqqi nudges me.

At the end of the third hour, Ghassan tries to wrap up the discussion.

"The conclusion here today is that the only entity that has saved Iraqi society is the tribes. Second, let's try to agree on a mutual policy about the following points: occupation, resistance, and the Kurds and Sunni participation. Can we cooperate or not? We should reconvene in two weeks and your mission is to find clerics who are on board with us and also female candidates. We don't have enough of those."

The chieftains break out into laughter.

The following week, I meet with a female candidate who's part of Ghassan's slate. A professor of constitutional law, Azhar al-Shakry is a forty-eight-year-old mother of three. She and her husband, a professor of political science, are both candidates on Ghassan's list, the Iraqi Independent Bloc. Of the sixty candidates, one third are women who are largely technocrats, seculars, and intellectuals: all amateur politicians who have joined at the behest of a scholar who has made it his life's mission to provide Iraqi voters with an alternative to the mainstream political parties.

Azhar agrees to meet me on the condition that the interview takes place in the privacy of my hotel room. She is too nervous to be seen in public giving interviews to a foreigner. She shows up impeccably dressed in tailored black pants, a red twin-set sweater, and a long black leather jacket. Her hair is styled in a bob, her long bangs curling near her thick eyebrows. Her briefcase contains some campaign notes and literature, cleverly hidden in between her students' term papers.

When Azhar and her husband signed up for politics, they envisioned something resembling the campaign activity of political power couples like Hillary and Bill Clinton. She imagined her husband and herself holding joint lectures and visiting different neighborhoods to meet voters. She thought she could focus on issues that mattered to her like women's rights, a secular-based justice system, and a constitution that offered equal rights to minorities. When she joined the Iraqi Independent Bloc, she imagined shaking hands with voters, posing for pictures with them, and listening to their woes.

"But that's just a dream. We quickly realized that such behavior would get us killed tomorrow. So now we campaign in hiding," Azhar tells me.

Unlike many of her counterparts, Azhar started out by publicly declaring herself a candidate and appearing on TV talk shows in which she spoke about the importance of democracy and voting from the viewpoint of a woman who had dedicated her entire career to defending secular laws. She was hoping to reach scores of people, like herself, who were interested in elections but were turned off by an increasingly religious, sectarian tone. Out of nowhere, the death threats arrived. Anonymous letters and strange phone calls warned her to stay away from elections if she wanted to live. When those threats mentioned the safety of her children, she was sufficiently spooked.

Since receiving these threats, she has not stepped outside her house with her children. "I don't want anything to happen to them in case they try to assassinate me. My younger one cries when I leave the house, saying, 'Mama, take me with you,' but I just can't. I can't risk it," she says.

Al-Shakry's husband kept the candidacy a secret even from his parents and siblings. Azhar's own sister, a doctor at a well-known hospital, claimed not to know when a colleague asked if her sister was running for office.

"Fear is on my mind all the time," says Azhar.

When you talk to Americans about Iraqi elections the attitude is strictly from an ideological point of view: they can vote, so democracy is on the march. But Iraqis admit that living under constant fear and utter chaos is just as frightening and repressive as it was to live under Saddam's dictatorship.

Across town in the Shiite suburb of Kadhimiya, the two junior clerics, Sheikh Nassrawi and Seyed Hashem, believe themselves to be on a holy mission for getting out the Shiite vote. Since I met them after the invasion, they have risen to prominent positions within the Shiite network. I now have to call days in advance to set up appointments and coordinate my visit to meet them at the head office. Recently, when I showed up for a meeting, they greeted me at the door of the main office to tell me that women were no longer allowed inside the building and its annexed library, where we have always had our afternoon teas.

"But I love that library. We have been meeting there for nearly two years now!" I protest.

"Yes, but it's full of men now; it's not appropriate for you to sit there," announces Sheikh Nassrawi. He leads me to a house directly across the street, reserved for meeting female patrons. We find a quiet unfurnished room where we sit on the floor to chat. I notice that the clerics leave the door open and put a twenty-minute limit on the interview because they must tend to election business.

Seyed Hashem is now the director of a new Shiite television station, Al-Salam, which is broadcast out of Kadhimiya and has been established with help and funding from Iran. Hashem utilizes the airwaves by running special election programs at peak evening viewing hours. There are hour-long speeches by authoritative clerics braiding equating elections with religious duty, strictly informative talks about the mechanics of casting a ballot, and nonstop advertisement of the favored Shiite bloc, list number 169. Seyed Hashem is candid about the influence he exuded simply by the fact that he is dressed in a clerical robe.

"All the Iraqi academics, seculars, and tribal leaders are doing their best to push people for election, but none of them have the same power as the *marjayat*. They have to go to great lengths to convince people why they should listen to them. But we just say it is the *marjayat*'s orders and people will listen. It's as simple as that," admits Seyed Hashem.

Sheikh Nassrawi is overseeing the overall voter drive in this section of the city and supervising a relentless door-to-door, mosque-to-mosque campaign. He says the clerics are playing an important role in helping the public get over its fear of violence on election day.

"We tell them voting is a holy duty; if you get killed while you are on a mission from God you go straight to heaven, you die for Islam, and you are a martyr. So there is nothing to be afraid of," he tells me.

At the advice of Sheikh Nassrawi, I visit a few voter education seminars at mosques around the city. The most interesting session takes place in Sadr City, at the house of a local cleric. Sheikh Shaker is Ayatollah Sistani's representative in Sadr City and under direct orders he has temporarily turned his house into a voting education center. The mosque where he used to preach every afternoon was taken over last month by Moqtada Sadr's militia along with seventeen other Sistani-affiliated mosques. Moqtada is ambivalent about whether he supports the upcoming election or not but he is systematically inserting control over his power base in Sadr City.

Sheikh Shaker al-Mousawi, a small, bony man with a shock of black hair that sticks out of his white turban, adjusts the microphone so it almost touches his chin. He yanks forward his thin brown robe so it covers the front of his body as he sits cross-legged. In row after row spread before him are women of all ages, dressed in head-to-toe black abayas. They look to me rather like a flock of blackbirds huddled together in the cold. We are at the sheikh's house in Sadr City, a modest three-room, cement-block building. There are no paintings of landscapes or family portraits that usually adorn Iraqi homes; unframed posters of revered dead clerics, frameless and the edges curled up, are stapled to the wall. Oil lanterns sit on the windowsills, ready to come to life when twilight and sporadic electricity interrupt.

The crowd at Sheikh Shaker's house spills out to the front yard, circling the two orange trees. Tall wicker partitions surround the compound wall, and effectively seal it off from the street. A red and blue striped carpet covers the bare ground. The sheikh invites me to sit beside him and Haqqi, the only man here other than the sheikh and his son. Haqqi tries not to look at the women, fixing his gaze on the carpet and whispering the translations so quietly that I must ask him to speak up. Munaf and his father, Abu Munaf, wait for us inside the armored car and surveillance car, ready to take off on the spur of the moment, in case something goes wrong. We now travel everywhere in a convoy of two cars; I sit in the armored car with Haqqi and Munaf while our armed bodyguards follow closely.

Sheikh Shaker's voice ripples through the microphone when he finally starts to preach. The audience is transfixed as he plays on the crowd's devotion and nationalism:

> Election is a historical time in Shiite history in Iraq. It marks a new beginning for us. For thirty years, we were not allowed to have a voice, we had no rights, and we were crushed. You were treated unjustly and not like a human being. We were always beggars. We never had a minister or even a general in the army. The dream of every Shiite was to have an important role in the government. Now is the time to be free. This is the time to move into a new phase of our history. I promise you that Shiites are going to be the majority with the biggest number of representatives. The period of Sunni dictatorship is over. With your vote you will decrease their numbers. The ruler of the new period will be from you and elected by you.

The crowd breaks into chants of "Inshallah."

The sheikh continues: "The *marjayat's* orders are very clear: Election is your religious duty. If you don't vote you will answer to God on judgment day. Voting is like praying and fasting. I repeat: it's your religious duty, not a political or national matter."

A sense of excitement permeates the air as the women stir in their seats, glancing at each other with anticipation of something greater. They raise their hands from under their coverings and sheepishly ask the sheikh questions after his sermon. A young woman in her twenties with a round, pudgy face complains that she is confused about which electoral slate she ought to pick.

"When the time nears, we will inform you of which list we support and who serves our best interests," answers the sheikh. "The *marjayat* says your vote is more precious than gold, so don't waste it on someone who doesn't deserve it. It has to go to the right person."

A middle-aged woman wants to know if she is religiously obliged to take her elderly bedridden mother to the polling station.

"Absolutely, it's your duty, even if you have to carry her there on your shoulders."

I make eye contact with a few of the women and they smile at me triumphantly. I edge myself closer to the crowd and start chatting with them. They are genuinely excited at the prospect of their opinions mattering, and at the public venue in which to cast a ballot. The details about the best candidates and how they serve the women's interests seem to be somewhat beside the point.

"But if they are telling you who to vote for, how is that choosing freely and independently?" I want to know.

"No, no, no. You don't understand," says Nahid Aboud, a forty-two-year-old mother of three, as she takes my hands into her own. "We follow whatever our *marjayat* says because we adore our clerics. When they say we must go, we will go. When they say pick this person, we obey. We don't ask questions and we have no doubts."

It's impressive how the Shiite parties are writing the practice of election and religion. They possess a certain level of political know-how that makes it easy to forget it's their first experience with democracy. They make no secret of the fact that Iran offers generous funding, hands-on advice, and training. With nearly three decades of experience with this hybrid style of government of elected officials supervised and endorsed by clerical authorities, Iran is an ideal role model.

The direct relationship between civic responsibility and Islamic duty offers a simple formula responsible for mobilizing the masses in Iran as early as the late nineteenth century, when the *marjayat* issued a fatwa against a royal decree by King Nasr el-Din Shah, who had given exclusive control of tobacco trade to the British. The religious edict, much like Sistani's fatwa over the election, took the country by storm. When everyone stopped smoking tobacco, including the Shah's wives, and his servants refused to prepare his pipe, he was forced to reverse his decision.

During the constitutional revolution, intellectuals enlisted the help of clerics to establish the country's first constitution in the early twentieth century. The symbolic relationship between secular and nonsecular camps was again called upon when revolutionaries deposed the monarchy of Mohammad Reza Shah Pahlavi in 1979. Shiites are now heading to the polls not because of lofty Western ideas of democracy but because they see it as an order from God, channeled through the clerics.

The two rather sentimental scenes at Sheikh Shaker's mosque and Ghassan's house embody the dilemma Iraqis face as it becomes clear that elections will be contested along sectarian and ethnic divides. Iraq's election is promised to be one of the greatest showcases of democracy in the Middle East and a model that the United States hopes it can uphold elsewhere in the region. But as the date nears, the election becomes the stage for confrontation in one of the greatest sagas unfolding in the region: the Sunni and Shiite divide.

The Shiites see the act of voting as the only way to solidify their new position while the Sunnis view boycotting elections as the surest way to reverse this power shift. Pitted against each other since the fall of Saddam, the Sunnis and Shiites are formally divided over the election.

My window into Iraqi elections is limited to the hotel and the three polling stations that are within walking distance. The countrywide vehicle ban means that we can't drive anywhere. As media organizations, we have special vehicle permits that were issued by the Ministry of Interior to allow the press to move about the capital and navigate the checkpoints and security rings set up around Baghdad. But given the ban, any car is an immediate signal of either a foreigner or a government official. We've seen reports of sniper insurgents taking positions on rooftops in neighborhoods right next to ours. The fear factor for this election is so grave that all of our Iraqi staff submitted forms with fake addresses and phone numbers in order to obtain election credentials from the Ministry of Information. The ministry is infiltrated with informants and there are rumors that the list of names of Iraqis working for foreign organizations may be leaked or sold to insurgents.

The Iraqi staff moves to the hotel for the duration of the four-day vehicle ban, hostage to our needs. They say goodbye to nervous relatives, who treat their departure with resigned fatalism. Munaf's mother held up the Quran near her husband's and son's heads, reading prayers to shield them from bad omens. There were tears and tight hugs and cautionary warnings.

"I told my mother, this is the day for democracy, not for war, but she said in Iraq every day is a day of war," Munaf tells me.

We strategize our reporting and pool our resources with both our staff and other news organizations. I require our staff to make a list of all the people, Shiite and Sunni, they know in Baghdad and to note their phone numbers. We combine the list and divide it by neighborhood. We call everyone three times during the day to find out how the election is faring in their corner of the city to get a picture from the outside.

The crowd streams into the polling station near the Hamra Hotel, where I've temporarily relocated to cover elections, by midmorning. I didn't want to be inside the Green Zone at the Rasheed Hotel and cut off from the Iraqi public on such a day, and I also needed to be near my staff. We allow a few hours to pass before walking to the neighborhood schools where polling is taking place. Jadriya, a largely Shiite area around the hotel, is thick with voters. The school has been encased in barbed wire and an amateurish security station has been set up to frisk voters. Men must empty their pockets onto a plastic table and leave cellular phones and pens behind. Women are searched behind a curtained booth that resembles the dressing room of a small boutique. Everyone is dressed up in their Sunday best.

The mood of the Shiites is decidedly joyous. Many have brought boxes of sugar cookies and sponge cakes layered with pink and blue confetti icing to pass around like an offering. Election monitors hover nearby, encouraging the crowd to vote and offering assistance when required. When the giant ballots are folded and dropped into a plastic box, the election monitor cheers, claps, and praises the voters with a teacher-like approval, "*Barak-Allah Eini* [Well done, my dear]."

Voters must dip their index fingers in purple ink, which as the day wears off is the ultimate symbol of the Iraqi vote.

The recorded number of attacks on the day of the election peaks at 175, more than double the usual 60 attacks per day. The number of casualties is estimated at 44, hardly the mass-murder scenario and spectacular bloodshed feared. We hear occasional booms of mortars falling in the distance and gunfire cracking and reports of suicide bombings targeting polling stations. Nonetheless, our Iraqi neighbors and many others across the country have successfully surmounted their fear in order to vote. When I ask people at the polling station in our neighborhood why they came to vote despite the risk, they tell me unanimously, "Because of *marjayat*'s orders."

When I call the Nassers in the middle of the day Ziad tells me Adhamiya is desolate; its polling stations never opened. "We would go and vote if we lived in another neighborhood," he tells me. "But here no one is leaving the house. The area is dead." In most of the Sunni Triangle, polling stations stay shut, while in places like Tikrit and Fallujah, voters number in the dozens. The election mirrors Iraq's sectarian tensions: a resounding success in the Shiite and Kurdish cities but a failure in the Sunni areas.

Throughout the day, we are continually surprised by unanticipated twists and turns: some Sunnis have defied their edict and headed to the polls. I watch in astonishment as Haqqi sheds his usual dismissive attitude and pleads with election workers to let him vote out of his district despite the fact that he has never bothered to pick up his registration form.

"I really want to vote," I hear him say. "I didn't before, but coming here today and seeing old people, handicapped, and women and men vote made me feel very nationalistic. I am Iraqi. I have a right to decide the future. Please let me vote."

The election worker smiles and hands him a ballot sheet.

When I ask him how it felt to vote for the first time, he beams.

"It was great," he says with a big grin before calling the rest of our staff at the hotel to encourage them to follow his lead. When we walk back to the Hamra Hotel, I spot other Iraqi employees of media organizations and some of our hotel staff, running in packs toward the polling stations. "We are going to vote!" shouts one of them as they pass us by. Haqqi shows them his purple finger. "*Yallah,* go, go, before it closes, hurry up. It's a great feeling."

There is something about this election that marks a new beginning for Iraq, not in the way that's being portrayed in the West as the birth of a great democracy, but in a practical sense. Iraqis have broken from their past. They have turned the page on the Saddam era. I've marked so many milestones since arriving nearly two years ago, but none has captured the attention and imagination of Iraqis as the elections have. No matter the side, the elections have stirred deep emotions in all Iraqis. The election is like a referendum for change in which the Iraqis are announcing that they are fed up with the status quo, and ready to move on.

The biggest question facing Iraq is whether the new polarized government will be able to translate its success into stabilizing the country and curbing the violence. It's hard to imagine how they can achieve this goal

234

without half of the country onboard. As I type my story, I listen to the staff argue about whether the Shiites will rig the vote in their favor, whether their vote actually means anything, and whether Sunnis and Shiites will be able to reconcile. When I look up, I notice Haqqi digging in our emergency first aid kit.

"What are you looking for? Did you hurt yourself?" I ask.

"No, I'm looking for some Band-Aids. I want to cover the purple ink on my finger. I don't want anyone in the street or in my neighborhood to see I voted. It would get me killed."

26

Every Good Muslim Woman
Must Think This Way,
My Dear

atima Yaqoub gives me a furious glare from behind her desk at
the Kadhimiya municipality where she has served as a councilwoman for the past two years working dutifully toward creating an
Iraq ruled by Islamic law. Rising abruptly, she clears her throat and
runs her black-gloved hands over the front of her gray, tailored
coat. She wears straight-cut pants that stop just above her fashionable kitten-heeled, suede pumps. Her hair is completely covered by
a silky scarf. A baby-faced woman, she is short, stocky, and looks
younger than her forty years. Circling her desk, she takes a seat
next to me and pulls my bare hands into her gloved palms, stroking
them softly. I can't tell if she is trying to overcome her anger at my
comments about how Islamic law curbs the rights of women or if
she is trying to convert me into her Shiite sisterhood. We smile
awkwardly at one another. After two years of holding public office
as a Shiite Islamist councilwoman, Fatima is still somewhat
stunned at her own prominent position in society and the reversal
of fortune that has empowered the likes of similarly devout
women. She is energetic and passionate about her beliefs and has
figured out that the harder she aligns herself with the clerical establishment, the faster she will get ahead. The days of the secular,
feminist-minded women are over.

"My dear, sweet sister," she says looking into my eyes. "We must not argue with the word of God. His orders for Muslim women are very clear, and we must obey him. Are you married?"

"No, but I'm engaged," I say, keeping in line with the usual explanation I offer when questioned about my marital status. As a Middle Eastern woman, introducing Babak as a partner with whom I live won't exactly sit very well.

"Well, I want to give you a lesson. When you get married you should not feel possessive of your husband. You don't have the right to own a man and want him only for yourself. God says that a married woman must make room in her heart to share her husband with unmarried women. I can tell from your face that you are mad but this isn't what I say, it's what God says. Therefore sharia is the law of God, and it's the best law for humankind."

"I'm sorry, but I just don't think this way," I say, as I free my hand from her grip.

"Every good Muslim woman thinks this way, my dear. Aren't you a good Muslim woman?" she replies.

The argument between rationalism and religious fanaticism is doomed to flounder. Reason and dogmatism are unequal partners in a free debate. You can argue to your heart's content about why implementing Islamic law, known as sharia, in Iraq's new constitution will be disadvantageous to women. But it's hard to argue with the retort that it is the word of God.

The elections provided the Shiite Islamist slate with 48 percent of the vote and secured them a little more than half of the 275 seats in the national assembly, and they are pushing to name Islam the definitive source of law. The first casualty under Islamic law is Iraq's secular family law.

Iraq's secular family status law, introduced in 1959 shortly after the republic was established, remains one of the most formidably progressive family laws in the Arab world. Women have the right to equal inheritance; they can divorce, receive alimony, and have child custody. Men are allowed to take more than one wife but only under very specific conditions; when, for instance, one wife is unable to have children, and only with the written permission of the wife.

Shiite Islamists want to overrule this ordinance in favor of a religious court ruled by clerics. This would not only institutionalize Islam in Iraq's constitution but would pave the way for officially segregating Iraq's sects. Iraq's factions—Shiites, Sunnis, and Christians—would no longer come together under the umbrella of one civil law. Each sect could allocate inheritance, and conduct the officiating parameters of family life, according to their religious codes.

Shiites seem to be unanimously in favor of institutionalizing Islam in the constitution while Sunnis are largely opposed to a move they fear will gradually head the country toward Iranian-style theocracy.

The things that bother secular women about Islamic law are not surprising—as a woman their rights are half those granted to men, and they are legally regarded as unfit to raise a child unless in special circumstances. By law, custody is awarded to fathers, and in their absence, to paternal grandparents. The mother's visitation right is completely subject to what her husband allows. A husband is free to take on a second, third, or fourth wife, and in Shiite practice, a "temporary wife" for as little as an hour. A husband can divorce a wife in a second, simply by repeating three times "I divorce thee." If the woman wants to divorce her husband she must prove a host of scandalous acts—medical proof of physical abuse, a criminal sentencing, or substance abuse. Without a male guardian's permission, a woman cannot be employed, receive education, or leave the country.

I can understand that the laws of God offer comfort to women like Fatima but I am stunned at the naïve view that holy laws are safeguarded by holy men and applied fairly, as God and the prophet intended. I've seen sharia law at work in Iran and have no illusions about how quickly laws are stripped of holiness and tainted by family battles.

Replacing civil family law with sharia has been a longtime wish of Shiite parties. Abdulaziz Hakim, the cleric at the head of the Supreme Council for Islamic Revolution in Iraq, first introduced this change to the

Governing Council in August of 2003. It drew fierce criticism and angry street protests from women activists, and when Paul Bremer threatened a veto, it was dropped. Now that Iraq is sovereign and the Shiite Islamists rule as a majority, nothing stands in the way. The Americans appear willing to live with sharia law in exchange for Shiite parties' support. The Kurds can similarly be persuaded to look the other way as long as they keep their autonomous northern corner of the country.

The rights of women in the new Iraq will send a crucial message to the world about the kind of country it wants to be. Will this new Iraq, the one that the U.S. is helping build, be a real democracy or a veiled theocracy? The fabric of a democratic society is not just free elections and an independent press, but an independent judiciary system that safeguards equal gender rights. Empowering women in postwar nation building is central to stability and transparency. Twenty-five percent of Iraq's parliamentary seats belong to women, a provision that was intended to enshrine their rights. But the rise of Islamist parties and the marginalization of secular technocrats have brought women like Fatima to power. Calling themselves Zeinab Sisters, a name given to devout Muslim women who follow the path of the prophet Muhammad's daughter, they fill most of the female seats in the parliament and are entrusted with decisions that impact the lives of millions of Iraqi women.

Fatima was raised in a strictly conservative religious family in which she was offered no possibility—other than through marriage—of a life of her own. She was the daughter of a water-tanker repairman, who had nine children and two wives. They all lived in a small house in Kadhimiya and spent the entire summer as religious pilgrims in Karbala. Fatima tells me that her father taught her how to pray and recite short verses of the Quran before she learned how to read and write. When she turned nine, the age that Islam considers a girl as reaching puberty, her father ordered her to wear the veil. Because religion was simply a way of life, Fatima didn't question her father's orders or get upset when he objected to her interest in attending college. He did not want Fatima mingling with boys, she says, "so my mind wouldn't get corrupted by 'modern' ideas." When Fatima stayed home, waiting for suitors to ask for her hand, no desirable candidates emerged, perhaps, she reflects, because she had a very strong will.

Iraqi culture viewed Fatima as an old maid and when her father died she moved into her older brother's house. With a gift for serving and an observant eye, she cut patterns from fabrics the neighbors brought her and soon began a small business sewing clothes for neighborhood women and children. She led a devout life, praying five times a day, reading the Quran before bed and upon waking at dawn, going to the neighborhood mosque every Friday for communal prayer. When she relays her life story, she strikes me as full of contradictions, a woman who wished to break out of a sheltered cocoon but who was unable to depart from religious tradition. In the same way that she can't stop speaking her native Arabic tongue, despite her improving English, she can't abandon Islam. She has found a social identity within the structure of religion.

The single most transformative event in Fatima's life was the fall of Baghdad to American troops when mosques suddenly became the only viable authority. Fatima volunteered at her local mosque to organize charity drives, health care, and neighborhood patrols. Her brother approved because she would be under the supervision of the mosque's religious leader, Imam Mohammad Baqir. Fatima bloomed in her new role, impressing the imam so much that he nominated her for the neighborhood council the Americans were establishing in Baghdad.

"You will make a very good role model for other women and young Muslim girls," the imam told her.

Fatima abandoned her sewing machine and spent all day at the neighborhood council offices. Soon after joining the neighborhood council she was appointed to oversee affairs for the district and served as its president for three months. She was part of the committee of council leaders that appointed Baghdad's mayor and governor. In the summer when the interim national assembly was being selected, Shiite parties scrambled to find female candidates to champion their Islamic cause. They went to Fatima, who gained a seat in the interim national assembly, becoming a lawmaker. She founded a social affairs committee that would help widows and divorced women claim their benefits and work through the paperwork in courts. As long as her work is within the framework of Islam, she tells me, she feels blissfully blessed.

"My mission is to improve women's rights within the framework of Islam. There is no other way," she says. In order to understand religious texts and be able to interpret their hidden meaning, Fatima has begun taking theological classes at the newly founded Kousar Institute, where religious teachings are on a par with the teachings of *hawza*, the Shiite seminaries of Najaf and Qom. In Islam, women can't become religious leaders although they can finish the exact same studies as their cleric counterparts. These female religious seminaries are a new phenomenon in Iraq and yet another import of Iran's regime, where such schools have been training "sisters of Zeinab" for a good two decades. The graduates move on to various government ministries, either as religious educators in the public school system or as public supervisors of morality. Funded by Ayatollah Sistani and free of charge, such classes are mushrooming. Under Saddam's regime, these classes existed underground, and few attended. Enrollment has more than tripled each semester in the past year.

Fatima recently traveled to Egypt for an American-funded course on constitution and human-rights law. She got into raging arguments with secular women activists, informing them, "If the constitution is not based on sharia law we will protest it and hold demonstrations. We are an Islamic country now." The secular women threatened that they, too, would hold protests and demonstrate against Islam as the rule of law. She complains that the secular women at the conference looked down on her, mocking her *hijab,* and in one case, going so far as to smirk that she looked like a "Shiite mujahid" who promoted backward laws.

"Secular women want to get rid of us. They don't accept that now we have the power over them. They can object but at the end, we control the government," she announces triumphantly.

The argument over family law in Iraq is unique in that the fight over women's rights is working in reverse. In Iran and many other Islamic countries where sharia is law, women's rights are always at the center of the struggle between traditionalists and reformists. Women activists have strived for years to reform the laws within the framework of Islam after it became clear that it was impossible to replace sharia law with secular law. This struggle has given rise to a group of Islamic feminists, women highly educated in Islamic jurisprudence who can match the arguments of male religious authorities about the intricate interpretations of the law in a manner that would offer more benefits to women. Some argue that for Iraqi women sharia law isn't as bad as it sounds: if they are determined, they can follow the footsteps of their fellow Islamic feminists and work within the system. This argument infuriates secular women activists who are outraged at the idea of reversing a perfectly progressive law only to have to fight for years to reform it.

I frequently discuss my insights on the matter with Amal, a pioneer in the field of women's advancement in her own right. She listens patiently while I discuss Fatima and the women Islamists defending sharia. I'm used to her interrupting me with angry comments about the state of affairs in Iraq, and her hushed reaction strikes me as more sad than outraged.

In this changed Iraq, Amal, too, is nostalgic. "In the 1960s, I went to Libya as part of a Red Crescent delegation from Iraq," she tells me. "We were all women and we were dressed in beautiful suits; we had high heels on and our hair was all done. When we got off the plane the Libyans said, 'Where is the Iraqi delegation?' They could not believe that we were representing Iraq. I am beginning to feel like a stranger in my own country, Iraq is changing so rapidly."

Some of the changes concerning women are already visible on the streets of Baghdad. It's true that the government has not imposed the *hijab* on women, like Iran, but a silent transformation is in the works. When I visited before the war, I first spotted a veiled woman in full body-length black abaya in the outskirts of the capital on the road to the south. Women wearing the headscarf were in the minority then. Now, almost nine out of ten women in the street are veiled. When I visit the headquarter offices of the two main Shiite parties, SCIRI and Dawa, I notice a sign at the entrance with a drawing of a veiled woman, which warns, "Only Women with Hijab Are Allowed Inside." In Basra, the local branch of the Ministry of Education has ordered all public middle and high schools to enforce *hijab* on female students. When the Ministry of Women's Affairs sent them an official letter of complaint, they were met with an unsympathetic response: "it's our policy and it's not your place to interfere." I've taken to wearing a big scarf and a full-length black abaya on top of my normal clothes because it makes me blend in with the crowd. Amal scolds me, "If you are wearing the *hijab*, then how can you expect Iraqi women to resist?"

I ask Amal if she knows Maysoon al-Damluji, a prominent female architect who returned to Iraq from Britain soon after the invasion. Maysoon is now serving as deputy minister of culture and the founder and head of the Iraqi Independent Women's Group, championing the secular women's rights movement. Maysoon was also one of the key players behind the idea of securing one fourth of the parliament's seats for women. When she pushed for it, it's unlikely she imagined women parliamentarians who would serve to block women's rights. After a few phone calls Amal secures me an interview with Maysoon at her office in the Ministry of Culture. Haqqi convinces the security personnel at the entrance to allow my guard to bring in his gun. Knowing that our guard Jamal, dressed in a loose gray suit with a 9mm handgun in his left pocket, is shadowing me is comforting and scary. When we reach Maysoon's office, she's not in. We wait for half an hour, an hour, two hours. I'm breaking one of our ground rules of security: never stay in one place longer than half an hour. Any longer might allow a kidnapping to be orchestrated and carried out. Jamal keeps whispering to Haqqi that it's time to go, but Maysoon's secretary, a woman in her twenties who's dressed in hip-hugging black pants and a tight white shirt adorned with little gold chains, insists that the deputy minister will arrive any minute. She flirts with Haqqi and offers us sugar cookies from a box inside her drawer.

Clutching a leather briefcase, Maysoon strides into her office around noon, walking several feet ahead of her bodyguards and assistant in long

243

forceful steps. Strikingly attractive, she is the kind of woman who exudes an air of confidence and authority. I'm startled by her outfit—a bright red coat, a midlength skirt, and flat riding-style black boots. A silver elephant charm dangles from her neck, and her hair is highlighted with blond streaks and cut into a fashionable bob.

In conversation she is frank and equally forceful, answering my questions with a flicker of impatience. She hails from a family with a long tradition of prominent politicians and intellectuals and left Iraq when she was nineteen because her parents refused to join the Baath party. As an Iraqi architect in London, she tried to promote her homeland's art and culture and slowly gained a foothold in the exiled opposition community. She returned a few weeks after his regime collapsed for a short visit that has extended into a two-year stay and a government position. Slowly she found her voice in the women's movement and began making acquaintance with activists. Preserving art and culture is her training but promoting women's rights is her passion.

"We would like to have a unified nation and one that is accommodating to everybody. I advocate separation of religion and state. I understand that this is a special time in the history of Iraq and people can resort to their kind of doctrine, but I really hope this mentality doesn't last."

She takes a deep breath. "Most of all, we feel that introducing sharia law will help divide our country along Shiite and Sunni lines. It will spread sectarian loyalty rather than Iraqi national identity."

I ask her about the Islamist women and how she plans to navigate around the fact that the Shiite Islamists now control the government.

"The reality is that they won by a landslide majority and they can add or subtract any law. I am concerned that we don't have enough backing from the international community to stop them. With some of these Shiite women, there's a red line. The conversation just stops. We don't speak the same language when it comes to women's rights. Their women think like their men; they say whatever the men tell them. They have no background in politics or activism and are completely overcome by religion, even if they are well educated."

The Iraqi Independent Women's Group, which Maysoon chairs, formed after a small gathering that included her and a group of like-minded women. They mobilized by inviting a dozen friends each to the next meeting, and in no time they drew five hundred women to their first official meeting in the Alawiya Club, an elitist members-only affair. In the mix: professors, doctors, teachers, engineers, lawyers, and former technocrats who were increasingly anxious that their voices were losing against the chorus of conservative, religious female lawmakers. They drew up a statement listing nineteen defining principles. At the top of the list were security and the reversal of family law to be modeled after the sharia.

"There is a lot of anxiety among women that all our achievements since 1959 are in danger. We are also in danger ourselves because of the work we do. There are a lot of people who can't stand active secular women and want to kill us. We all know that by getting involved we are risking our lives," she tells me.

Two prominent members of the organization have been murdered, and the husbands of two others have been killed. As I walk out the door with two oil canvases I purchased from her assistant under my arm, Maysoon tells me to be careful; the roads around the ministry are often targets of random suicide car bombs. Maysoon and Fatima are worlds apart in their role in the new Iraq but circumstances have pitted them against each other. The only commonality they share is the intense fear for their lives and their loved ones. As a rule, Maysoon never shows up at her office at the same time, and she travels on different roads and in a different car every single day. She has escaped close calls and threats not to carry out her mission. For her part, Fatima has received several death threats, her nephew has been threatened with kidnap, and her home has been at risk of an RPG attack. Yet none of these factors will keep either woman away from a mission she believes in.

My visits to both of these women were frightening. Entering the ministry to interview Maysoon, we attracted unwanted attention when the information booth required that we leave our picture IDs with them and register our names. While Haqqi argued on my behalf that doing such a thing was suicidal because it would inform everyone that a foreigner, a perfect kidnap target, was in the house, the man would not budge. Dozens of people overheard the argument. While we waited for Maysoon, every time someone entered her waiting room my heart skipped and I wondered if this was the point where the gun would be brought out and I would be dragged away, kicking and screaming. Jamal, while trying to be inconspicuous, paced the room and poked his head into the hall. In fact, the kidnapping attempt came on the way back to the hotel from my interview with Fatima at the Kadhimiya city council. I have always been comforted by the notion that if something bad is about to happen, I'd know it in my gut. But it isn't true. I am lost in my thoughts as our car crosses the Jadriyah Bridge when a message comes from our surveillance car. I detect the panic in Abu Munaf's voice warning us from behind. He uses our code radio name and then says, "We are being followed. I try, but can't lose them. Roger. We are being followed. White Toyota with two men, they have been tailing us for a while. They picked us up shortly after we came out of the city council.

"I think they want to kidnap her. Escape."

What follows next is a blur. Abu Munaf hits the brake to slow down the Toyota, as our drivers have been instructed in hostile training courses for defensive driving. The Toyota tries to pass us, perhaps to block our way, or to turn in our direction. Munaf puts his foot on the gas; I instinctively slump in the backseat, my heart racing a million beats a minute as we embark on a crazy chase and run. Munaf crosses traffic lines, and exits the highway so fast that I'm certain our car will flip off the bridge. Here I am face-to-face with what I most fear. My mind races as fast as my heart. What will they do to me? Will they have mercy on my Iraqi staff? Will they shoot at us or drag me out at gunpoint? Will they rape me, cut off my head, or let me rot in a cell? Oh, God, what will this do to my family and Babak? I don't know how many wild turns we take until I see the white tower of the Hamra Hotel, where we have maintained a suite that serves as our office. When Munaf hits and brakes, he yells, "Thank God, they are not behind us. Get out of the car and run inside."

I run straight to the door of our security advisers at AKE and collapse on their sofa. Rick gathers my staff, pulls out a map, and interviews each one of them to piece together information. Yes, it was a kidnapping attempt, he determines. I'm very lucky to have escaped. But our cars are identified and so is the staff. The kidnappers could linger around, waiting for a second chance to nab me. Any movement for us is banned for at least three days. We need to switch our surveillance car for at least a month and the staff must take taxis home. I'm a prisoner once more inside the hotel.

27

You Are Next;
Leave the House
as Soon as You Can

Munaf and Abu Munaf are camping on relatives' floors, bouncing from house to house like a pair of fugitives. Once every other day or so, one of them goes back just long enough to check on the family, and to leave money for groceries and bills. When they come to work every morning they look haggard and anxious.

Every morning I ask, "Did you go back home last night?"

And every morning, Munaf replies, "No, it's not safe yet. Actually, our house may never be safe for us again."

My drivers live in the Abudishir area of Dora, a sprawling middle-class community of simple, one-story or two-story buildings. A mixed neighborhood of Sunnis and Shiites, it is a notorious trouble spot for Americans. Rockets are launched from Dora aimed at the American military base across the highway and roadside bombs frequently blow up their convoys. Still, Shiite and Sunni residents say that until the formation of the new Iraqi government, tensions were low. Everyone focused on their mutual dislike of the U.S. occupation.

Dora is fast becoming the frontline for sectarian tit-for-tat killings. It's where the seeds of civil war are being sewn. Shiite militias detain or murder Sunnis, and Sunni insurgents massacre Shiites. About a week ago a car bomb ripped through a crowded produce market, killing and injuring scores of bystanders, mostly Shiites. Abu Munaf was on his way home, a few feet away from the blast, when the windows of his car blew out, and he felt something sharp and warm pierce the flesh of his arm. Blood oozed from a shrapnel wound. Abu Munaf abandoned his car amid the chaos and got himself to the emergency room of a nearby hospital. Doctors and nurses had no time to treat his wound. The hospital was short-staffed and short-supplied and dozens of more serious casualties from the blast demanded immediate attention. "Go home and come back in three days," a nurse told him. Another doctor told him to only return to the hospital if his arm swelled or he had a serious infection.

Within days of the market bombing, Shiite squads from the Wolf Brigade showed up in the neighborhood. The Wolf Brigade is an elite unit of about two thousand special commandos at the Ministry of the Interior. It is rumored to be an offshoot of the Shiite militia Badr organization, funded and trained by Iran's notorious Revolutionary Guard Forces. Evoking the name of the Wolf Brigade in front of a Sunni man has the same terrorizing impact Saddam's name once had on Shiites. In Dora, the Wolf Brigade's units began knocking on doors of Sunni residents in the middle of the night and arresting men. The squad's behavior mirrored the early raids of the American troops in search of insurgent cells. Munaf says that most of the Sunni men who are being detained are those who wear their Sunni sect like a badge of honor, attending Friday prayers at the neighborhood Sunni mosque, helping with charity drives for people of Fallujah, and openly supporting the resistance fighters attacking Americans.

"They capture anyone who is proud he is a Sunni," says Munaf. "Why this campaign against us? They think all the Sunnis are Baathists, Wahabi, or terrorists."

The raids continued night after night, stirring the neighborhood and creating deep distrust among Sunnis and Shiites, people who had lived, worked, and socialized alongside each other for decades. At first, Abu Munaf told his family they had nothing to fear; they had committed no crime, there was no cause for panic. But then three Sunni men, one whom Munaf knew, vanished from the neighborhood. Two days later, their bodies were found in a heap of garbage on an empty lot a block away from Abu Munaf's house. The men had been blindfolded and cut. The next night, a Shiite neighbor came to the family's house with a warning, "They are coming after all the Sunnis. You are next. Leave the house as soon as you can."

Munaf and Abu Munaf fled late in the night, leaving behind Munaf's mother and four other siblings. They feared that if they all suddenly evacuated, Shiite militiamen from the Mahdi army would take over their house, as they had done with other homes abandoned by Sunni families. When I ask Abu Munaf whom he blames for the sectarian tensions simmering to the surface, he says, "The new government is dividing the country. It's making me hate Shiites and making Shiites hate me."

It's a simplistic answer, but it reflects how rapidly the violence is turning inward in Iraq. Abu Munaf's house was raided by Americans looking for weapons not so long ago. They left when Munaf took one American soldier to the side and whispered to him that he and his father worked for *The Wall Street Journal* and showed him ID cards issued by the American military. When the American soldier asked Munaf why he hadn't said so in the first place, Munaf urged him to be discreet: "I don't want any of the Iraqi soldiers and translators with you to find out we work for Americans. They may come back and kill us or inform on us." Munaf says that Sunnis are now far more fearful of Iraqi forces, which are mostly Shiites and Kurds, than of American troops and believe the Shiites are utilizing the forces and militia to take revenge on Sunnis.

May was the most violent month in Iraq since the U.S. invasion. There were 148 car bombs and more than 750 civilian deaths, many of them sectarian related. Dozens of bodies are discovered each day, decaying in empty lots or floating down the river. Most corpses show signs of torture: slashed flesh, drilled skulls, nails hammered into fingers, limbs mutilated. Many are found blindfolded or handcuffed and almost always grouped according to their sects. The sectarian clashes, which no one will call a civil war, have spared no place and no one, not even schools and mosques. Several cleric aides to high-ranking Shiite and Sunni religious leaders were recently kidnapped and murdered. Students at Baghdad University clashed after gunmen assassinated a Shiite student after he hosted a party celebrating the formation of a new Shiite government.

Munaf says, "We are like animals in the wild. We eat, sleep, and try not to get killed each day."

I'm also grieving for a dear friend, Marla Ruzicka, an American aid worker who championed for the rights of civilians harmed by the war. Marla, twenty-eight years old, was killed in April by a suicide car bomb on the airport road. Every time I take the road to and from the airport, Marla's face, with her big smile and hair the color of summer sunshine, comes to my mind and I fight back tears. She was such a fixture in the tight-knit tribe of war correspondents that it's impossible not to miss her when we have a party or when we reminisce about our adventures. Marla is the second friend I've lost in the Iraq war. In the early days of the invasion, when we were still up in Kurdistan and Saddam had not yet fallen, Iranian photographer and BBC cameraman Kaveh Golestan was killed when their car drove into a minefield.

Sometimes I find myself wanting to cry while I'm interviewing people and other times I feel detached, like a machine recording misery and death. I have days when I open a Word document on my computer and stare at it for a long while without being able to write a story until I've had a good cry. Other times I just crank out the sentences, burying myself in work on days that stretch fifteen hours or more. I no longer see any of my Iraqi friends, because they are too fearful for me to visit them in their homes. Even on the phone they speak quietly, and I sense an eagerness to hang up. Several times Sabah Nasser, my Christian friend whose family I've known since before the war, has abruptly hung up on me in the middle of the conversation because he heard footsteps in the street outside the window and doesn't want to be heard speaking English. Sometimes when I ring friends or Iraqi staff, they hear my voice and say in Arabic, "*Ghalat nomreh* [Wrong number]," and hang up on me because they are out in public, in a taxi or shop, and don't want to be overheard speaking to a foreigner.

Sabah tells me that the sectarian tensions are getting in the way of old friendships and neighborly relations. Although the Christians aren't involved in the Shiite-Sunni clashes, they are constantly targeted by Sunni Islamists. The Nassers are keeping to themselves and avoiding contact with their Sunni neighbors. This year, for Christmas, none of their neighbors came over for coffee and Marie-Rose's homemade marble cake, a ritual that had been a tradition for as long as they have lived there. During the Muslim Eid celebrations, the Nassers avoided eye contact and conversations with neighbors. Sabah hasn't seen his oldest and best friend, Adel, a Shiite antique dealer he's known since elementary school, for over three months. Until recently, a week would not pass without the two friends meeting or talking on the phone.

When I ask Marie-Rose over the phone if she is seeing any of her Muslim friends, she tells me she would not know what to talk about with them anymore. "All we talk about now is terrorism and violence. I don't want to see them because I'm worried I may say the wrong thing and make them upset. We don't think the same way anymore."

Everyone seems to be pulling more tightly into their own sectarian cocoons, looking for protection and revenge. The tensions spill into our home and office more than we like. The Shiite guards don't trust the Sunni drivers and translators, whom they suspect of sympathizing with the insurgency. The Sunni staffs don't trust our young Shiite cook, suspicious that he has links to the Mahdi army militia. When our staff refuses to cross sectarian lines for reporting, I'm extremely frustrated. Managing the Iraqi staff is becoming impossibly taxing. I have to constantly walk the fine line between demanding work and knowing when my demands are life-threatening. Haqqi suggests that it might be time for two sets of translators and drivers—one for Sunni areas and one for Shiite.

The sectarian killing in itself is nothing new. Shiites have been targeted almost daily in assassinations, kidnappings, and bomb attacks aimed at civilian day-to-day places like religious festivals, funerals, schools, police stations, markets, mosques, and so on since 2003. But now the Shiites are finally striking back at the Sunnis. The violence against Shiites, compounded by a history of suffering under Sunni regimes, has strained the Shiite community's patience. Sometimes explosions are totally random, other times perfectly synchronized. When one bomb explodes in a popular gathering place, it attracts a bigger crowd of spectators who rush over to help, only to be torn apart by a second blast.

For a while, Shiite officials and religious leaders like Ayatollah Sistani managed to tap into the Shiite culture of suffering and martyrdom in their call for restraint. The idea behind holding back vengeance was that suffering was endured because of a greater cause: the impending possibility of having a Shiite-dominated government. The attacks were blamed on terrorists with links to al-Qaeda rather than a homegrown Sunni resistance. Ordinary Shiites enthusiastically believed that election would lead to a Shiite government capable of resurrecting rights and protecting them against Sunni insurgents. But that didn't happen.

It's taken the interim government, which has only a yearlong term in office, six months to name a cabinet and get on with official state business. Half of its time in office has been thus far spent bickering and horse-trading instead. For six months, there's been no defense minister, no interior minister, and no policy against dealing with militia, insurgents, or American troops. Furthermore, sectarian representation is lopsided because Sunnis didn't vote and although the Shiites and Kurds say they want Sunni participation, they hold out on giving them key ministerial posts. Sunnis say they are not interested in token cabinet posts and feel they don't have a stake in either politics or security. As Abu Munaf points out, among the general public, anger is mounting at Iraqi authorities and Americans for their failure to prevent innocent gatherings from turning into spectacular tragedies. There is an overwhelming realization that the government is incapable of protecting its citizens. In a lawless world, justice must be taken into one's own hands.

The Americans are cautious about getting caught up in sectarian warfare, which they see as a distraction from their main purpose in Iraq: fighting al-Qaeda and building a nation. The question will rise: is the U.S. military fighting to establish freedom and democracy in Iraq or preventing Iraq from collapsing into an all-out civil war? I notice a lot less American convoys in the streets of Baghdad, and increasingly security of neighborhoods is being handed over to Iraqi forces. But violence thrives with a more or less predictable pattern.

I dispatch our staff in small groups to mixed neighborhoods where Shiites and Sunnis live alongside each other, to find people to interview. It's the same neighborhood my drivers, the father-and-son team of Munaf and Abu Munaf, live and were warned by Shiite neighbors to leave.

I can't go to Dora and many more neighborhoods in Baghdad. In fact, outings have become few and far between. When I venture out, I follow a strict security process by telling at least two reporter friends the details of my travel—time, roads taken, and the people I'm seeing. In the event of a kidnapping, someone will have an idea about roughly when and where I disappeared.

In order to still stay in touch with the Iraqi public's mood, I often ask the staff to bring people back to our office at the Hamra Hotel to be interviewed. For the story on Dora, over a course of a week, I sit in the cafeteria of the Hamra Hotel as an assortment of characters parade in and out. Their stories paint an alarming picture of deterioration.

Amer Mohi Ismaeel is a twenty-seven-year-old who runs his father's grocery store in Dora. His income sustains fifteen people who live crammed together under one roof. One night in early May, Amer was arrested with his father and three brothers when their house was raided by Wolf Brigade forces at 3:30 AM. They shot at the hallway floor; the bullet punctured the mosaic tiles and bounced off the wall. They put a gun to Amer's mother's head and ordered her to shut up. They rounded up the men and asked which Sunni tribe they belonged to; they said they were after members of the Dulaimi and Jaburi tribes. One of the soldiers said, "You Sunnis are dogs, you are terrorists, you are killing our people." He handcuffed them and shoved them into the car.

That night the Shiite forces of the interior ministry raided thirty-five homes and arrested forty Sunni men.

Amer was released a week later but his father and brother are still in detention at prisons run by the Ministry of the Interior. He says he was tortured and shows me burn scars on the skin of his calf. "They put a hot rod against my skin," he says and adds, "I don't trust any of the Shiites on my street anymore. They are cooperating with the Americans or working for one of the militia. They pretend to be friendly and then stab you in the back."

In a way, Amer saw this coming. After the explosion in Dora that killed scores of Shiites, a young Shiite man came into his shop and told him, "See what your people are doing?" and then a warning, "One day it will be the Sunnis' turn. Wait until we have the power. You will all be paid back."

A week later, graffiti in bold red Arabic letters appeared on their street: "*Jaburi, Arhabi, Wahabi* [Jaburis are terrorists and Wahabi extremists]."

Omar Falleh Hassan is a twenty-three-year-old barber who mans a shop from the ground floor of his house in Dora. He wears baggy acid-washed jeans and a loose, checkered shirt and chain smokes throughout our interview. He has brought his mother, Hadiah Hassan, an outspoken and opinionated woman despite her traditional dress. The Hassans are a Sunni family who live near Munaf and Abu Munaf. When they come for the interview, my drivers hide in our office at the Hamra Hotel.

Omar's story resembles Amer's, a nightly raid by the Wolf Brigade and mass detention of all the men in the house. He was released the next morning but his father and cousin are still in custody. When the Ashura blast hit the Shiite Husseinyieh Mosque in Dora last January, Omar and his family were at home. Their windows rattled and the children ran inside from the street where they were playing. A few minutes later, one of Omar's neighbors and customers, a middle-aged Shiite man, approached their house. The man stood in the street and began shouting in Arabic: "Terrorists! . . . All Sunnis are killers. They are killing us. We will take revenge!" After that day, most of his Shiite clients stopped coming to him for haircuts, and those who do, avoid small talk. "I hate them," he says, echoing a widespread sentiment. His mother tells me that since the explosion and subsequent raids, even the camaraderie between neighborhood women, who relied on each other for help with cooking and child care, has ceased. A lot of Sunni families are migrating from the neighborhood, and Omar's family has put their house up for sale. In the meantime, he won't go back home.

Hussein Hamoud Suraybet is a thirty-two-year-old day laborer with five children whose income supports two families. Before he answers my first question, he recites a brief passage of the Quran, and throughout our interview rolls prayer beads between his fingers. He is wearing a chunky silver ring with a brown stone that he says is a blessed prayer stone from Najaf. Hussein is among the Shiite residents of Dora and among the dozens who have been injured in powerful bomb blasts carried out by Sunni insurgents and aimed at Shiites. He recalls the moment of the explosion with painful clarity. He walked through the courtyard of the Husseinyieh on Ashura with his friend and took off his shoes and socks in preparation for washing before noon prayers. He was splashing cold water on his elbow and massaging it down to his fingertips when a loud *boom* flung him onto the ground. A suicide bomber had blown himself up at the gate.

Hussein remembers the burning smell and the air swirling with debris. Blood and flesh were clinging to his clothes. The explosion instantly killed Hussein's friend and twenty others. Hussein was rushed to the hospital, semiconscious from shrapnel wounds. He shows me scars on his head and his arms. Two pieces of shrapnel are still embedded in the bone of his right leg and pieces lodged in his skull give him headaches and blur his vision. His doctors lack the technology to remove them without causing greater harm. The injury has deprived him of his livelihood and made him dependent on his brother for small handouts and stipends. "I think the Sunnis are helping the terrorists. I was injured only because I went to pray. Why? Who is doing this to us? They are trying to create a civil war and if things continue this way, they will get their wish."

He is elated that the Wolf Brigade is arresting neighborhood Sunni men, who, he says, "deserve it. They must have evidence that they are terrorists and our new government and our new police will deal with them."

He doesn't hesitate when I ask him if he would ever consider informing on one of his Sunni neighbors. "If I am suspicious of them, of course I will."

28

If the Teacher Asks,
Tell Her
I Was Kidnapped

The sectarian war is bleeding into Mohanad and Fatin's marriage. He is Sunni. She is Shiite. They have four children, ages three to thirteen. Mohanad is *Newsweek*'s office manager and my translator Jabbar's brother. Two weeks ago on a sunny afternoon, Fatin's twin brother, Saddiq, was gunned down and murdered on his way home from work. Thirty-five years old, Saddiq was an up-and-coming surgeon at one of the city's best hospitals and the father of a six-month- old baby boy. His assassination is a symptom of a bigger campaign to murder Shiite doctors.

After her twin's assassination, Fatin travels the stages of grief one by one. First it's the denial that her twin brother is gone. Then rage at Americans, at Sunnis, at the Iraqi government, at God, at herself for being alive. After anger, she sinks into a deep depression that makes getting through the hours of the day and taking care of her four children seem almost insurmountable. Mohanad takes days off from work to help out, as do cousins, sisters-in-law, and siblings. But nothing consoles her. She has vivid dreams about her brother at night; sometimes she sees the two of them as children chasing one other in the garden; in other dreams, Saddiq holds Fatin, telling her not to cry. Often knowing he will soon be leaving, she begs him to stay. One night he appears in a dream floating above her. Pointing to the sky, he says his spirit will always be with his sister.

As Fatin and Mohanad struggle to come to terms with their loss, other violent incidents deliver the family blow after blow: A bomb explodes twenty meters from their house, damaging a nearby elementary school and smashing the windows of their older son's middle school. They watch in horror as children run screaming in bloodstained school uniforms. The Sunni father of Hassan's best friend is kidnapped, and several days later his corpse is dumped in the neighborhood. Another friend's uncle is assassinated.

The children begin showing other signs of trauma. When they hear an explosion, they rush to Fatin's side, tug at her clothes, and ask worriedly, "Where is *baba*? Where is *baba*?" They are paralyzed with fear that Mohanad, who is often shuffling between the Green Zone and the *Newsweek* office, may be harmed. After one explosion, Omar, thirteen, begs his teacher to let him use his cell phone to check on his dad. When Mohanad hears this, he buys his older sons their own mobile phones. The children have recurring nightmares, and wake up screaming for help in the middle of the night.

Every day Fatin's children return home from school with stories that make the hair on her neck prickle with fear. Nine-year-old Hassan cries that his buddy Ali Shaker, a Shiite, teased him for being a Sunni and bullies the rest of the Shiite kids not to speak or play with Sunnis. On the bus ride home from school, he shoves Hassan off his seat, announcing loudly, "I don't want you to sit with me because you are Sunni."

Their youngest son, Azouz, a first-grader, declares one night that he will not attend school. He is too scared that something will happen to his parents in his absence. Mohanad takes Azouz to the nicest stationery store he can find and picks out colorful notebooks, crayons, and a school bag emblazoned with a cartoon character. But he won't be swayed. Mohanad coaxes him, "School is fun, *hababi;* you learn how to read and write. You play with the other kids. What should I tell your teacher when she asks me why Azouz is absent?" The little boy's answer shocks his parents: "Tell the teacher Azouz is kidnapped by mujahideen and we have no news of him."

When they finally persuade Azouz to return to class, Fatin has to stay with him, sitting on a chair in the hallway outside his classroom to prevent him from bursting into tantrums.

Fatin finally announces to Mohanad she thinks they should move from Dora to a neighborhood that's either all Sunni or all Shiite. She can't endure any more threats of violence. They migrate to a house in Mansur, in a Sunni neighborhood where there is less of a threat for Mohanad and where the kids won't be in the minority at school. When I visit them, Mohanad is waiting for us outside. The garage door is half open. When we pull into the driveway, he motions for us to park the car inside. He doesn't want to take a chance with any of the neighbors spotting our armored car. He puts his finger on his mouth, instructing me not to speak until we are inside the house. To my left is a small kitchen without cabinets and a large deep sink made of steel better suited to an industrial space than to a home. All of the family's pots and pans are piled on the floor next to a red plastic bowl in which freshly washed plates and glasses are stacked. The untiled floor is covered by a thin gray carpet.

In the living room, Fatin and the children are waiting for me. The room's lace curtains are drawn, but a warm light shines through them, reflecting intricate shadows on the carpet. Matching sofas line the room and a big coffee table rests in the middle. A computer flanked by two joysticks sits in the corner. The two younger boys are playing a shoot-and-kill game when I walk in, until the electricity cuts off. When Mohanad shows me the house, I sense his embarrassment at displaying their refugee home. Several times he repeats that their old house in Dora, where they had lived for years, was twice the size and better furnished. This isn't, he seems to be saying, the way of life. This is not his home.

I am served tea and small spongy cakes and a bowl of perfect oranges. Fatin sits on the sofa in front of me and speaks slowly of her grief. When I look at her beautiful brown eyes, her pale skin, lush lips, and her elegant mourning dress, it's difficult to hear her anguish. Her two-year-old daughter, Sarah, lies on the couch, her head in her mother's lap. She is dressed in a pretty pink party dress and white lace-trimmed ankle socks. But her body seems devoid of energy and childhood joy. She doesn't look at me when I talk to her and she won't smile back, turning her head to the wall.

With Ahmad, Mohanad's brother, as our translator, Fatin tells me about her dreams, her children, and the impossible insecurity that haunts them. She feels like a refugee in her own city. It's incredibly hard for her to leave the neighborhood she lived in for a decade, her friends, shop owners who knew her children by name. In this new house in a borrowed life, she doesn't know anyone and doesn't want to make new friends. She doesn't trust anyone anymore. She won't let her kids visit friends' homes for play dates.

When Fatin sends her three sons to school, she squeezes each of them tightly and lingers on the doorstep until the school van carrying them disappears around the curve of the road. Some days, her eyes fill with tears and she has to restrain the urge to run after the bus and retrieve her boys to keep them near her, out of harm's way.

"It breaks my heart that this is my children's reality. Kidnappings, murders, death, explosions are part of our daily chitchat," she says as her eyes glance over to her boys, and after a small pause she continues, "Saddiq's death has been very hard on my children. They were very close to him; he visited us every few days and played football and video games with them."

At the mention of Saddiq's name, Omar shows me a smiling photograph of the slain uncle. When I ask the children how they see their lives, Omar tells me, "I don't mention my uncle, because if I do, I can't stop crying. I can't believe he is dead. I loved him so much, I wanted to be a doctor like him, but now I don't want to be a doctor, because all the doctors get killed."

Nine-year-old Hassan talks about his friend whose father was kidnapped and killed. "He is always sad. When we play in school, he doesn't want to play with us. When we ask him why he doesn't answer us, we know it's because of his dad. He doesn't laugh when we make funny jokes. We can't make him forget it no matter how hard we try. Now, I always think of these things. I fear for my dad when he goes to work."

Neither of the boys lets slip to anyone that their father works for the American press. They stick to the line that he is an engineer who runs a computer shop.

When I ask Azouz, the six-year-old with chubby cheeks and a naughty grin, why he doesn't like school, he stares at me for a while pursing his lips together, before asking his mother in Arabic if he should answer me. When she gives him the green light, he tells me in a barely audible whisper, "Because I want to be near my mom. Maybe if I leave something bad will happen to her."

My eyes sting from tears at his answer. Mohanad breaks the long silence that follows: "You see how hard life has become for us, Farnaz? Even my children can't escape the war."

I can understand now why Mohanad often talks about leaving Iraq for Canada or Australia—anywhere far from here. I've often spotted him working after hours at the office, surfing websites, and reading about the paperwork required for applying for Canadian immigration. He seeks advice from me and Babak. He believes that leaving Dora is a first step. He is willing to do anything to get his family out.

A few days later, after meeting with Mohanad's family, I am working in the office when my translator, Jabbar, knocks on the door. Although he has a college degree in English, his conversation is just passable; but he comes from a family we know and trust. Although Jabbar didn't like Saddam, he takes great pride in being Sunni and his criticism of the Americans is quiet but frank.

Today, he says he has news, both good and bad. He grabs a chair and sits in front of me and says without a smile or a trace of real joy, "We just found out that my wife is pregnant."

I know that he and his wife have been trying for a child, and I congratulate him on his news.

But Jabbar looks down in silence. When he looks up, his eyes are welling with tears. He reaches out and grabs a tissue from my desk, trying hard to gain control of his emotions. After a long pause, he says, "No, I feel guilty. I can't raise a child in this situation. I'm worried that I will get killed like Saddiq, then who will take care of my wife and child? You know we really wanted to have a child, but in this terrible situation I am very afraid."

After a pause he blurts out, "I'm really sorry. I'm so sorry, Farnaz, I know this is a very bad time but I have decided to leave Iraq. I'm quitting."

"That's a big decision. Are you sure?" I ask.

He is sure. He and his wife plan to leave Iraq for Damascus at six the next morning.

When I ask why they're departing in such haste, he responds that he simply can't take it anymore. Now that he's convinced his wife, there's not a moment to lose.

"What does she say?" I ask.

"She is crying nonstop. She doesn't want to leave her family but she doesn't want to raise our child here either. She is now packing. I told her to only pack one suitcase for each of us."

From where I sit, Jabbar could not have picked a worse time to quit. With Saddam's trial and elections coming, we are already short-staffed. But I can't ask him to stay an extra few days until I find a replacement. I don't want to be responsible in case something dreadful happens to him in the interim. I sympathize with his desire to leave Iraq and make a life elsewhere for his family.

He has little money, and no place to stay or work in Damascus, where he will join the first wave of Iraqi refugees streaming into neighboring countries. I open up the safe and bring him a stack of $100 bills, paying him three months in advance as severance. He hands me his three ID cards and we shake hands, embrace, and say goodbye.

Iraqis face daunting dilemmas that show no sign of easing despite the political machinery marching ahead. On one single day in September there are twelve separate attacks targeting crowds of Shiite civilian day laborers, Iraqi police, and American convoys that kill 150 people and wound over 600. The attacks were claimed by al-Qaeda's branch in Iraq, and the group's leader, Abu Musab al-Zarqawi, calls for all-out war against Shiites, Iraqi troops, and the country's government-recorded message. The attacks coincide with an announcement by Shiites and Kurds of the finalization of the constitution without amendments that address Sunni demands. It calls for a loose federal state with a weak central government and some semiautonomous regions like the Kurdish north. It allows the remaining three provinces to form semiautonomous groups. The constitution calls for Islamic sharia law as the governing legislation. Though Sunni political parties urged constituents to reject the document in the national referendum, it passed with Shiite and Kurdish support. Sunni leaders have since vowed to win enough seats in the next government to completely revise the constitution, though any change or amendment to the draft will entail a lengthy process.

There has been a steady exodus of Iraqis and internal displacement of families like Mohanad's who are taking shelter in segregated sectarian communities. I visit a number of schools in Shiite neighborhoods where principals tell me that Shiite enrollment has quadrupled for the academic year as families move in. When Haqqi checks in Sunni neighborhoods, he finds the same scenario. But there, a surge of displaced people fleeing cities like Fallujah and Samarra where the security situation is particularly dire have also been added to the mix. Some Arab families, particularly Christians, are moving to Kurdistan. Those with enough means or connections are fleeing across the border where refugee life awaits them.

In November, my guard, Jamal, comes to the office early in the morning and tells me he has received a death threat. His cell phone rang early in the morning on his way to work and a Sunni militant who identified himself as Haji Abu Mugeira threatened to harm him and his family unless he quit working for Americans. He tells me that Abu Mugeira is a nom de guerre for an insurgent cell leader in the Seyediaya neighborhood.

The caller warns Jamal of a plot to blow up his house, adding that there is a bundle of explosives planted in his doorway. His wife and teenage son and daughter are at home. Jamal appears surprisingly in control and more outraged than frightened, but I feel the color drain from my cheeks, and my knees tremble. Jamal sits down and I go and get Babak from our bedroom. I call AKE, our security advisers, and within minutes one of their personnel, a British man named Jed, comes down to our office at the Hamra. Haqqi arrives soon after. Jed asks Jamal to repeat everything several times. Small details in his story keep changing with every recollection, which adds to our confusion. His phone rings again. The room grows silent as we stare at the phone.

"I don't recognize the number," Jamal says.

"Answer it," Jed commands. "Engage him in a conversation and try to get as much information as you can. Everyone else must be completely silent in the room."

Within minutes Jamal is shouting and cussing at the caller, accusing him of being a terrorist. We are nervous that he's exacerbating the situation. Haqqi takes notes and translates the conversation on a piece of paper that we pass from Jed to me to Babak. The man is saying something about tailing Jamal's brother, who used to work for the United Nations and whose car Jamal has been driving around town. He gives Jamal three days to quit his job and show up at the local Sunni mosque to promise never to be a traitor again. He claims that a Greek journalist in his custody has told them about Jamal. The man quotes the prophet Muhammad and comments on Jamal's weapon as indicative of his relationship with the Americans. The conversation is lengthy and bizarre.

In bold letters Jed writes, "ASK HIM ABOUT THE BOMB PLANTED AT YOUR HOUSE."

The caller backtracks on the bomb, which he claims to have removed after realizing Jamal has children in the house. He says he is from a militant group called Jihad al Sunna, which is unlike the violent cells showcased beheading people on TV. They are real mujahideen, people who make sure a person is guilty before killing him.

I write a note to Jamal, "DO THEY WANT MONEY?"

To which the reply is no, they want only revenge against American collaborators. They are receiving orders from above.

Jamal raises his voice again, shouting at the top of his lungs and making us nervous. I hold up more signs, this time in capital letters, "DON'T YELL. STOP YELLING. IT WILL MAKE THINGS WORSE FOR YOU."

When Jed tells Jamal to call back the number after hanging up, he gets a message that the phone is disconnected. Our meeting, in which we try to piece the information together, lasts nine hours. Jamal receives several phone calls of this nature and frantic calls from his wife, who has gotten two threatening calls from the same man. I want Jamal to stay at the hotel and his family to leave his house immediately. But Jed thinks it's risky for Jamal not to return home. He must act normal, as if nothing he's heard holds any truth. We ask Jamal to leave his weapons, his license issued by the American military, and all of his IDs behind. If he is kidnapped, it would be far worse were he found with any identification linking him to Americans. He feels vulnerable without a gun, but we see no other choice.

Jed offers to enlist the help of his contacts at the interior ministry to track down the phone number, and to find out whether there is an insurgent leader named Haji Abu Mugeira. But Jamal doesn't want to involve the interior ministry or the police, because they are Shiites and could target him. After some inquiries, Jed and I find that there is no Greek reporter missing. Jed warns me that although Jamal could be telling the truth, it's not out of the realm of possibility that he is staging the threat in exchange for assistance in an asylum case abroad. Several other Iraqis working for other organizations have pulled this tactic. Over an emotionally agonizing couple of days, the drama continues with more threatening phone calls. Jamal claims that his car is shot at in a drive-by shooting by masked highway gunmen. When he shows me pictures of a bullet-riddled car, I wonder how he has escaped from injury. He also shows me a police report that he filed in a dangerous area, in which Haqqi mentions he has friends at the precinct. I ask Haqqi if he thinks Jamal is telling me the truth. Jamal is married to Haqqi's aunt.

"I honestly don't know. Maybe he is, and maybe he isn't," Haqqi says.

Within days, Jamal asks if we can help him get asylum in a Western country. I say we can't because of company policy, but we will help in other ways. We start arrangements to evacuate Jamal and his family to Syria, and put up money for several months of expenses until he can find work and resettle. I can't know if he is telling the truth, but I know we can't gamble with his life. Iraq has become a place where a phone call from a stranger can carry a death sentence and where people are so desperate for escape that they are willing to stage their own kidnapping and murder threats.

29

Our Life Here
Is Not
Real Living

T*he Hamra Hotel*, the classic war-hack lodge, has two front-desk receptionists who have each worked here for more than fifteen years. Abdul
Salaam Khuteer and Mohammad Jabber, both Shiites, are welcome fixtures in a chaotic land. They know all of us by our first names and follow
our movements closely. They keep score of which reporters are in and
which are out, who ordered room service, and who has company. Salaam
sits on a stool in tower one, eyeing everyone entering the hotel lobby and
making passing comments to me. "Miss Farnaz, are you on a regime?" he
asks (Arabic for "diet"). "Because you are now too much thin."

Salaam is forty-eight years old, short and stocky, with a receding hairline. He speaks with a coarse voice that makes him sound grumpy even
when he is cheerful. Poor eyesight requires him to wear thick glasses. If
you ask him for someone's room number, he reaches under the counter
for a small notebook, each page of which is covered with only two or three
giant-size letters. He holds the notebook up close, an inch away from his
eyes, and flips the pages quickly until the giant letters fall into words, a
record of all our names and room numbers.

Mohammad, who mans tower two where our office is located, is always standing on watch like an officer or poring over the day's newspaper
spread on the counter. He is fifty-two, a man of medium height and
weight, with thinning black hair that he combs to the side, and a thick

black moustache that curls upward. He dresses up every day in neat formal clothes and well-shined shoes. Mohammad is soft-spoken and good-humored and has taken it upon himself to teach me an Arabic phrase a day, in Iraqi dialect, making a point to have me practice every time I pass reception.

In a way, Salaam and Mohammad experience Iraq's transformation through the eyes of the journalists they service, who run screaming past them on any given day. I will never forget the ghastly expression on Salaam's face the day a bomb exploded at the United Nations. When I ran past him yelling the name of a friend in sheer panic, he quickly reassured me, "She just left ten minutes ago with some other people. Run, run. You will catch up with them." Or Mohammad's gleeful shouts of *"Alhamdullah, alhamdullah!"* as I skipped the steps and ran past him when Saddam Hussein was captured. On the day of Iraq's first election last January, I encountered Salaam and his wife, who live just around the corner from the hotel, on their way home from the polling booths. Salaam proudly introduced his wife before both of them held up ink-stained index fingers. On the same day, when I returned from reporting, Mohammad greeted me with a triumphant laugh and a box of sugar cookies. "This is the best day of my life. It's victory day for Iraq."

They are old friends and colleagues who often eat lunch together in the back room of the hotel or catch the afternoon news on a small black-and-white television set. They exchange stories about their families, particularly their sons, who are close in age. Both have two daughters and one son. They are proud that in these circumstances their sons have jobs. Mohammad's son sells prepaid mobile SIM cards and Salaam's son works at the hotel's bakery. Salaam often says he is happy his son works at the hotel, because he doesn't have to worry about him being kidnapped. Mohammad is proud that his son brings home a small income, contributing to the family's expenses.

In November, within a space of two weeks, both of their sons are killed.

Mohammad's nineteen-year-old son, Hayder Jabbar, is murdered outside the family's home by Sunni insurgents who accuse him of selling mobile SIM cards to Americans. Salaam's son, eighteen-year-old Ali Khuteer, is blown to pieces as he walks toward the hotel on his way to work when a van packed with explosives detonates near him. Our hotel is its target.

These cruel murders cripple Mohammad and Salaam and cast a thick gloom over the Hamra.

Mohammad's son Hayder Jabbar hustled to make a small living and contribute to his father's meager salary. He bought SIM cards in bulk for wholesale prices, and sold them to shops and locals for $20 each. Last summer, he saved enough money to take his first trip outside of Iraq. He took a rickety taxi to the Iranian border and a bus to the outskirts of Tehran, where his uncle has lived as an Iraqi refugee for almost two decades. He went sightseeing, mountain hiking, rode a motorcycle, and strolled through parks late at night eating ice cream. When he came back, he vowed to save enough money to allow his family to take a vacation to Iran.

"He came back from Iran and told me, now I understand that our life here is not real living. I am happy that he had at least the chance to taste this," Mohammad tells me, his voice traced with grief as he shows me a stack of pictures from Hayder's trip to Iran.

He keeps the pictures hidden under the reception desk, removing them every fifteen minutes to look through them. He arrived at work, dressed fully in black, for weeks after his son's murder. "In the house, everywhere I look I see him." In the half-lit, cold reception hall of our hotel it's unbearable to watch Mohammad's sadness. He no longer smiles when we greet him, or converses. Our cheerful exchanges over the day's news and hotel gossip, and our practice of Arabic phrases, are shelved in my memory. When I ask, "How are you today?" without looking up he answers, *"Al hamdollelah* [Thank God I am alive]."

Hayder Jabbar was kidnapped from his neighborhood. Within twenty-four hours, someone called to demand that Mohammad go to the neighborhood mosque to denounce his son as a traitor and beg for forgiveness from the mosque's imam. Mohammad reiterated that his son had no connection to the Americans, but he and his brother nonetheless followed the kidnappers' orders. He suspects the kidnapping may be the work of Sunni neighborhood gangs who were jealous of his son's lucrative business, or of Sunni jihadis hungry for the blood of young Shiites. After he carried out the kidnappers' orders, he was told that his son would be released in front of his house at 9 AM the following day. It was a Thursday. Mohammad got dressed for work and paced his living room. Minutes after 9 AM, Mohammad heard the screech of brakes outside the door, followed by the crack of a gunshot. When he ran outside, his son was lying on the doorway; a bullet had ripped through his heart. Blood gushed from his chest; he was straining to breathe. The kidnappers had already fled. Mohammad kneeled on the ground and held his son's head on his lap and howled; his wife beat herself unconscious. A crowd formed around them as neighbors screamed for help. Before the ambulance arrived, Hayder bled to death in his father's arms.

Salaam refused to watch his son die. The moment was captured on the hotel's closed-circuit security cameras set up to film any movement near the security blast walls that surround the compound. It was Friday shortly after 8 AM. Ali was casually strolling toward a door-size opening in the blast wall that allows passage between the Hamra complex and the neighborhood when a white van packed with four hundred pounds of explosives approached the wall. On the recorded film, there's a glimpse of Ali passing the van before a ball of smoke, fire, and debris explodes. Ali's body parts were later found and taken to the area's hospital.

A second massive explosion followed within moments. A pickup truck loaded with barrels filled with a thousand pounds of explosives tried to enter the compound through the big crater created by the first blast. The hotel guards shot at the truck, but it wouldn't stop. It lodged in the hole and blew up with a loud roar. At the moment his son was killed, Salaam was standing on his roof talking to construction workers. His wife, brother, sister-in-law, and daughter were eating breakfast downstairs. The house shook with the first boom. Salaam remembers thinking, "Where is Ali," before reassuring himself that his son had already reached the bakery safely. The second explosion collapsed the Khuteers' house on their heads. Emergency workers freed them from the rubble after what seemed like an eternity. His brother's wife was dead, as was their ten-year-old daughter. Salaam broke his leg and his wife broke her back. At the hospital, a relative told them that Ali's image was caught on a security tape and he was believed dead. On top of this insurmountable loss, they've been rendered homeless in the space of several hours.

The attack on Hamra demolished several other apartment buildings near the hotel and ripped off the front of the second tower. It killed eight people and injured over sixty. Our office was closest to the attack. My bedroom is a stone's throw away from the truck's designated entry point. The blast demolished our office: ceiling tiles and chunks of plaster collapsed on my bed and the wall facing the street has been punched open. The furniture is a mangled mass of wood. The kitchen cabinets have been blown off. Chunks of glass blanket our suite. It's impossible not to contemplate what would have happened had I not been out for a two-week break and had the bomb not occurred on a Friday, when the staff has the day off. The damage to our office was so extensive that if we hadn't been killed, we'd have been seriously injured. When Munaf and Haqqi arrive at the scene a few hours later, they rummage through the debris in an attempt to salvage what little they can. Haqqi tells me that he spotted a foot in the hotel's courtyard and a scalp on the tiles next to the swimming pool, where in the bygone early days of the war we partied with journalist friends, and I celebrated two birthdays. Since then, *The Wall Street Journal* has only maintained an office inside the Green Zone.

I return a week after the attack to cover the final election for a new government that will rule Iraq for four years. There is no question that the majority of the votes will still be counted for the Shiites, and the next prime minister will be from one of the main Islamist Shiite parties. But this time around, the Sunnis have vowed to participate in the voting with a sense of conviction to counter the growing influence of Shiites and Kurds. In this sense, the election does not have a spirit of cooperation. It is marked instead by division and confusion. The United States army remains the dominant source of security here and it's doubtful that will change in the near future.

Iraq has become cruel and unforgivable. The stench of death surrounds Baghdad, the smell of destruction and of a failed power. Every outing is now a form of Russian roulette. Iraqis ask themselves every day: Will we survive this trip to the vegetable market? Will my child make it home from school or the university? Will my spouse return from work? Or will they die or disappear?

I ask to be driven to the Hamra so I can see the destruction. "Trust me, Farnaz, you don't want to see it. It's very, very sad," Munaf warns in advance. Nothing can prepare you for the moment you see a place you once called home in ruins. I am shocked to see the extensive damage to the hotel. The windows and doors of the restaurant are all blown out. There is nothing left of the bank branch, where I have an Iraqi account for the bureau, and the business center and bakery are also completely gone. The lobby, where Mohammad stood, is in ruins. I stand frozen in the doorway of our room and stare at the rubble and debris piled into several mounds in the middle of the living room. Here, I have conducted many of my interviews, written my stories, shared laughs and moments of frustration with my Iraqi staff, cooked dinner for journalist friends, and shared intimate moments with Babak. I can't step inside. Tears stream down my face. "I've seen enough," I say quietly and turn around. Haqqi and Munaf follow me silently.

I wake up early in the new house in the Green Zone to watch the sun rise on my last day in Iraq at the end of December 2005. I tiptoe upstairs, unlock the iron door leading to the roof, and step into the morning chill. A mist hangs over the palm trees as the sun slowly rises from behind the groves, a splendid orange globe illuminating the gray sky. Watching the sun set and rise are my favorite moments here. Unlike everything else, they are serene and magnificent. I lean forward on the rail and reflect on my time here. A rush of memories comes to me. I've borne witness as people's lives have unraveled around me. I recall a poignant quote from Martha Gellhorn, a pioneer female war reporter, from her book *The Face of War*: "War happens to people, one by one." War doesn't just happen to the military, whose soldiers are fighting, or to the government, who wages it. It happens to people, one by one, house by house, and family by family. I have not met a single Iraqi whose life hasn't been touched by the war or altered because of everyday violence. I have heard this sentence from Iraqis over and over, "Until now, we are still waiting." What are they waiting for, I wonder. Perhaps just for an ordinary day.

Epilogue

At the Chaotic Departure Lounge of Baghdad International Airport passengers anxiously pushed and elbowed through a long security line. I lingered behind, shoving my suitcase forward to hold my place while I stepped away to steal a few last words with Haqqi and Munaf. Twice, the loud *boom* of mortars shook the building, rattling windowpanes, and interrupting our conversation. I'm not going to miss this, I joked. When it was finally time to part, Haqqi whispered to me that although I was leaving Iraq, the country would never leave me. It would stay, he said, pointing to my chest, in my heart.

Leaving a war zone behind is an emotionally complicated endeavor. I could be dining in a New York restaurant, lying on a Caribbean beach, or cooking at home in Beirut when a sudden flash of memory, as instantaneous and brief as lightning, would hit me with vexing intensity. Sometimes nostalgia filled my heart, but most often grief, anger, and guilt weighed upon me. Haqqi was right.

Since my departure, I've followed the lives of our Iraqi staff members closely, and kept in touch with each of them. But I have been less lucky with Iraqi friends, many of whom have left no trace in the inherent chaos of displacement.

Babak, and many journalist friends who have continued to cover the ongoing conflict, offer firsthand accounts of the deteriorating situation in Iraq.

In January 2007, Babak returned to Iraq full time as *Newsweek*'s Baghdad bureau chief. On assignment, he spends two months in Baghdad and one month on a break. Iraq, once again, has been thrust back into my life. We speak at least three times a day and I monitor the news of Iraq closely. Although I wrote this book from Beirut, I could never escape Iraq. I spent most of my days dwelling in my memories of the country, as I re-read a suitcase full of notebooks. When I allowed myself a break, I listened as Babak told me about his days. His accounts were no less than heart-wrenching.

At the peak of the civil war in 2006, a dozen male Sunni staff members took refuge in the backyard of *Newsweek*'s Green Zone house, where they slept in a tiny, crowded room to avoid the dangers of their own homes. Later, one of Babak's translator's brothers, an elementary school teacher, was assassinated by gunmen. On the day of the funeral, the masked men arrived at the cemetery on motorcycles and opened fire on the largely Sunni crowd. Four more family members were killed in one fatal swoop. Little by little, Iraqi friends and staff began to leave, joining a massive exodus of middle-class Iraqis fleeing the civil war for Jordan and Syria. Throughout this period, my conversations with Babak were often interrupted as he cut off the phone to take shelter. Once, a rocket hit the house next door; on another day, the house across the street. The worst day of all was when Babak called to tell me that his colleague's fiancée, 28-year-old Andrea Parhamovich, was killed in an ambush.

For the first time I discovered how difficult it was to live in relative safety while a loved one was working in Iraq. Quickly, I gained perspective for what I'd put my family through during years of war reportage.

Iraq was unraveling with alarming speed. In February 2006, a month after I had left, a massive attack on the al-Askariya Shrine in Samarra officially sparked the civil war between Sunnis and Shiites. The explosion ripped apart the shrine's golden dome, a monument revered as one of the sacred sites of Shiite Islam. Within hours, Shiite militia had taken over the streets, mortars rained down on Sunni neighborhoods, and Sunni mosques were set on fire. Vengeful killing engulfed the country for much of the year. By July 2006, the average daily death toll from war-related violence topped 100 in Baghdad alone. The number of attacks on Americans and Iraqi forces more than doubled, reaching an average of 960 attacks each week from August to November 2006.

American military commanders publicly warned that the situation was untenable. The Shiite-dominated government of Prime Minister Nuri al-Maleki had no control over the militia. In early 2007, America announced it would deploy 30,000 additional troops to Iraq to curb sectarian violence in the capital, and as part of their effort to turn the tide, reached out to Sunnis, even those former insurgents who were killing American soldiers. By the middle of 2007, the American military began arming former Sunni militant groups, who proclaimed themselves ready to fight al-Qaeda in Iraq. The Sunni tribal chiefs formed the Sunni Awakening Council, a committee aimed at deterring tribesmen from siding with terrorists. In exchange, the American military added 80,000 Sunnis to its payroll for a monthly salary of $250 a head. For their loyalty, the Sunnis demanded positions in the Shiite-dominated government and Iraqi forces. The Sunnis have threatened to call off the deal if the American military fails on its promise.

The militant Shiite cleric Moqtada al-Sadr declared a six-month cease-fire and recalled his Mahdi army militia from the streets in August 2007 before returning to Najaf to train as an Ayatollah. But Moqtada's cease-fire has been an on-and-off game. Several times, he has breached the truce, and violent battles have ensued in Sadr City and Basra. The heavily fortified Green Zone, seat of the Iraqi government and the American forces and embassy, remains in the line of mortar and rocket fire.

Gradually, the combination of the surge of American troops, Sunni cooperation, and Shiite cease-fire began to take effect. The number of casualties fell from its civil war zenith, and relevant calm was restored in some Baghdad neighborhoods. In an effort to contain violence in the city and to segregate sects, walls have been erected around entire neighborhoods.

Five years have passed since the United States led a military invasion into Iraq and George Bush declared a mission accomplished. But America's proposed goals remain elusive. Iraq's fragile stability hinges on deals brokered with Sunnis and Shiites. Ordinary Iraqis caught in the midst of open-ended war struggle to survive.

In considering the state of Iraq, it's necessary to remember that the reasons for which the United States declared war have proven false: Iraq did not have weapons of mass destruction, and Saddam had no ties to al-Qaeda. As these reasons faded from the public's mind, the American administration banked on the "democratization" of the Middle East to justify the war. If Saddam were replaced by a democratic regime, so the logic went, a domino effect would result in the rest of the region. This too has proven false.

As Iraq has faltered, sectarian Sunni-Shiite tensions have spilled over to the rest of the region. Islamic militancy has gained a new breeding ground in Iraq and Syria, and in Palestinian refugee camps in Lebanon. Equating change with sheer chaos, autocratic Middle Eastern leaders have tabled reform and democracy. When free elections are held, candidates affiliated with Islamist movements routinely sweep into office.

As of this writing, 175,000 American troops are on the ground in Iraq; more than 4,000 American soldiers have died and tens of thousands have been injured; war-related Iraqi civilian deaths are estimated at anywhere between 180,000 and 1 million; 14 percent of Iraq's population (4 million) is displaced: 2 million people have been displaced within the country, 2 million are living as refugees in neighboring countries. The war has cost the United States approximately three trillion dollars, and the effect of its psychological trauma on Americans and Iraqis is just beginning to surface.

In the summer of 2006, Haqqi left Iraq for the United States at the invitation of the *Journal*. He did not return. Instead he applied for asylum, which was granted to him eleven months later. Today he is married to an Iraqi-British woman named Noor, and works as a car salesman at a Honda dealership in Detroit. Recently he and his wife have been forced apart by U.S. immigration law that denied his wife reentry to the U.S. after she visited her family in Jordan. As a foreigner married to a green-card holder, she must apply for the appropriate visa from outside of the U.S., where she must remain until her application is approved. This process could take years. Haqqi's mother and younger sister are refugees in Syria. His father and brother remain in Baghdad. In his last e-mail to me, he despondently summed up his situation, "So I will wait for my green card and see which place on earth will hold an Iraqi man with his wife whom the war destroyed his dream, his life, his country and separated his family."

Munaf remains in Baghdad, where he continues to work for the *Journal* as an office manager and a reporter's assistant. Recently he completed his master's degree in chemistry at the University of Baghdad, despite the formidable hurdles that arise on a campus divided by civil war. In the summer of 2006, Munaf's family abandoned their house in Dora, a mixed Sunni-Shiite neighborhood, after Shiite neighbors warned that they would be murdered if they remained. Until they were able to buy a new house with the help of a generous loan from the *Journal* in a safer, all-Sunni neighborhood in Baghdad, they stayed with relatives. In a dispatch he wrote for the newspaper's blog, Munaf reported in April of 2008, "Now, life in Baghdad is better than the past year. But, there are still car bombs and unknown bodies found in the city. Yet we hope that life will get better, which gives us the energy to continue on."

Jabbar, our translator who left for Syria with several hours' notice, returned to Baghdad after nearly a year of living in Damascus without a job or a work permit. He has resumed his former post as a translator for the paper, and takes joy in his baby daughter, whom he calls "my little angel." Although he and his wife were safe in Syria, they were lonely, and when their savings ran out, they headed back to Iraq.

Mohanad, *Newsweek*'s office manager, left Iraq in 2007. After making his way to Ireland, he was granted refugee status when he applied for asylum. Fatin and their four children are in Syria. When he can, Mohanad visits them. (Currently he works at a refugee center helping newly arrived refugees settle in Ireland.) Their separation as a family is devastating for each of them. As he tells me in one of our recent exchanges, "I bet you can imagine the tragedy scene every time I leave the kids and Fatin and go back to Dublin. They cry a lot . . . they make me cry every time and make it really sad and complicated." Fatin and the children are waiting to join Mohanad. (Approval could take as long as two years.)

Ayad, who frequently traveled with Babak and me as a translator, is in Damascus with his wife and daughter. They registered as refugees with the United Nations High Commission for Refugees requesting relocation in a Western English-speaking country. After several lengthy interviews with UN and American officials, Ayad's application was approved. He and his family were settled in Houston, Texas, in May.

Amal al-Khudeiry, the art gallery owner, left her house and belongings in Baghdad in 2006 for Jordan. She was unable to refurbish Beit al-Iraqi, her glorious art and cultural center. To date, I have been unsuccessful in my attempts to contact Amal directly. My news comes from her friends in Jordan, who report that refugee life has been hard on her. She was alone and without income. Last winter, she moved to the United Arab Emirates to live with her son.

The Nasser family has been widely scattered as a result of war. They too fled their ancestral home, in the Sunni-dominated enclave of Ad-hamiya. When the neighborhood park where their children once played was transformed into a makeshift cemetery to accommodate civilian deaths, Sabah knew that it was time to leave. He and Marie-Rose, along with their younger son Ziad and his wife Rana, now live in a relative's house in Karada, a Christian neighborhood. According to Sabah, they rarely leave the house, and their days are spent caring for their two grand-children. Sabah's deaf brother Nosrat and his wife Theresa now live in Beirut with members of her family. Recently Sabah told me over the phone, "I wish I could leave Iraq but I have no money. It's very expensive to live in Jordan. I have sold all the antiques and all of Marie-Rose's jew-elry. When I think about the days when we lived in our big house with all of my children around me, I think it was a dream."

Ayad, the Nassers' oldest son, his wife Aseel, and their two young chil-dren live in Jordan, where Ayad works as an accountant. They have re-cently registered with the UNHCR as refugees in hope of attaining placement elsewhere, but they have been told that their chances are slim because they didn't work for Americans. Sabah pleads with me over the phone, "Can you please help them? Can you do something for them? Do you know anyone in the refugee office?"

The tribal chieftain from Fallujah, Sheikh Khamis al-Hasnawi, has become a key member of the Sunni Awakening Council, the committee that cooperates with Americans to dissuade tribesmen from joining the resistance in exchange for a position in the police force or the army. The tribal chiefs, including Sheikh Hassnawi, are under threat from Sunni extremists, particularly those affiliated with al-Qaeda in Iraq. In March 2007, a truck bomb filled with chlorine and explosives blew up outside his home near Fallujah, killing three members of his family and sickening scores of passersby.

The two junior Shiites clerics I befriended after the invasion have risen to the top ranks of religious and political prominence. Seyed Hashem Mousawi is now the Dean of Al-Kadhimiya religious university and a member of the Haj Committee, a powerful and ultra-wealthy government body that oversees Iraqi pilgrimage to Mecca. Sheikh Hayder Nassrawi is now Grand Ayatollah Sistani's representative in Kadhimiya, one of the most important postings in Shiites hierarchy. He is also the Imam of the Kadhimiya shrine, leading Friday prayers and delivering political sermons every Friday. He also lectures at Shiites seminaries.

Abdul Salaam Khutheer and Mohammad Jabber, the two hotel receptionists who lost their only sons within two weeks of one another, still work as receptionists at the Hamra Hotel. Mohammad returned to work after the second tower, demolished in an explosion attack, was refurbished. Since their sons' murders, they have tried to find solace in their faith but both admit that their losses are unbearable. Mohammad tells me, "I believe in destiny but what happened made a deep wound in my heart." Salaam concedes, "I feel sad when I see someone talk to his son or when I want to move something heavy because my son used to help me."

I keep asking myself: What justifies the enormous costs of this war and the wounds it has inflicted? I am at loss for an answer. This is the story of war.

—JUNE 12, 2008, BEIRUT

E-MAIL TO FAMILY AND FRIENDS,
SEPTEMBER 2004

BEING A FOREIGN CORRESPONDENT IN BAGHDAD these days is like being under virtual house arrest. Forget about the reasons that lured me to this job: a chance to see the world, explore the exotic, meet new people in faraway lands, discover their ways, and tell stories that could make a difference.

Little by little, day by day, being based in Iraq has defied all those reasons. I am housebound. I leave when I have a very good reason to and a scheduled interview. I avoid going to people's homes and never walk in the streets. I can't go grocery shopping anymore, can't eat in restaurants, can't strike up a conversation with strangers, can't look for stories, can't drive in anything but a fully armored car, can't go to scenes of breaking news stories, can't be stuck in traffic, can't speak English outside, can't take a road trip, can't say I'm an American, can't linger at checkpoints, can't be curious about what people are saying, doing, feeling. And can't and can't. . . .

There has been one too many close calls, including a car bomb so near our house that it blew out all the windows. So now my most pressing concern every day is not to write a kick-ass story, but to stay alive and make sure our Iraqi employees stay alive. In Baghdad I am a security personnel first, a reporter second.

It's hard to pinpoint when the "turning point" exactly began. Was it April when Fallujah fell out of the grasp of the Americans? Was it when Moqtada and Jish Mahdi declared war on the U.S. military? Was it when Sadr City, home to 10 percent of Iraq's population, became a nightly battlefield for the Americans? Or was it when the insurgency began spreading from isolated pockets in the Sunni Triangle to include most of Iraq? Despite President Bush's rosy assessments, Iraq remains a disaster. If under Saddam it was a "potential" threat, under the Americans it has been transformed to "imminent and active threat," a foreign policy failure bound to haunt the United States for decades to come.

Iraqis like to call this mess "the Situation." When asked, "How are things?" they reply, "The situation is very bad."

What they mean by situation is this: the Iraqi government doesn't control most Iraqi cities; there are several car bombs going off each day around the country, killing and injuring scores of innocent people; the country's roads are becoming impassable and littered by hundreds of landmines and explosive devices aimed to kill American soldiers; there are assassinations, kidnappings, and beheadings. The situation, basically, means a raging, barbaric guerilla war.

In four days, 110 people died and over 300 got injured in Baghdad alone. The numbers are so shocking that the Ministry of Health—which was attempting an exercise of public transparency by releasing the numbers—has now stopped disclosing them.

Insurgents now attack Americans eighty-seven times a day.

A friend drove through the Shiite slum of Sadr City yesterday. He said young men were openly placing improvised explosive devices into the ground. They melt a shallow hole into the asphalt, dig the explosive, cover it with dirt, and put an old tire or plastic can over it to signal to the locals that this is booby-trapped. He said on the main roads of Sadr City, there were a dozen landmines per every ten yards. His car snaked and swirled to avoid driving over them. Behind the walls sits an angry Iraqi ready to detonate them as soon as an American convoy gets near. This is in Shiite land, the population that was supposed to love America for liberating Iraq.

For journalists the significant turning point came with the wave of abduction and kidnappings. Only two weeks ago we felt safe around Baghdad because foreigners were being abducted on the roads and highways between towns. Then came a frantic phone call from a journalist female friend at 11 PM, telling me two Italian women had been abducted from their homes in broad daylight. Then the two Americans, who got beheaded this week, and the Brit were abducted from their homes in a residential neighborhood. They were supplying the entire block with round-the-clock electricity from their generator to win friends. The abductors grabbed one of them at 6 AM when he came out to switch on the generator; his beheaded body was thrown back near the neighborhood.

The insurgency, we are told, is rampant, with no signs of calming down. If anything, it is growing stronger, organized, and more sophisticated every day. The various elements within it—Baathists, criminals, nationalists, and al-Qaeda—are cooperating and coordinating.

I went to an emergency meeting for foreign correspondents with the military and embassy to discuss the kidnappings. We were somberly told our fate would largely depend on where we were in the kidnapping chain once it was determined we were missing. Here is how it goes: criminal gangs grab you and sell you up to Baathists in Fallujah, who will in turn sell you to al-Qaeda. In turn, cash and weapons flow the other way from al-Qaeda to the Baathists to the criminals. My friend Georges, the French journalist snatched on the road to Najaf, has been missing for a month with no word on release or whether he is still alive.

America's last hope for a quick exit? The Iraqi police and National Guard units we are spending billions of dollars to train. The cops are being murdered by the dozens every day—over seven hundred to date—and the insurgents are infiltrating their ranks. The problem is so serious that the U.S. military has allocated $6 million to buy out thirty thousand cops they just trained to get rid of them quietly.

As for reconstruction: firstly, it's so unsafe for foreigners to operate that almost all projects have come to a halt. After two years, of the $18 billion Congress appropriated for Iraq reconstruction only about $1 billion or so has been spent, and a chunk has now been reallocated for improving security, a sign of just how bad things are going here.

Oil dreams? Insurgents disrupt oil flow routinely as a result of sabotage and oil prices have hit the record high of $49 a barrel.

Who did this war exactly benefit? Was it worth it? Are we safer because Saddam is holed up and al-Qaeda is running around in Iraq?

Iraqis say that thanks to America, they got freedom in exchange for insecurity. Guess what? They say they'd take security over freedom any day, even if it means having a dictator ruler.

I heard an educated Iraqi say today that if Saddam Hussein were allowed to run for elections, he would get the majority of the vote. This is truly sad.

Then I went to see an Iraqi scholar this week to talk to him about elections here. He has been trying to educate the public on the importance of voting. He said, "President Bush wanted to turn Iraq into a democracy that would be an example for the Middle East. Forget about democracy, forget about being a model for the region, we have to salvage Iraq before all is lost."

One could argue that Iraq is already lost beyond salvation. For those of us on the ground, it's hard to imagine what, if anything, could salvage it from its violent downward spiral.

The genie of terrorism, chaos, and mayhem has been unleashed onto this country as a result of American mistakes, and it can't be put back into a bottle.

The Iraqi government is talking about having elections in three months while half of the country remains a "no-go zone"—out of the hands of the government and the Americans and out of reach of journalists. In the other half, the disenchanted population is too terrified to show up at polling stations. The Sunnis have already said they'd boycott elections, leaving the stage open for a polarized government of Kurds and Shiites that will not be deemed as legitimate and will most certainly lead to civil war.

I asked a twenty-eight-year-old engineer if he and his family would participate in the Iraqi elections, since it was the first time Iraqis could to some degree elect a leadership. His response summed it all: "Go and vote and risk being blown into pieces or followed by the insurgents and murdered for cooperating with the Americans? For what? To practice democracy? Are you joking?"

—FARNAZ

Doonesbury

NEXT UP ON OUR **HONEST VOICES READING LIST!** AN ANALYSIS OF BUSH'S WAR IN IRAQ! LOOK FOR IT AT: www.poynter.org/forum/?id=misc

BUT I DON'T **WANT** TO READ SOMETHING FROM A LIBER-AL DEFEATIST PERSPECTIVE!

NO WORRIES, SECURITY MOM...

10-12

THIS ASTONISHING LETTER FROM BAGHDAD WAS WRIT-TEN BY A REPORTER FROM THE ARCHCONSERVATIVE WALL STREET JOURNAL!

PERFECT! SO IS FREEDOM ON THE MARCH?

JUDGE FOR YOUR-SELF – IT'S YOUR **RIGHT!**

ACKNOWLEDGMENTS

EVER SINCE I CAN REMEMBER, I wanted to write a book. For making this dream come true, I have many people to thank and acknowledge.

I am deeply indebted to the Iraqi staff of *The Wall Street Journal*'s Baghdad bureau. Our small team of translators, drivers and guards is an example of courage, loyalty and friendship and without them, working and living in Iraq would be impossible. We rely on them for everything—from buying groceries to guarding our lives with guns. They carry out their tasks while braving considerable risks and violence. I particularly cherished the companionship and assistance of Haqqi Hamoudi and Munaf Mustafa, my team of translator and driver who traveled all over Iraq with me and helped me better understand the places and people I was covering. My appreciation to Haqqi, Munaf, Amar Abdullah (Abu Munaf), Jabbar Yaseen, Muthana Hamed, Amer Saleh, Nahid Saadollah, and Jamal Naji.

I have been on the road with America's war on terror since September 11, 2001, following the story from the foot of the collapsed towers of the World Trade Center in Manhattan to the mountains of Afghanistan and the deserts of Iraq. A special gratitude is extended to the brilliant editors who sent me to far flung places and under whose stewardship I flourished as a journalist: Bill Spindle, formerly at *The Wall Street Journal*, sent me to Iraq and oversaw the war coverage with tremendous wit and compassion; Fran Dauth and Jim Willse, at *The Star-Ledger*, assigned me to some of the biggest international stories and said "go" whenever I raised my hand; Joel Rawson and Andy Burkhardt, formerly at *The Providence Journal*, let me pursuit the story of EgyptAir Flight 990, which crashed off the coast of my suburban beat, all the way to Cairo.

I couldn't have written a book without the generous support and encouragement of my editors at *The Wall Street Journal*, both during my Iraq assignment and on book leave. I thank them for their commitment to continue covering Iraq, despite the perils and costs. The *Journal*'s environment is unique in our competitive business; it holds you to the highest standards while being incredibly nurturing. Bill Spindle consistently urged me to keep my eye on the big picture as events unfolded around me and to find compelling stories about how Iraqis were coping. He also called every single day—often as soon as he woke up in New York and before he got to the office—just to check on how I was faring. It was a reminder of the *Journal*'s tremendous concern for our well being and safety above every thing else. Editors in New York always made time to see me and hear firsthand about Iraq. My deep appreciation to Paul Steiger, Marcus Brauchli, Dan Hertzberg, Alix Freedman, Jim Pensiero, Laurie Hays, Cathy Panagoulias, Michael Miller, Michael Williams, Michael Allen, Matt Murray, John Bussey, and Chip Cummins and my colleagues Yochi Dreazen, Philip Shishkin, Steve Stecklow, and Joshua Prager.

My colleagues and friends in the Baghdad press corps demonstrated solidarity and camaraderie of the highest kind. They included Hannah Allam, Jon Lee Anderson, Anne Barnard, Kate Brooks, Mohamad Bazzi, Molly Bingham, Annia Ciezadlo, Thanassis Cambanis, Rajiv Chandrasekaran, Borzou Daragahi, Thomas Dworzak, Hassan Fattah, Dexter Filkins, Scott Johnson, Larry Kaplow, Quil Lawrence, Matthew McAllester, Delphine Minoui, Jim Muir, Rod Nordland, Evan Osnos, Ilana Ozernoy, Catherine Philp, Louise Roug, Alissa Rubin, Anthony Shadid, Liz Sly, Vivienne Walt, Ivan Watson, Ed Wong, and Robert Worth. And a heartfelt thanks to Ranya Kadri in Amman for securing my first Iraq visa and for her formidable assistance and friendship on countless transit trips in and out of Iraq.

I marvel at the courage of all Iraqi employees of media organizations who risk their lives in order to facilitate telling their country's story. Because we shared a house with *Newsweek* and I often traveled with Babak, the magazine's Iraqi staff repeatedly went out of its way to help me. My gratitude to all of them, especially: Mohanad Obeidi, Ayad Obeidi, Ahmad Obeidi, Munib Obeidi, and Salih Mahdi.

The willingness of countless ordinary Iraqis who generously opened their lives to me and shared their stories made this book possible. The Nasser family welcomed me into their home at a time when most Iraqis wouldn't dare speak to foreigners. They made me feel at home by feeding me delicious meals and showering me with kindness amidst the bitterness of war. Thank you to Marie-Rose and Sabah, Nosrat and Theresa, Ayad and Aseel and Ziad and Rana. I was lucky to befriend Amal al-Khudeiry, whose feisty energy to survive inspired me during taxing times. I would also like to express my appreciation for a number of individuals who always made time to share their insights so I could better understand Iraq: Ghassan Attiyah, Fareed Ayar, Sheikh Kashef al-Ghatta, Dr. Salamah al-Khafaji, Hania Mufti, Huda al-Nuami, Wamidh Nadhmi, and Sheikh Ali al-Waezi.

I lost two dear friends to the war in Iraq. Iranian photographer and BBC cameraman Kaveh Golestan died in a landmine explosion and American aid worker Marla Ruzicka was killed in a car bomb attack. Their spirit runs through the pages of this book.

Over the years I've been privileged with the mentorship and friendship of some of the best names in our business. Neil MacFarquhar helped me navigate the world of American newspapers. Nora Boustany taught me precious reporting lessons. Geraldine Brooks urged me to attend journalism school at Columbia University. David Unger shared his encyclopedic knowledge of U.S. foreign policy over sushi lunches. G. Wayne Miller influenced me to trail narrative journalism and Christopher Dickey advocated branching out of my comfort zone to tackle book writing.

I would like to thank Columbia University's Graduate School of Journalism for granting me an invaluable education and for its staunch support and cheerleading. My appreciation to: Dean Nicholas Lemann and Professors Samuel Freedman, Sig Gissler, Stephen Isaacs, Sandy Padwe, and Seymour Topping. I would like to point out that in addition to being a world class instructor, Professor Gissler and his wife, Mary, are like family to me. They took me under their wings when I was a young student dealing with a family tragedy and I never left their shelter. My N.Y. Mama and Papa, thank you for everything.

Peter Osnos, the founder of PublicAffairs, was instrumental in the conception of this book. He convinced me during a garden party at his house that I had a book in me about Iraq and it was important that I write it. Clive Priddle honed my ideas, offered skillful advice at every turn and edited my manuscript with brilliant insight. Morgen Van Vorst patiently smoothed out the drafts and accommodated my concepts. Tessa Shanks handled publicity affairs with tireless enthusiasm.

A special thanks to my agent, Flip Brophy, for her fierce belief in this project and for guiding me through every step of the publishing maze. Her assistant Sharon Skettini diligently accommodated logistical details while still finding time to fire off cheerful e-mails.

At home in Beirut, several people worked hard so that I could carry out my writing with as much ease as possible, chief among them was my phenomenon assistant, Nada Raad, who read over the manuscript and helped with the proofreading in a crunch.

Shortly after leaving Iraq, I had a fluke accident while skiing in Lebanon and injured my neck. It was a frightening ordeal and compounded with the emotional traumas of Iraq, my recovery was slow and long. My deep appreciation to Dr. Jack Saul who gently helped me processes the war memories and persuaded me that writing this book would be therapeutic. Dr. Michael Daras, Dr. Arash Emami, and Dr. Kristjan Ragnarsson are gifted physicians with an abundant amount of positive energy and hope.

My friends and cousins scattered across three continents nourished me with endless encouragement, support, and humor. I must single out Claire Allistone and Erika Dionisio in New York and Sara Dolatshahi and Afrooz Tavakoli in Tehran for always lending an ear despite crappy phone connections and differing time zones and for consistently reassuring me that I will pull through any challenge. My deepest thanks to Nasim Alikhani, Andrew Lee Butters, Shahrzad Daneshmand, Sahar Dolatshahi,

ACKNOWLEDGMENTS

Anthony Elia, Thomas Erdbrink, Houri Etesam, Mariam Fakhimi, Scheherezade Faramarzi, Nazila Fathi, Rana Fil, Susan Ghafari, Roshanak Ghahremanpour, Parand Ghobadi, Pooneh Ghodoosi, Melanie Lefkowitz, Maryam Majd, Eva Marer, Andrew Mills, Jon Naso, Sharif Nezam-Mafi, Karim Sadjadpour, Leena Saeedi, Niloufar Safavieh, Kamand Shaibani, Delly Shirazi, Rory Stewart, Ali Tavakoli, Mahzad Tavakoli, Reza Tavakoli, Newsha Tavakolian, Abigail Walch, Jeff Whelan, and Amir Ali Zolfagharia.

I am blessed with a wonderful family and extended relatives whose unconditional love and support keeps me grounded despite my affinity for a nomadic life. My grandmother Etty, from whom I inherited the love for news, spoils me endlessly while secretly agonizing over my safety. Uncle Hamid Tavakoli and aunts Farzi and Fariba Tavakoli have been a primary source of affection and friendship ever since I can remember. I am extremely fortunate to have found a second home among Babak's family. I'm especially indebted to his parents, Elaine and Hassan Dehghanpisheh, his brother Dr. Keivan Dehghanpisheh and his lovely wife, Terez, for their unwavering love, support, and encouragement throughout the years.

Above all, I must thank my parents for giving me a unique upbringing filled with love and a healthy dose of risk and adventure. I am deeply sad that my father, Ali Fassihi, is not with us to see that my constant chattering and storytelling finally amounted to a book. We lost my father to a battle with cancer nearly a decade ago but I still feel his love and wisdom with me every day. My mother, Fereshteh Tavakoli, has been a source of support and strength through out my life. I credit her for becoming a writer because she turned me into an avid reader from a very young age and saved all my essays in a shoe box under her bed. I admire the graceful and courageous way she handled my war reportage and for understanding why I did it. Thank you to Shapour Javadizadeh for his support and for getting her through the difficult days.

I cannot be grateful enough for having Tannaz Fassihi as my sister. She is my best friend and rock. I like to tell the story of how I named my little sister after my favorite doll; she turned out to be just as adorable and more. I regard her husband, Ali Joulaee, as the brother I never had and would like to thank them both for their constant love, tender care, and generous hospitality during good times and bad. They truly define the meaning of family.

Last and most important, I have to thank Babak Dehghanpisheh. Because of him, war zones felt like home and crazy adventures turned into romance. I am forever grateful for his solid calm and steadfast support all these years but especially during the writing of this book. Babak read every word, over and over, with the precision of a dedicated editor despite his busy schedule in Baghdad and on occasions when it felt as if I could never finish the project, he lovingly reminded me that I would. I feel tremendously lucky for his love and companionship.

Kate Brooks

FARNAZ FASSIHI is *The Wall Street Journal*'s deputy bureau chief for the Middle East and Africa. From 2003 to 2006 she ran the *Journal*'s Baghdad bureau, prior to which she was a roving foreign correspondent for *The Star-Ledger* of Newark and a reporter for *The Providence Journal* in Rhode Island. An award-winning journalist, she has covered three wars and reported extensively from the Middle East. Her essays on the Iraq war have appeared in several publications and books and an e-mail she wrote from Baghdad was included in an anthology of historical letters written by American women. A graduate of Columbia University's Graduate School of Journalism, she is based in Beirut, Lebanon.

PublicAffairs is a publishing house founded in 1997. It is a tribute to the standards, values, and flair of three persons who have served as mentors to countless reporters, writers, editors, and book people of all kinds, including me.

I.F. STONE, proprietor of *I. F. Stone's Weekly*, combined a commitment to the First Amendment with entrepreneurial zeal and reporting skill and became one of the great independent journalists in American history. At the age of eighty, Izzy published *The Trial of Socrates*, which was a national bestseller. He wrote the book after he taught himself ancient Greek.

BENJAMIN C. BRADLEE was for nearly thirty years the charismatic editorial leader of *The Washington Post*. It was Ben who gave the *Post* the range and courage to pursue such historic issues as Watergate. He supported his reporters with a tenacity that made them fearless and it is no accident that so many became authors of influential, best-selling books.

ROBERT L. BERNSTEIN, the chief executive of Random House for more than a quarter century, guided one of the nation's premier publishing houses. Bob was personally responsible for many books of political dissent and argument that challenged tyranny around the globe. He is also the founder and longtime chair of Human Rights Watch, one of the most respected human rights organizations in the world.

·   ·   ·

For fifty years, the banner of Public Affairs Press was carried by its owner Morris B. Schnapper, who published Gandhi, Nasser, Toynbee, Truman, and about 1,500 other authors. In 1983, Schnapper was described by *The Washington Post* as "a redoubtable gadfly." His legacy will endure in the books to come.

Peter Osnos, *Founder and Editor-at-Large*